PUBLIC RELATIONS
AND THE
MAKING OF MODERN BRITAIN

Manchester University Press

Public relations and the making of modern Britain

*Stephen Tallents
and the
birth of a progessive media profession*

Scott Anthony

Manchester University Press

Manchester and New York

*distributed in the United States exclusively
by Palgrave Macmillan*

Published by Manchester University Press
Oxford Road, Manchester M13 9NR, UK
and Room 400, 175 Fifth Avenue, New York, NY 10010, USA
www.manchesteruniversitypress.co.uk

Distributed in the United States exclusively by
Palgrave Macmillan, 175 Fifth Avenue, New York,
NY 10010, USA

Distributed in Canada exclusively by
UBC Press, University of British Columbia, 2029 West Mall,
Vancouver, BC, Canada V6T 1Z2

British Library Cataloguing-in-Publication Data
A catalogue record for this book is available from the British Library

Library of Congress Cataloging-in-Publication Data applied for

ISBN   978 0 7190 8457 7   hardback

First published 2012

Typeset
by Carnegie Book Production, Lancaster
Printed in Great Britain
by TJ International Ltd, Padstow

For my parents

Contents

List of illustrations

Acknowledgements

This book could not have been written without the guidance and support of Adrian Gregory and Peter Mandler. Stephen Tallents's daughter, Miranda Pemberton-Pigott, and her extended family have also been incredibly supportive of the project – I can't thank them enough for their interest and generosity. I also want to thank Emma Brennan for being such a creative, enthusiastic and flexible editor and Max Jones for being a benevolent mentor. Among my many intellectual creditors I particularly want to thank Ruth Artmonsky, Tim Boon, Stephen Eeley, Jo Fox, Jose Harris, Jonny Hoare, Melanie Horton, Jacquie L'Etang, John Lloyd, Tamson Pietsch, Margaret Timmers, Patrick Russell and Jean Seaton. I also owe a lasting debt of gratitude to Wolfson College, Oxford, for offering financial support when this project was at a low ebb.

Any work of history is a work of archival labour, and I would like to thank Barry Attoe, Siobhan O'Leary and Adrian Steele at the British Postal Museum and Archive, Helen Beardsley and Karl Magee at the Grierson Archive, Els Boonan at the BBC, Bryony Dixon, Mark Duguid and Janet Moat at the BFI, Sue Filmer at the History of Advertising Trust, Julie McCaffery at the Institute of Commonwealth Studies, Rain Soosaar at Valga Museum and the staff of the Bodleian, for all their assistance, guidance and patience.

After the Great War:
The origin of public relations

Public relations today has an image problem. Seen through the prism of popular works such as Adam Curtis's *Century of the Self* and Nick Davies's *Flat Earth News*, public relations is a profession that has endowed sectarian interests with the ability to manipulate entire populations. Scholars tend to share this scepticism. British historians invariably track the development of propaganda techniques and systems of censorship against exceptional media flashpoints of the early twentieth century such as the Great War, the General Strike or the abdication crisis, while social scientists under the influence of various strands of media sociology and Frankfurt School post-Marxism tend to view public relations as a mechanism for engineering social consent.[1] Starkly put, public relations is widely understood as a tool that allows dominant power groupings to keep the radical compromises necessary for 'real' mass democracy at arm's length. At best public relations is seen to serve established interests, at worst it is tinged with conspiratorial malice.

By contrast, this book argues that the development of public relations in Britain was a product of the Great Depression that was animated by the same liberal ideals that inspired William Beveridge and John Maynard Keynes. Initially prompted by the slump, the wider ethos of British public relations in the interwar period would directly inform the creation of postwar organisations such as UNESCO. It can even be argued that public relations in early twentieth-century Britain operated as a kind of cultural Keynesianism.

Sir Stephen Tallents (1884–1958) stands at the centre of this story. From the documentary film movement to the establishment of Listener Research at the BBC and the staging of the Festival of Britain, Tallents's career in the Civil Service (as well as his more personal interventions in public life) touched every significant public relations innovation in early twentieth-century Britain. As well as Tallents's pre-eminence as a practitioner (he was to become the inaugural President of the Institute of Public Relations), he was also a well-connected proselytiser, a status that embroiled him in the high political, organisational and administrative development of public relations in Britain, as well as the production of its unique material culture.

The aim of this book in tracking the development of public relations through the peaks and troughs of Tallents's career is to build a holistic understanding of the discipline's political, professional, organisational and personal genesis.[2] It's an approach that understands that public relations straddles the personal and the professional, and recognises that by using Tallents as an archetype it becomes possible to examine the private calculations as well as the public mythologies that are crucial to understanding the profession.[3] Taking a humbler human-eye view also usefully conveys the excitement, chaos and contingency of the revolutionary social and technological challenges that the pioneers of public relations in Britain struggled to understand.

Although the image of ideological extremism dominates our perception of politics during the interwar years, Britain was run by national government for the larger part of the period. High political debate may have stagnated but economic and social hardships combined with breakthroughs in areas such as agro-science, communication technologies and mass transportation demanded an organisational response. For a brief moment, as some of the edge was taken out of party politics, problems of governance came to the fore. Thus alongside political division and 'disagreement', as Arthur Marwick argued, there co-existed 'a very large groundwork of social and political "agreement" in the 1930s [from which] there arose the ideological structure which brought Britain safely through the forties and brought her to rest in the fifties'.[4] Public relations in Britain was a byproduct of this interwar effort to voluntarily co-ordinate pockets of 'progressive' government and third-sector practice in a time of financial austerity. Hoolger Hoock wrote recently about the interrelationship between the 'cultures of power' and 'the power of culture' in eighteenth- and nineteenth-century Britain. In a similar vein, 'public relations' would be shaped by the preoccupations and sensibility of an emerging bureaucratic stratum. The expanding role of the state in the twentieth century, and the increasing numbers of powerful officials employed to administer it, were fundamental to the formulation of public relations in Britain.[5]

My argument is a challenge to the template of British public relations history popularised in the 1960s by Professor Sam Black and little questioned since.[6] According to Black, Britain's first Professor of Public Relations, public relations had primarily been an American innovation.[7] He posited Ivy Lee and Edward Bernays as the fathers of the profession and saw an echo of the American Revolution in Lee's 'founding principles of public relations'.[8]

Without denying that Lee and Bernays are significant figures, the account retrospectively canonised by Black and his contemporaries is rather skewed.[9] There are material reasons for this. When Black published *Practical Public Relations* in 1962 it was the first mass-market work on the subject available in the UK. As a senior figure in both the Institute of Public Relations (IPR) and the International Public Relations Association (IPRA), Black had already begun a long campaign to win charter status for the profession (eventually granted in 2005) and to establish international standards of behaviour (enshrined as the IPRA's Code of Athens in 1965). From a contemporary perspective it's clear that *Practical Public Relations* was but one strand of Black's efforts to increase both the size and status of the profession.

Interestingly, *Public Relations Practice* attempts to raise the profession's status by almost completely ignoring past British practice. It was a book aimed at practitioners and the purpose of its 'history' section was to provide role models that appealed to the private sector.[10] Hence Lee is celebrated for converting John D. Rockefeller from 'a "greedy old capitalist" to a kindly old man who gave dimes to children and millions of dollars to charity'.[11] Black mythologises (some would argue distorts) Lee's personal story and in the process enables his DIY book to conclude with a hopeful vision – by judicious use of his craft a humble public relations professional can transform the actions of the world's most powerful people as well as the public's perception of them. Such a myth, mixed with an entreaty not to allow British business to fall further behind its transatlantic counterparts, provided the active core of the appeal of *Practical Public Relations*.

While Black overtly promoted public relations as an American profession with universal application, it is also possible to see the threads of a different narrative emerging from the pages of

Practical Public Relations. In Black's book, only a handful of
the sixteen examples given of good public relations practice in
Britain could be firmly classified as private sector. 'In support of
sales' illustrates how organising country fairs in urban locations
(replete with games of polo and sheepdog trials) had boosted the
sales of a margarine brand, while 'using stunts in public relations'
demonstrates how the strength of Wedgwood bone china was
promoted in the press by placing tea cups underneath the tyres of
a four-tonne lorry. Elsewhere public relations activity in Britain
is summed up under subheadings such as 'public relations in the
community', 'for a new food', 'Local Government', 'securing
acceptance for an increase in price of gas', 'public relations for
town' and 'world-wide publicity for art'. The outstanding example
of British public relations practice in 1960, according to Black,
was the organisation of World Refugee Year. What is interesting
about the projects listed in *Practical Public Relations* is not only
that it is difficult to imagine Ivy Lee or Edward Bernays employed
on any of them but that it is almost impossible to credit that
Bernays and Lee were role models to Black's provincial town
counsellors, nationalised industry administrators or humanitarian
campaigners. Indeed, while Lee and Bernays worked as consultants
to outré millionaires and the entertainment industry, Black himself
had moved into public relations from ophthalmology.

When Black's book does briefly (and grudgingly) touch upon
the history of British public relations practice, it posits Lloyd
George's National Insurance Act of 1911 as a starting point before
moving on to Lord Northcliffe's War Aims Committee and then
the interwar appointment of Press Officers by the Air Ministry
and the Ministry of Health. It mentions the importance of local
government initiatives, the launching of the BBC Empire Service
and the second Ministry of Information in laying the ground for
the industry's postwar expansion. Strikingly, not only do Black's
earliest examples of British public relations practice predate his list
of American innovations but the emphasis in Britain was firmly on
the public sector.[12] Black would later admit what is immediately
apparent to twenty-first-century eyes:

> In the private sector public relations continued to remain largely
> a mystery until the 1970s, so the early post-war momentum
> was maintained mainly in the public sector, notably in national
> and local government and in the nationalized industries.[13]

'Tallents and others formed the Institute of Public Relations in

1948', Black recalled in another telling aside; 'its early membership was very largely comprised of civil servants and bureaucrats, who attracted formidable public figures to their events'.[14] This book is an attempt to restore and comprehend a significant episode in British history that was for the most part studiously passed over by Black's generation and has been all but forgotten since.[15]

The pre history of public relations in Britain

When Stephen Tallents joined the Civil Service on 2 April 1909 the function of government was fast changing (as Graham Wallas conceptualised it) from the safeguarding of citizens' rights to the active direction of national development.[16] Reflecting this shift, the British Civil Service grew in number from 280,900 to 387,400 during the interwar period as the percentage of the British population employed in government service gradually increased from 3.5% to 14.1% between 1891 and 1950. This expansion had initially been driven by two prongs of state-sponsored social welfare – the National Insurance Act and the Pensions Act.[17] 'I was entering, though I little suspected it at the time', Tallents reflected, 'a Civil Service on the eve of revolution'.[18]

Working in a junior capacity with Sir Hubert Llewellyn Smith and William Beveridge on the establishment of a nationwide network of labour exchanges, Tallents was to gain first-hand experience of brokering creative compromises between employers, trade unionists, local councillors, social workers and educationists. He answered complaints, promoted the exchanges on speaking tours and administered National Insurance contributions. It was a kind of work that, although Tallents did not realise it at the time, would influence early conceptions of public relations in Britain. The development of 'public relations' was a mass-media consequence of the expansion of centralised social welfare provision.[19]

The First World War prompted further rapid developments in public relations. First World War propaganda immediately calls to mind fabricated atrocity stories, but Tallents's work at the Ministry of Food exposed him to a very different type of mass-media campaign. The introduction of rationing, believed the Secretary of State Lord Rhondda, required public consent and he demanded that a comprehensive media programme should accompany its introduction.[20] At one level this simply meant the employment of Sydney Walton as a press agent, but it also entailed – among other initiatives – the release of nutritional statistics, the production of a twice-weekly journal and the release of recipe booklets.[21] The Ministry also created a short-lived advisory Consumer Council, which in theory ensured that Whitehall was kept in touch with the average citizen's experiences. The perceived 'fairness' of the Ministry of Food's scheme subsequently became a much-trumpeted success of the war and turned Lord Rhondda into a public figure of some esteem.[22] Tallents remembered:

> Not without deliberate skill, and yet without falsehood, he created in the public mind a portrait of himself as a benevolent man who has understood its [the public's] difficulties and has no personal ambitions to serve. He gave millions of his humbler citizens something of that sense of care and concern for the under-dog which Mr Roosevelt in a later day has given to the yet more numerous millions of the United States.[23]

Jose Harris has convincingly argued that William Beveridge's work at the Ministry of Food would influence his later approach to the administration of social insurance.[24] Less widely appreciated is how important Lord Rhondda's publicity work at the Ministry of Food was in establishing a particular style of government publicity. Paternalistic, but even-handed, Lord Rhondda and Sydney Walton had demonstrated that the construction of an information infrastructure could be as uncontroversial, urgent and necessary as the distribution of food. Invalided from battle, Tallents had been reunited with his mentor William Beveridge at the Ministry of Food in 1918 to organise the introduction of rationing, and he would later often make rather naive literal equivalences between the parcelling out of food (or other material commodities) and the rationing of information.[25] The Ministry of Food's work helped establish a belief that good publicity was an integral part of good administration.[26]

Over the coming decades the precedent provided by the Ministry of Food would continually prove useful to Civil Servants struggling to cope with a widening remit. Defence and security had been the key functions of the Victorian state, but by the early twentieth century the majority of Civil Servants were employed in the provision of social services.[27] Although the progress of this change was not linear during the interwar period, Civil Service norms were profoundly affected by the range and complexity of the social, economic and technological challenges faced by the nation in the aftermath of the First World War. One Civil Servant explained:

The first essential then is to build up public understanding and an appreciation of the services rendered to them [the public] and thus obtain their goodwill ... I believe more effective results would be obtained at no great cost by the addition of training for the staff in what might be termed 'public relations.'[28]

Historians have traditionally scorned what they characterise as the amateurism and inflexibility of the British Civil Service during the interwar period, but newly established journals such as *Public Administration* (created in 1923) illustrate how unfair these judgements can be.[29] In magazines and meetings Civil Servants vigorously debated how they could best fulfil their new obligations to the public.[30] Tallents's lengthiest article on the subject contended that public relations must lead 'the public to take the most economic advantages of the facilities which they have caused to be provided for themselves'.[31] His previous experience of administering labour exchanges had underlined his conviction that the Civil Service frequently failed to deal either efficiently or sensitively with the ordinary citizen. The belief that officials needed to be trained in skills variously termed 'correspondence', 'intelligence', 'personal relations', 'salesmanship' and, eventually, 'public relations' was widely shared.[32] Indeed, Tallents's standard defence of public relations, drawn partly from his frustrations with the tortuous practices of the Civil Service, was that it facilitated the flow of life-enhancing information. He wrote in *The Projection of England*:

It is commonly said that applications of science lag at least twenty years behind its discoveries. In the field of medicine alone, a host of simple facts, of the utmost importance to the daily life of whole peoples and long familiar to the worker in the laboratory, remain outside not merely the practice but the knowledge of the populations whom they might profit ... Yet England, with her great traditions in scientific research, her close contact with the thought and work of Europe is well fitted to convey that knowledge to the whole of her Colonial Empire and far beyond it. It is her plain duty to harness the new methods of international projection to the vital bridging of the gulf between scientific discovery and its application – a gulf which at present divides hundreds of millions of her fellow peoples from well-being and happiness.[33]

The newly created Ministry of Health appointed the first government press officer in 1918. Its distribution of leaflets detailing proper hygienic practice, for example, was the kind of apolitical, socially beneficial 'information' that legitimised the government's media capabilities. Public relations as practised by these Civil Service idealists was an odd hybrid of scientific promotion, advertising, political diplomacy, education and philanthropy. It has been argued that under the direction of Warren Fisher the Civil Service became imbued with a distinctive moral ethos and an analogous interwar faith that educated opinion (as distinct from elite opinion) could mediate between competing social and economic demands; this faith was central to the development of public relations in Britain.[34]

Public relations versus propaganda

While Civil Servants began to develop ideas about the necessity of public relations, state use of 'propaganda' during the War had been a controversial intervention that cast a grim shadow across the postwar period.[35] Not only did defeated German generals attribute the Allies' victory to their mastery of psychological warfare but postwar publications such as Arthur Ponsonby's *Falsehood in War-time: Propaganda Lies of the First World War* revealed how misinformation had been spread in order to incite hatred of Germany and win support for British intervention. Where Arthur Ponsonby led, Adolf Hitler followed, praising the efficiency of British wartime communications in *Mein Kampf* and excusing the Nazi regime's enthusiasm for propaganda by reference to previous British practice.[36]

The excitable tenor of intellectual discussions on the effectiveness of 'propaganda' is best exemplified by the work of the American sociologist Harold Lasswell. Laswell's was the most realised of a tranche of interwar studies that attempted to analyse the new disciplines' impact. Laswell quoted *The New York Times*:

> The public mind to the trained propagandist is a pool into which phrases and thoughts are dropped like acids, with a foreknowledge of the reactions that will take place, just as [a biologist] ... can make a thousand crustaceans stop swimming aimlessly about in the bowl and rush with one headlong impulse to the side the light comes from, merely by introducing into the water a little drop of a chemical.[37]

Over the course of the interwar period, the perceived malleability of the masses in tandem with the roll-out of powerful new media technologies would further test the faith of the intellectual and political elites in the average citizen. Tallents's early career encapsulates in microcosm the tension between democratisation and control. On the one hand, Tallents was part of a new bureaucratic intake tasked with improving the service that central government offered to the ordinary citizen. Serving at the Front, Tallents had noted, 'larger scale losses depend to a much greater extent even that I would have supposed, on good management'.[38] From this point of view Tallents's development of various public relations techniques represented a kind of managerialist idealism.[39] Less idealistically, Tallents would also become engaged with more nefarious propaganda activities. He succeeded Sydney Walton on the Supply and Transport Committee, an innocuous-sounding organisation that had been responsible for smearing trade-unionists in the aftermath of the War. 'The octopus created may', according to Keith Middlemass, 'not unfairly, be compared with the Nixon apparatus at the time of Watergate, without the denouement of exposure.'[40] Whatever the truth of Middlemass's accusation, it's clear that the rise of public relations and 'transparency' also generated a corollary governmental need for secrecy.[41] The mass mobilisation entailed by the First World War brought this tension in 'public relations' work to the surface. As Tallents rationalised it, a necessary function of governmental public relations was to 'justify public action based on considerations too technical, too complicated or sometimes necessarily too secret to be fully comprehended by the public'.[42]

In Britain, official attitudes to 'propaganda' were ultimately played out in the arena of high politics. As corruption, propaganda and press manipulation became synonymous in the public mind with Lloyd George's coalition government, Stanley Baldwin began to make political capital out of the issue. When Baldwin succeeded Bonar Law as Prime Minister in 1923 he did so as part of a Conservative drive to rescue the body politic from 'moral degeneracy' and restore the nation's 'constitutionalism'.[43] Rebuilding the Chinese walls between government and fourth estate was symbolically crucial to this. Lloyd George had ennobled the newspaper barons and ostentatiously courted their favour; in pointed opposition Stanley Baldwin forbade his ministers from publishing articles on contemporary issues.[44] Although this rule was relaxed in 1928 to enable ministers to write newspaper pieces to supplement speeches delivered to Parliament, this concession was not extended to other forms of media. For the greater part of the interwar period politicians' opportunities to broadcast were limited to apolitical discussions and items of a non-party-political nature.

Similarly, by adopting an outwardly emollient attitude to the BBC during the General Strike, Baldwin increased his popular standing, whilst Winston Churchill's maverick *British Gazette* newspaper appeared a throwback to the excesses of the Lloyd George era.[45] Baldwin's calm and unruffled, if rather sancti-monious, positioning against the media became a crucial part of his public image.[46] This was a development shrewdly observed by Tallents:

> Only a few weeks ago, Mr Baldwin, responding to a leader in *The Times* in which the subject of projection had been discussed, said that 'perhaps in some ways the Englishman is a man who never grew up, preserving till late life that intense reticence of masculine adolescence' ... I felt not a little discon-certed by his opinion. But on reflection I remembered that these somewhat discouraging words were spoken, not like poetry, to be overheard, but before an ample and international table of Press reporters, with Press photographers waiting outside the door, and with a microphone in front of him through which his modest statements were being relayed to all parts of the United Kingdom. I recognise in Mr Baldwin a master and not a critic of the art of projection, and I pressed on with renewed courage to press for national candour in place of national sheepishness.[47]

Taking their rhetorical marker from Baldwin, public relations professionals tended to self-depreciate, downplay and understate. This domestication of propaganda into public relations was hastened by the reform and modernisation of the Conservative Central Office undertaken by J. C. C. Davidson.[48] Davidson expanded his party's own media capabilities and in doing so temporarily freed what remained of the governmental wartime media machinery from sustained party-political pressure.[49] Although this freedom allowed Civil Servants to begin their experimental ad hoc development of the state's media capabilities, the price of this freedom was chronic underfunding, duplication of effort and political marginalisation.

The development of public relations in Britain

While high political crosswinds battered the reputation of 'propaganda', British public relations pioneers began to search for models of good practice. The work of Frank Pick at the Underground was to be particularly influential.

The appointment of Albert Stanley (later Lord Ashfield) as Managing Director of the Underground Electric Railways Company in 1907 had ushered in a period of mergers and massive expansion that would eventually result in the formation of the London Passenger Transport Board. Frank Pick, who was to be a crucial influence on Tallents, had been appointed to unify the disparate management structures, staff and timetables of the previously independent railway companies into a cohesive whole.[50] This radical change demanded new management techniques, as the business world of the interwar years was re-defined by mergers and the increasing separation of ownership from management.[51] After the General Strike the result was a management culture that sought to soothe conflicts between workers and capital.[52] Research organisations such as the Industrial Welfare Society, the National Institute of Industrial Psychology and Seebohm Rowntree's Management Research Group came to the fore. Frank Pick's career exemplified this trend. In an effort to instil pride, Pick issued staff with redesigned uniforms, enlarged training opportunities and encouraged 'democratic' interventions from the workforce.[53] These considerable administrative achievements were overlaid with an idiosyncratic imaginative vision.[54] The introduction of Edward Johnston's lettering, the Underground's 'bulls-eye' logo and Harry Beck's famous 'circuit' Tube map, as well as Charles Holden's modernist stations, saw the Underground become a leading patron of contemporary art and design.[55] Moreover, Pick saw his aesthetically advanced commissions as a way of imaginatively unifying London as well as the Underground. He believed that high-quality commercial art could animistically uplift the populace. For Pick the London transport network was the nervous system of the metropolis and by disseminating high art through its well-ordered stations, tunnels and trains the city could be respiritualised.[56]

Transferred to the Empire Marketing Board (EMB), Tallents saw an imaginative correlation between Pick's co-ordination of the existing underground railway companies with Britain's relationship to its Empire. Disillusioned by the 'old' imperialism of war and economic exploitation, Pick was to become an enthusiastic collaborator with the EMB. He shared his contacts with Tallents as they began to utilise modern art to propagate the co-operative ideal of Commonwealth.[57] He counselled Tallents:

> I count the imagination the chief bond of Empire. Self-interest will serve, but is unsafe. Self-interest plus imagination would be an alloy of immense tensile strength. At some moment our publicity must make a venture of an imaginative kind if we are to be a success. I believe the Roman Empire was largely an imaginative creature. It lived on tangible experience of common material progress in civic buildings. There was little else.[58]

Pick further brought Tallents into the orbit of the Design and Industries Association (DIA), an organisation which Tallents would serve as President in 1955. Like public relations, Britain's design industry depended heavily on government patronage.[59] Jacquie L'Etang has already identified the curious overlap between the nascent design and public relations industries (Sam Black, for instance, was the brother of the designer Misha Black) but it is worth briefly exploring how Tallents's attitudes to design were further reflected by his developing philosophy of public relations.[60]

Broadly put, the DIA's mission was to reconnect the concerns of the arts with the aims of industry. Indeed, the organisation's books, lectures and lobbying would eventually be successful in prompting government action.[61] However, the DIA's patriotic enthusiasm for 'modern' production was considerably more complex than this summary implies.[62] Whereas the Department of Overseas Trade's uncomplicated aim was to stimulate trade, the DIA pursued idealistic, almost socialistic aims.[63] It was as interested in the 'human factor' of reconstruction as in the commercial one.[64] The DIA was essentially pursuing a new design of society.[65] It aimed to transform everything from the layout of conurbations to the design of cakes, from the operation of dustcarts to the building of churches.[66] Just as the DIA expressed ideals of a self-appointed 'design' elite intent on aesthetically reshaping society, a cadre of communications specialists determined to 'educate' public opinion were responsible for defining early public relations practice.[67]

Frank Pick and Tallents were unique in that their work combined the economic and organisational elements of corporatism with a cultural equivalent. Considered abstractly, some of their theories of design and public relations might appear more proto-fascist than paternalistic.[68] The reality, however, was a kind of low-church small-scale philanthropy.[69] Pick bemoaned the fact that so many Londoners faced 'a life sentence of hard labour for the crime of being poor', while Tallents was fond of drawing a comparison between his duties as a public relations officer with the relief work carried out by the Order of St John.[70] Despite the DIA's fondness for Masonic symbolism (its logo was a cross inside a triangle inside a circle) its industrial backers pledged to follow a Ruskinian mission to become 'guides, counsellors, and rulers – wielding powers of subtle but gigantic beneficence'.[71] Artful design and public information were, in both Pick's and Tallents's estimation, the elegant pursuit of a socially worthy goal.

While Pick represented the acceptable face of public relations activism, British pioneers publicly set themselves against 'American' practices. Superficially, the self-conscious 'Britishness' of early public relations practitioners merely meant adopting a cautious tone. Tallents repeatedly wrote of his disapproval of 'personal boosting'. Sir William Crawford prided himself on belonging to the 'school which believes in the effectiveness of understatement'.[72] A. P. Ryan argued that, while he did not believe that the British 'were less self-satisfied than their neighbours', it had to be recognised that for the average citizen, 'blowing one's own trumpet, like wearing one's heart on one's sleeve or being kissed by one's general on parade is a cheap exhibition not to be stooped to'.[73] Gervas Huxley wrote, 'more rubbers are lost by overplaying rather than underplaying a public relations hand, exhibitionism is no more attractive in an institution than in a person'.[74] John Grierson believed that part of the reason 'documentary' took root in Britain was the national tendency to understatement.[75]

The 'Britishness' of public relations reflected the pioneers' roots in the public sector. Having worked alongside businessmen and trade-unionists during the War, they contrasted the lack of transparency and 'shoddy carelessness' of the private sector with the openness of government.[76] Public relations in Britain was pioneered by large organisations that had long-term strategic goals, which Tallents and his followers felt encouraged them to develop a wider perspective than was usual in American practice.[77] Rather than being beholden to prominent entrepreneurs they were tightly bound into the national fabric. Hence public relations practice in America was dismissed as the 'creation of synthetic incidents'.[78] American practice was criticised from both the conservative flank of British opinion (it was accused of being a homogenising product of 'the American semi-socialist ideal') and the progressive one.[79] During the interwar period British practitioners distanced themselves from their American counterparts as surely as Baldwin positioned himself against Lloyd George.

According to Peter Mandler, the interwar period saw a sharp rise in the stock of the British national character.[80] Many of the debates among British practitioners were certainly superficial and self-congratulatory. The belief that the British were an inherently stable, democracy-loving, common-sense people led many British public relations practitioners to conceptualise their work as uniquely sophisticated. 'It is possible on the one hand to over-estimate the value of propaganda', wrote Tallents, 'but there are areas of Europe where people are susceptible to this kind of influence'.[81]

Nevertheless, as well as cultural and institutional differences, British and American practitioners were separated by a contrasting set of values. Tallents characterised public relations – like all public administration – as an ongoing infinite process of social development.[82] His aim was to create new democratic forums rather than serve short-term business objectives.[83] By contrast, Edward Bernays saw public relations as 'the conscious and intelligent manipulation of the organized habits and opinions of the masses [and] the executive arm of the invisible government'.[84] Thus while Tallents's reading list included Edward Bernays and Ivy Lee, he also drew on Cecil Stuart Emden's *The People and the Constitution* and F. R. Leavis and Denys Thompson's *Culture and Enlightenment*.[85]

The schism between public relations practice in Britain and America was not just between Bernays's partisan media advocacy and the administrative neutrality espoused by Tallents but between a results-orientated approach and a process-orientated one. Before the Second World War, the term 'public relations' in Britain was used interchangeably with projection, publicity, advertising, intelligence, salesmanship and propaganda. Discreetly expanding in number at the innovative edges of the Civil Service, British public relations practitioners were less interested in codifying the profession than in ensuring it was conducted in the proper manner. As one official argued:

> We English are an illogical nation, we have built up our civilisation without any attempt to reduce our constitutions to writing, and we have, as our critics tell us, an incurable habit

of trusting to muddling through all the problems that confront us ... The spirit is more than the letter or the written word and the problem of the [public relations] specialist in public administration depends far more upon cultivating in all ranks of the service a spirit of goodwill and mutual co-operation than any precise delimitation of functions.[86]

This mentality partially explains why 'public relations' was not properly defined in Britain until after the Second World War when the creation of the second Ministry of Information necessitated tighter bureaucratic order.

There is a sizeable and worthwhile scholarly literature that has attempted to define the exact nature of public relations.[87] However, the Civil Servants, scientists and business administrators who developed public relations defined their interventions by doing it. Mariel Grant noted that British public relations practice achieved a stylistic and organisational consistency despite the lack of any centrally directing organisation.[88] This consistency is explained by the informal network of interesting and innovative thinkers bound together by Tallents. Indeed public relations in interwar Britain was best described as a social movement. Its emergence as a profession cannot be understood without recourse to a small group of individuals and the economic, political and cultural interests which tied them together.

Stephen Tallents and the development of public relations

Tallents had already reached middle-age when he began his media innovations (discussed in more detail in the next chapter) at the Empire Marketing Board (1926–1933). Tallents recalled his appointment as Secretary of the Board:

Suddenly, about halfway through my life, I was called upon to assist the distribution of ideas ... I'd had no previous experience in that line and looked hopefully round for advice. But I quickly discovered that scarcely any British government department had ever thought about publicity and that most departments despised and were inclined to resent it. I had to go outside for counsel – into the business and advertising worlds; and to quite an extent my colleagues and I had to improvise methods of our own.[89]

The Colonial Secretary, Leo Amery, had appointed Tallents to the

EMB because of Tallents's success in hazardous ambassadorial roles in Poland, the Baltic States and Ireland.[90] It was in Estonia that Tallents first recalled encountering 'foreign propaganda', noting that the German army generals' aggression was tempered by the state of their troops 'who had been affected by Bolshevist and Spartacist propaganda'.[91] Having taken responsibility for drawing the disputed Estonian/Latvian border through the border town of Walk and served briefly as Governor of Riga, Tallents developed diplomatic expertise that would inform the rise of public relations in Britain.[92] Collaborative international efforts at securing peace after the First World War, along with the experience of working in Ireland during partition, were imprinted on the strategic and research-driven conception of public relations developed by Tallents and his collaborators.[93]

Tallents's ambassadorial experience was supplemented by his scientism. Working with ophthalmic experts such as Edward Nettleship at the marine department, Tallents deduced that the Board of Trade's colour-blindness test was unreliable.[94] He further came to his superiors' notice for his work on the prevention of beri beri amongst Malay sailors. After taking advice from a visiting lecturer at the London School of Tropical Medicine, Tallents prepared a series of recommendations that eventually eliminated the ailment amongst Lascar seamen. This experience caused him to reflect 'that there must be something wrong with the machinery for circulating important and tested scientific research if so vital a discovery depended upon a purely chance encounter by one of its most junior clerks at a week-end country house party'.[95] From that moment onwards Tallents showed a marked deference to scientific expertise. Dismissing the role of Private Secretary as 'a parasitic type of employment', he blended an idiosyncratic career in the Civil Service with personal ventures – such as the breeding of guinea pigs for scientific experiments – that reflected his personal enthusiasms.[96] The restlessness that further compelled him to work on novel bureaucratic ventures such as the creation of the labour exchange and the introduction of rationing at the Ministry of Food also compelled him continually to seek out new sources of expertise. American public relations pioneers such as Bernays posited themselves as experts; British practitioners more often saw themselves as bringing hitherto squandered resources into the public arena. The Head of the Civil Service wrote of Tallents, 'he combines literary gifts, a varied experience of administration & *the art* of managing men in authority'.[97]

Retrospectively, Tallents's scientific interests, willingness to experiment and experience in mediating diplomatic conflicts can be seen to have informed the early practice of public relations in Britain. However, the network of personnel relations that underpinned the professional practice of these amateur media professionals was even more important. A period Tallents spent at Toynbee Hall appears to have been particularly formative. Not only would figures such as Clement Attlee, Leo Amery, J. J. Mallon, William Beveridge and Hubert Llewellyn Smith prove crucial in furthering Tallents's career, but there is also the sense that Tallents's conception of public relations, with its documentary films, thoughtful consumer exhibitions and artistic school pamphlets, could be construed as an enacted criticism of the staid exhibitions of model gardens, schools and houses organised at the East End mission. Toynbee Hall had been established with the Arnoldian brief of 'bringing into one harmonious and truly humanising life, the whole body of English society'; the pioneers of public relations similarly attempted to put new technologies to the reforming service of national unity and international harmony.[98] Accordingly, there is a substantial overlap between Tallents's cabal of early public relations experts and the kind of bleeding-heart establishment figures later demonised by the Thatcherite historian Correlli Barnett.[99] Towards the end of his career, Sam Black would reflect that 'the essential difference between public relations and marketing is not in the techniques employed, since they are somewhat similar, but in the ideology'.[100] Public relations in Britain began with Tallents's attempt to systemise the innovations of contemporaries who had begun to creatively rethink the manner and method of public administration.

Notes

1 J. Habermas, *The Structural Transformation of the Public Sphere: An Inquiry into a Category of Bourgeois Society* (Cambridge, 1989), influenced by The Frankfurt School is a classic statement of the neo-Marxist 'false consciousness' interpretation of public relations. A recent and more rooted criticism of the British profession (with particular reference to structural changes in PR since the 'Big Bang') is A. Davies, *Public Relations Democracy: Public Relations Politics and the Mass Media in Britain* (Manchester & New York, 2002).

2 Just to be clear, the aim is not to provide British PR history with

its own 'Great Man' story. If anything, it is a method of piecing together fragmented sources inspired by *1599*, James Shapiro's 'partial biography' of William Shakespeare. See J. Shapiro, *1599: A Year in the Life of William Shakespeare* (London, 2005).

3 Previous historical works by Mariel Grant and Philip Taylor have outlined this, although their focus has been on public relations as privately discussed by officials and politicians rather than how it was practised. See Mariel Grant, *Propaganda and the Role of the State in Inter-war Britain* (Oxford, 1994), and P. M. Taylor, *The Projection of Britain: British Overseas Publicity and Propaganda 1919–1939* (Cambridge, 1981).

4 A. Marwick, 'Middle Opinion in the Thirties: Planning, Progress and Political "Agreement"', *The English Historical Review*, Vol. LXXIX, No. CCCXI, 1964, p. 285.

5 H. Hoock, *Empires of the Imagination: Politics, War and the Arts in the British World, 1750–1850* (London, 2010). This development was also noted with characteristic astuteness by Dan LeMahieu. D. L. LeMahieu, *A Culture for Democracy: Mass Communication and the Cultivated Mind in Britain between the Wars* (Oxford, 1988), p. 140.

6 An honourable academic exception is the work of Jacquie L'Etang. See J. L'Etang, *Public Relations in Britain: A History of Professional Practice* (London, 2004). There is a large scholarly literature that attempts to analyse *how* public relations works: J. L'Etang, *Public Relations: Concepts, Practice and Critique* (Los Angeles & London, 2008), S. Harrison, *Public Relations: An Introduction* (London, 1995) and R. Tench and L. Yeomans (eds) *Exploring Public Relations* (Harlow & New York, 2006).

7 The year 1960 marked a boom in public relations publications. Alongside Black were books by Herbert Lloyd, Frank Jefkins, Pat Bowman and Nigel Ellis. See H. Lloyd, *Teach Yourself Public Relations* (London, 1963), F. Jefkins, *Public Relations in World Marketing* (London, 1966), and P. Bowman and N. Ellis (eds) *The Handbook of Public Relations* (London, 1963).

8 This is an interpretation that Black might have borrowed from an early edition of *Effective Public Relations*. See S. Cutlip and S. Center, *Effective Public Relations* (New York, 1952).

9 Contemporary American scholars have recently begun to challenge the 'Great Man' version of public relations history. See, for example, K. Gower, 'US Corporate Public Relations in

the Progressive Era', *Journal of Communications Management*, Vol. 12, No. 4, 2008, pp. 305–318.

10 Jacquie L'Etang advised me that Black derived much of his 'history' from secondary sources such as the *IPR Journal*. One likely source is Fife-Clark's early history. See T. Fife-Clark, 'The Administrator and the PRO', *Public Relations*, Vol. 9, No. 2, 1957, pp. 7–17; L'Etang, *Public Relations*, pp. 4–5.

11 S. Black, *Practical Public Relations* (London, 1962), p. 229.

12 Indeed, Britain's 'backwardness' in the fields of advertising and public relations is increasingly being challenged. See, for example, S. Schwartzkopf, 'Who Said "Americanization"? The Case of Twentieth-century Advertising and Mass Marketing from a British Perspective', in J. Gienow-Hecht (ed.) *Decentering America* (New York & Oxford, 2007).

13 S. Black, *Public Relations* (London, 1992), p. 9.

14 Black, *Public Relations* (London, 1992), p. 9.

15 Tallents's contemporaries were more open to the idea of there being a 'progressive' tradition of public relations. See J. A. R. Pimlott, *Public Relations and American Democracy* (New York & London, 1951).

16 See G. Wallas, *Human Nature in Politics* (London, 1908). Tallents frequently quoted Wallas. See S. Tallents, *Man and Boy* (London, 1943), p. 161.

17 See M. Abramovitz and V. Eliasberg, *The Growth of Public Employment in Great Britain* (Princeton, 1957).

18 Tallents, *Man and Boy* (London, 1943), p. 161.

19 See Grant, *Propaganda and the Role of the State*.

20 Lord Rhondda's innovative approach is detailed in W. Beveridge, 'The Ministry of Food under Lord Rhondda', in *DA Thomas: Viscount Rhondda as Remembered by His Daughter and Others* (London, 1921), pp. 218–248. See also W. Beveridge, *British Food Control* (London, 1928).

21 As well as serving an obvious propaganda purpose, the calculation and comparison of national diets excited much interest in Beveridge, for example. See NA, MAF60/11, 'Report by Departmental Committee on Rationing and Distribution as to Scale of Rations'.

22 Rhondda's premature death – precipitated by overwork – added a further martyr-like dimension to his personal legend that Lloyd George fully exploited. See J. Grigg, *Lloyd George: War Leader 1916–1918* (London, 2003).

23 *Man and Boy*, p. 248. Tallents further referred to the inspiring

example set by Sydney Walton and the Ministry of Food while President of the Institute of Public Relations. S. Tallents, 'Who Goes There?', *The Journal of the Institute of Public Relations*, Vol. 5, No. 2, January 1953.

24 See J. Harris, *William Beveridge: A Biography* (Oxford, 1997), pp. 228–240.

25 Working on the establishment of a national network of labour exchanges had recommended Tallents's to William Beveridge. Tallents's administrative ability impressed Beveridge and they struck up a close working and social relationship. They subsequently worked together again – notably at the Ministry of Munitions and at the Ministry of Food – and often walked together at the weekends as part of an occasional group that included James Bone, Julian Huxley, Humbert Wolfe and the Webbs.

26 It perhaps also goes some way to explaining the sly competence of Beveridge's future promotion of his famed report into the co-ordination of social services.

27 This analysis owes much to Grant's *Propaganda and the Role of the State*.

28 H. Whitehead, 'Salesmanship in the Public Service', *Public Administration*, Vol. XI, No. 3, July 1933, p. 275.

29 'It recruited its new young blood', Peter Hennessy wrote of the interwar Civil Service, 'and kept it until well stale'. P. Hennessy, *Whitehall* (London, 1989; 2001), p. 86. See also C. Barnett, *The Collapse of British Power* (London, 1972).

30 Created by free-thinking Civil Servants such as G. H. Stuart-Bunning – a key figure in establishing Civil Service Whitleyism – *Public Administration* quickly became the forum favoured by officials of a progressive outlook. Tallents, Grierson and many other EMB and GPO publicity employees would frequently grace its pages. *Public Administration* tended to make the argument – betraying its Whitleyist roots – that the treatment the public suffered at the hands of lower- and mid-ranking officials mirrored the treatment that lower- and mid-ranking officials received at the hands of their superiors. The Civil Service communicated poorly with the public because, 'to put it bluntly', the seclusion of the senior Civil Servants from their humbler juniors 'made it possible for the whole organisation to go stale'. See for instance, A. P. Ryan, 'Intelligence and Public Relations', *Public Administration*, Vol. XIV, No. 1, January 1936, p. 64.

31 S. Tallents, 'Salesmanship in the Public Service: Scope and

Technique', *Public Administration*, Vol. XI, No. 3, July 1933, p. 262.

32 See the debate develop in, for example, H. Finer, 'Officials and the Public', *Public Administration*, Vol. IX, No. 1, January 1931, pp. 22–36, H. Whitehead, 'Salesmanship in the Public Service', *Public Administration*, Vol. XI, No. 3, July 1933, pp. 267–276, S. H. Wood, 'Intelligence and Public Service', *Public Administration*, Vol. XIV, No. 1, January 1936, pp. 41–48, and W. D. Sharp, 'Correspondence with the Public', *Public Administration*, Vol. XIV, No. 3, July 1936, pp. 41–48.

33 S. Tallents, *The Projection of England* (London, 1932), pp. 20–21.

34 See E. O'Halpin, *Head of the Civil Service: A Study of Sir Warren Fisher* (London, 1989) Also J. R. Greenaway, 'Warren Fisher and the Transformation of the British Treasury, 1919–1939', *Journal of British Studies*, Vol. 23, 1983, pp. 114–125.

35 During the War the appointment of *The Daily Express* owner Lord Beaverbrook as Minister of Information and *The Times* and *Daily Mail* proprietor Lord Northcliffe as director of propaganda had been questioned in the House of Commons.

36 A. Hitler, trans. R. Manheim, *Mein Kampf* (London, 1992), pp. 165–179.

37 *New York Tribune*, 12 July 1918, quoted in Harold Lasswell, *Propaganda Technique in the World War* (New York, 1927), p. 209.

38 LSE Archive, Beveridge papers, BEV2/B/14, 'Tallents to Beveridge', 19 February 1915.

39 'This sort of war', he wrote to Beveridge while recuperating after injury at the Front, 'should be run just like a scheme of unemployment insurance'. LSE Archive, Beveridge papers, 'BEV2/B/14, 'Tallents to Beveridge', 21 June 1915.

40 K. Middlemass, *Politics in Industrial Society: The Experience of Britain since 1911* (London, 1979), p. 352.

41 See D.Vincent, *The Culture of Secrecy, Britain 1832–1998* (Oxford, 1998).

42 S. Tallents, 'Salesmanship in the Public Service: Scope and Technique', *Public Administration*, Vol. XI, No. 3, July 1933, p. 262.

43 See P. Williamson, *Stanley Baldwin: Conservative Leadership and National Values* (Cambridge, 1999).

44 National Archive, CAB 24/166, 'Cabinet Ministers and the Press', Note by Lord Privy Seal, 24 April 1924.

45 On Baldwin's handling of the BBC during the General Strike, see A. Briggs, *The History of Broadcasting in the United Kingdom Volume 1: The Birth of Broadcasting* (Oxford & New York, 1995).

46 For more on the 'traditionalism' of Baldwin's modernity see D. Cannadine, *In Churchill's Shadow: Confronting the Past in Modern Britain* (Harmondsworth, 2001).

47 Institute of Commonwealth Studies, University of London, Tallents papers, File 34, S. Tallents, 'Projecting the Empire: Candour Must Replace Sheepishness: The Englishman's Habit of Adolescent Reticence', *Ceylon Observer*, 10 June 1932.

48 See J. C. C. Davidson, *Memoirs of a Conservative* (London, 1969).

49 The Conservatives were very quick to recognise the potential of film, for example. See T. J. Hollins, 'The Conservative Party and Film Propaganda between the Wars', *English Historical Review*, Vol. 96, No. 379, April 1981, pp. 359–369.

50 See C. Barman, *The Man Who Built London Transport: A Biography of Frank Pick* (Newton Abbot, 1979).

51 By 1930 the top 100 British companies accounted for 26% of net manufacturing output as compared with 17% in 1919. See J. F. Wilson, *British Business History, 1720–1994* (Manchester, 1995), pp. 144–157.

52 See H. Perkin, *The Rise of Professional Society: England since 1880* (London & New York, 1989).

53 Pick's legal training introduced him to the work of the lawyer and anthropologist Henry Maine, whose thought appreciably feeds into Pick's conviction that the development and modernisation of London's transport system went hand-in-hand with the 'civilisation' of the population it served.

54 For a deeper exploration of Pick's enthusiasm see M. Saler, *The Avant-garde in Interwar England: Medieval Modernism and the London Underground* (New York & Oxford, 1999). See also W. Olins, *The Corporate Personality: An Inquiry into the Nature of Corporate Identity* (London, 1978) and A. Forty, *Objects of Desire: Design and Society 1750–1980* (London, 1986).

55 The Danish architect Steen Eiler Rasmussen described the Underground as one of the Seven Wonders of the World. S. E. Rasmussen, *London the Unique City* (London, 1935), pp. 339–364. Also see Nikolaus Pevsner, 'Patient Progress: the Life Work of Frank Pick', *The Architectural Review*, Vol. XCII, 1942, pp. 31–48.

56 See, for example, Frank Pick papers, London Transport Museum, B6 Box 4, 'An Edinburgh Address on Design and Industry', July 1917.

57 Pick supplemented the Board's commissions with Underground posters advertising EMB initiatives (including an athletics meeting between the British Empire and the United States) and attractions such as the Imperial Institute ('The Empire under one roof').

58 Tallents papers, 'Empire Experiment', File 26, 'The Start'.

59 The explosion of national and international trade fairs and exhibitions in the interwar period tied designers to the state and encouraged the Ministry of Information to employ pre-eminent talents such as Milner Gray and Misha Black during the Second World War.

60 See J. L'Etang, *Public Relations in Britain: A History of Professional Practice* (London, 2004), pp. 80–83.

61 The Council for Art and Industry (chaired by Pick and also served by Crawford) was established out of the Gorell Report of 1932, and paved the way for the post-Second World War Labour government's Council of Industrial Design (run by Clem Leslie, a protégé of Tallents) which was created to bolster the nation's export drive. During the Second World War, Tallents would attempt to use the BBC Overseas Service to enhance the reputation of British design. He explained: 'It was impressive on the borders of Russia fifteen years ago, to find how thoroughly the best English prints and English tableware of the late eighteenth century had by their quality found their way into the remote country houses of the Baltic. Today good design is the one passport into foreign markets that tariffs can not refuse.' S. Tallents, 'Introduction', *TREND: Design of Everyday Things*, Vol. 1, No. 1, Spring 1936, p. 2.

62 The DIA had been inaugurated in 1915 at an 'Exhibition of German and Austrian articles typifying design' at Goldsmiths Hall. Against the backdrop of the First World War and associated anxieties of national decline, the DIA argued that the German technological innovations made evident by the conflict were a result of that nation's success in unifying art and industry into the new discipline of design. It credited the Art and Crafts tradition of William Morris as responsible for German innovations, recognising that by embracing the machine age that Morris had rejected, the British movement's German disciples had paradoxically managed to keep its principles alive. The

aim of the DIA was to return Britain to pre-eminence. This interpretation of design history was canonised a decade later by Pevsner. See N. Pevsner, *Pioneers of Modern Design: From William Morris to Walter Gropius* (London, 1936).

63 Some younger members of the DIA (such as Pick's protégé Bassett-Lowke) were associated with the Fabians. Herbert Read described Pick as being 'almost the peculiar kind of Socialist I was'.

64 It has been argued that the DIA's version of modernity was already outdated, as the introduction of new plastics, for example, meant that form could be freed from function. For a further critique of DIA theory and practice see S. Hayward, '"Good design is largely a matter of common sense": Questioning the Meaning and Ownership of a Twentieth Century Orthodoxy,' *Journal of Design History*, Vol. 11, No. 3, 1998, pp. 217–234.

65 Pick argued that art and learning ought to be an expression of common existence ('Art galleries', he believed, 'are alive to the same degree as tinned salmon') and that the atomising pressures of the modern world had separated them from their proper function. Frank Pick papers, PB10, F. Pick, 'Art in Modern Life', *The Nineteenth Century and After*, Vol. XCI, No. 540, February 1922, pp. 256–264.

66 Pick and Tallents shared interests in such developments as the maturing town-planning movement, for example. Both aspired to a future where housing was built strategically, to mitigate the unsanitary conditions of industry and to enable all citizens to have access to the recreations of the countryside. Tallents would later work for the MTCP, while Pick was a Garden City enthusiast.

67 There is an echo of Coleridge's call for the establishment of a 'Clerisy' to safeguard culture here. See R. Williams, *Culture and Society 1780–1950* (London, 1958), pp. 63–68.

68 Although, ironically, the DIA has often been dismissed by modernist art historians for its timidity. Fiona MacCarthy wrote, 'Pleasant and straightforward, civilised and sensible, a reasonably idealistic, gentlemanly clique … Tolerant and gentle, unpretentious and careful, in friendly and predictable agreement with Frank Pick that national design should be: "modest and not too grandiose in scale … not too logical in form … a reasonable compromise between beauty and utility, neither overstressing beauty till it degenerates into ornament, nor overstressing utility until it becomes bare and hard."' F. MacCarthy, *All Things*

Bright and Beautiful: Design in Britain 1830 to Today (London, 1972), p. 110.

69 Pick's final work is strident in its argument that Britain has failed the average citizen. 'The pedagogues have held sway for far too long, they are ensconced in the Board of Education. Education is much more than extending the years at school ... The poverty of leaders that makes any reconstruction of government a mere game of musical chairs must be remedied by encouraging and unfolding talent wherever they may be.' F. Pick, *Paths to Peace: Two Essays in Aims and Methods* (London, 1941), p. 66.

70 Frank Pick papers, PB8, 'Man – A Forgotten Factor in Reconstruction', 1918. In *The Projection of England*, Tallents compares the EMB's publicity practitioners to the Order's 'secluded guilds'. See Tallents, *The Projection of England*, p. 23. Other connections between Tallents and the Order are legion. In 1949 Tallents would complain bitterly that the BBC was ignoring the Order's 850th anniversary. Indeed, before turning the property over to the National Trust in 1943, Tallents and his family actually lived at (and maintained the chapel of) St John's Jerusalem, Sutton-at-Hone, the Order's headquarters between its suppression by Henry VIII and its official revival in 1831.

71 J. Ruskin, *The Two Paths: Being Lectures on Art and Its Application to Decoration and Manufacturing Delivered in 1858/9* (Orpington, 1887), pp. 131–132.

72 BBC Archive, Caversham, P382, Box 2, Propaganda General Policy, W. Crawford, 'Letters to the Editor', *The Sunday Times*, 16 February 1941.

73 A. P. Ryan, 'Intelligence and Public Relations', *Public Administration*, Vol. XIV, No. 1, January 1936, p. 59.

74 Tallents papers, File 34, G. Huxley, 'PR – A Talk Given to the Empire Tea Bureau in 1947'.

75 Grierson said, 'Documentary cinema was an essentially British development. Its characteristic was this idea of social use, and there, I believe, is the only reason why our British documentary persisted when other aesthetic or aestheticky movements in the same direction were either fitful or failed ... If it came to develop in England there were three good reasons for it. It permitted the national talent for emotional understatement to operate in a medium not given to understatement. It allowed an adventure in arts to assume the respectability of a public service. The third reason was the Empire Marketing Board and a man called Tallents.' Grierson archive, G3/14/5, personal notes, 1935–39.

76 'Civil Servants, who found themselves between 1914 and 1920 working side by side in wartime departments with the elite of the business world', remembered Tallents, 'came away with no sense of inferiority but with the conviction that they were involved in a sweated trade and often with attractive offers to abandon it'. *Man and Boy*, p. 165 and p. 177.

77 Although it is acknowledged that the information programmes of American railroads and utilities predated the innovations of Lee and Bernays. See A. Raucher, *Public Relations and Business, 1900–1929* (Baltimore, 1968).

78 Huxley gleefully remembered that Harry Reichenbach had hired an actor to check into a hotel under the name T. R. Zan with a pet lion in tow, while for the *Virgin of Stamboul*, 'he got hold of eight Turks and had them go round all the New York hotels, saying they were looking for a missing virgin called Sari. The rare spectacle of eight Turks in their national costume (aided perhaps by the rarity of virgins in New York in the early twenties) produced front page news stories.' Tallents papers, File 34, G. Huxley, 'PR – A Talk Given to the Empire Tea Bureau in 1947'.

79 Interestingly, American practice would be criticised later in the postwar period for serving the interests of monopoly capitalism. See M. N. Olasky, *Corporate Public Relations: A New Historical Perspective* (Hillsdale, 1987).

80 Britain's avoidance of totalitarianism apparently led to an 'orgy of anatomizing, congratulating and self-congratulating upon the English national character.' P. Mandler, *The English National Character: The History of an Idea from Edmund Burke to Tony Blair* (New Haven and London, 2006), p. 151.

81 BBC Archive, P574, 'Telling the Foreigner', *The Nottingham Guardian*, 13 October 1937.

82 After Lord Summerhayes, 'The danger of public business is that it never ends. A man may kill himself at it.' Tallents, *Man and Boy*, p. 163.

83 R. T. Lang, 'Empire Advertising', *Advertising World*, Vol. XLIX, No. 4, February 1926, p. 484. Indeed, despite the fame of individuals such as Lee and Bernays, the most influential (perhaps only influential) American public relations practice on Britain was that of Theodore Newton Vail's American Telephone and Telegraph Company (AT&T). AT&T's unique position as a privately owned public utility forced it to take the kind of conciliatory, long-term strategic approach that was

to become dominant in Britain. There is a fuller discussion of AT&T's influence on Tallents's work at the GPO in Chapter 4.

84 E. Bernays, *Propaganda* (New York, 2005), p. 48. However, it is often overlooked that Bernays's coarse attention-grabbing rhetoric conceals a relatively sophisticated argument. Much of *Propaganda* (originally published in 1928) deals – in a fashion not wholly removed from Tallents – with the necessity of publicising the arts and scientific developments. The biggest difference is between Tallents's patriotism and Bernays's cynicism.

85 These examples come from an unpublished list held by Tallents's surviving family. 'Notes from Tallents private papers', 22 July 2006. After the War, Tallents's understanding of public relations was shaped, at least in parts, by the equally esoteric Frances Donaldson's *Four Years Harvest* and T. S. Eliot's introduction to *The Dark Side of the Moon*. See Tallents papers, File 34.

86 F. Floud, 'The Sphere of the Specialist', *Public Administration*, Vol. 1, No. 2, 1923, p. 122.

87 See, for example, M. Pieczka, and J. L'Etang, 'Public Relations and the Question of Professionalism' in R. L. Heath (ed.) *Handbook of Public Relations* (London, 2001), pp. 223–237.

88 Grant, *Propaganda and the Role of the State*, p. 9.

89 Stephen Tallents, 'What I Believe', *BBC Radio*, 2 September 1956.

90 Tallents wrote intelligence reports on diplomatic developments in Estonia. See, for example, Churchill College, University of Cambridge, Winston Churchill Papers, CHAR 16/14, 'Tallents to Churchill', 13 December 1919.

91 Tallents, *Man and Boy*, p. 281.

92 Tallents's border was reinstated when Estonia and Latvia gained independence from the USSR in 1991, though Walk is now known as Valga and Valka respectively.

93 It is interesting to speculate whether Tallents, who served as Secretary to the Last Lieutenant of Ireland and worked in Northern Ireland after partition, had any connection with the British propagandist Basil Clarke. See M. Walsh, *The News from Ireland: Foreign Correspondents and the Irish Revolution* (London & New York, 2008), and B. P. Murphy, *The Origins and Organisation of British Propaganda in Ireland 1920* (Aubane, 2006).

94 This was actually a serious admission of failure for the Board of Trade, and resulted in its losing in an expensive and high-profile legal appeal. See J. Bailkin, 'Color Problems: Work, Pathology

and Perception in Modern Britain', *International Labor and Working Class History*, No. 68, Fall 2005, pp. 93–111.

95 Tallents, *Man and Boy*, p. 172.

96 Tallents, *Man and Boy*, p. 178.

97 LSE Archive, Beveridge papers, Beveridge/5/36, 'Fisher to Beveridge', 24 March 1926.

98 Qtd in S. Meacham, *Toynbee Hall and Social Reform 1880–1914: The Search for Community* (New Haven and London, 1987), p. 10.

99 Interestingly, Barnett began his professional career as a press officer to the gas industry. See C. Barnett, *The Audit of War: The Illusion and Reality of Britain as a Great Nation* (London, 1986).

100 S. Black, *Public Relations* (London, 1992), p. 11.

2

Beginnings:
The Empire Marketing Board,
1926–1933

'No one can successfully manage over a long period of time even the smallest estate without a definite plan', wrote Tallents at the inception of the Empire Marketing Board, 'yet at present we are making no real attempt even to frame, still less execute, any plan for the organised development of the Empire's economic resources'.[1] The Board had been created by Stanley Baldwin to promote Empire goods, but the delicacies of imperial politics and a lingering suspicion of state propaganda prevented the Board from articulating an aggressively 'imperialist' vision.[2] Instead, over the course of its existence the Board's idealism gradually shifted from Leo Amery's 'Constructive Imperialism' to Malcolm MacDonald's broader enthusiasm for the Commonwealth. Under Tallents's management the Board became a haven for a brand of liberal technocrat.[3] These bureaucrats were convinced both that the sun was most assuredly setting on the Empire and that international economic, technical and scientific interdependence was accelerating.[4] The inadvertent consequence of the EMB's attempt to encourage the pooling of scientific and commercial knowledge was to blend advertising, diplomacy and market research into the new discipline of public relations. At the EMB Tallents created a public relations infrastructure that he was to spend the rest of his career building upon.

The EMB and Empire shopping spectaculars

Empire Shopping Weeks were characteristic of the EMB's early promotional approach. Patriotic shopping weeks had been a feature of the First World War and there is a degree of continuity between the EMB's promotions and wartime appeals for public goodwill. The wartime popularity of 'Soldiers' Christmas Pudding' perhaps created a residual cultural memory that explains the EMB's later efforts to promote the 'King's Empire Christmas Pudding'. In 1928, for example, the EMB invited press photographers to capture Leo Amery's wife cutting a seven-foot-high pudding baked at the Olympia Cookery Exhibition. The EMB built upon this stunt by releasing posters, recipes and a film, *One Family*, which attempted to popularise the same theme.[5] Although the EMB's shopping weeks did not initiate the practice of patriotic shopping events, the Board's events did coincide with an upturn in the fortunes of Empire goods. While the 'Empire Cookery' section of the Ideal Homes show catalogue of 1927 chided visitors for holding the 'silly prejudice' that buying from the Empire meant making 'some sort of patriotic sacrifice', by the end of the interwar period the Empire was producing 37% of Britain's imports.[6]

At first glance the Empire Marketing Board's shopping weeks appear to vindicate the received wisdom of imperial historians such as Stephen Constantine. For Constantine, the EMB's sophisticated posters, films and shopping events illustrated how old-fashioned political ideas of Empire could be popularly redeployed in a flashy modernistic idiom.[7] By contrast, my argument is that the Board was unable (and ultimately unwilling) to repackage old ideas of Empire. Indeed, the fate of the EMB's Empire Shopping Weeks provides an instructive example of why the Board struggled to assert any kind of directive influence. It also helps demonstrate, at a remove, why Tallents would in future stress that public relations needed to be understood as a series of overlapping co-operative processes rather than the simple propagation of a message.

Empire Shopping Weeks 'failed' because large retailers had only a superficial interest in Empire. Over the course of the interwar period macroeconomic factors pushed down the price of goods and thus increased the popularity of Empire Shopping Weeks among price-cutting stores. Thus the EMB's ethical initiatives ('Remember the Empire, Filled with Your Cousins') were apt to be elbowed aside in a business environment which focused on attracting shoppers with opulent and outrageous publicity stunts.[8] London's taste-making retailers organised personal appearances by celebrities such as the film actress Anna May Wong, the record-breaking racing driver Colonel Seagraves, Arsenal's all-conquering footballers, a question-answering robot and a Himalayan bear.[9]

Retailers were interested in spectacle rather than imperialist ideology or the theory and practice of international co-operation. Selfridge's was primarily interested in the sensory appeal that Canadian hosiery and Indian bedspreads could provide, and space taken up in Harrods' by Empire Food Stuffs one week would be filled by Swiss yodellers selling Gruyère the next.

Harrods' major exhibition of Empire foodstuffs – held in October 1929 – highlighted the irrelevance of the EMB's ethos to the organisation of Empire Shopping Weeks. Among the highlights of Harrods' successful display were meat and fish pastes 'made under modern hygienic conditions', free samples of Empire cigarettes and Australian champagne. On the face of it, this initiative demonstrated the wisdom of offering Sir Woodman Burbidge a seat on the EMB Publicity Committee. However, as Gervas Huxley recalled of Burbidge: 'His remarks were always very much to the point, though it seemed that the sole criterion by which he judged the importance of any subject was whether it was of interest to Harrods.'[10] Huxley's observation is borne out by Harrods' October event. In Harrods' exhibition there is absolutely no mention of the organisational debt that it owed to the Empire Marketing Board.[11] Indeed, Burbidge later boasted to *The Daily Express*, 'in our [Harrods'] exhibition of empire foods we have hit on a new idea'.[12]

Despite the success of EMB-sponsored consumer events such as the Belfast Empire Week, the Edinburgh Imperial Exhibition, the Liverpool Commerce and Industry Exhibition, the Cardiff Empire Exhibition and the Norwich Grocers Exhibition, the public were equally ignorant of the Board's imperial mission. Although the EMB participated in seventy regional Empire exhibitions during the interwar period, shoppers struggled to differentiate the produce of their 'cousins' in the Empire from anything appealingly exotic. The Malayan delegation at the North East Exhibition complained, 'on no occasion was a single child able to answer this preliminary question – "where is Malaya?"' Regional shopping events saw representatives from the Women's Institute decry the EMB's failure to stock Chinese tea and Californian grapefruit.[13] One EMB official admitted that 'most of the visitors were merely sightseers', attracted by the novelty of lychees, mangoes and curry cooking demonstrations. Evidence that the EMB's shopping events either consciously or accidentally reformulated imperial consciousness amongst the wider population is scarce. Several months after the North East Exhibition 481 local grocers were

questioned about the effects of the event on sales and more than
half – 291 – registered no increase of interest in Empire goods. The
public enjoyed the EMB's events primarily as spectacle.[14]

The EMB's lack of standing with retailers and consumers
also points to practical failings. Tallents was fond of reciting
an anecdote about a presumably fictitious businessman who,
on the grounds of propriety, wanted to change the slogan of his
company's dog food from 'Dogs like 'em' to 'No more appetising
or nutritious fare was ever offered to the canine tribe'.[15] He might
have been describing the EMB's early efforts at shop displays. The
artistic pedigree of the EMB's posters has long been recognised
but the stern display of these images is less commented upon.[16]
The modern posters commissioned by the EMB were exhibited
in multi-panelled wooden frames that resemble museum display
casings. Or, as one MP put it, 'they look like something from
the *Encyclopaedia Britannica*'.[17] The flaws that hampered the
EMB's posters similarly affected its shop furniture. Even Edward
McKnight Kauffer's range of displays (which included a striking
blackboard emblazoned with the words, 'to-day's pick of the
Empire basket') were not exempt from criticism. Buried amongst
lengthy text and statistics, too much of the EMB's store furniture
was, as one businessman had it, designed for 'careful students of
goods' rather than the 'footsore and mind-weary, whose eyes can
only take in things that are shown with dramatic force'.[18] In EMB
shop windows reproductions of arresting posters by the Nash
brothers are lost amongst poorly presented stacks of Empire food
and the sharp modernist images jar with handwritten signage such
as, 'There is not an article of food produced within the Empire
that is inferior to Foreign Produce'. Compared with competing
patriotic slogans of the age like Shredded Wheat's 'Britons Make It
– It Makes Britons', the EMB's shop displays were not impressive.[19]

EMB information in the era of 'scientific shopping'

As the bulk of the Board's work revolved around the administration of agricultural grants it is not surprising that the EMB
lacked the skills and resources to direct and initiate aggressive
media campaigns. However, the Board's administrative responsibility did lead it to begin developing a series of mechanisms for
disseminating research throughout the Empire. Over time the
EMB was to build up a fund of knowledge that enabled it to excel
in less contested sections of the media.

The EMB had first commissioned a series of pamphlets detailing the main products and trade routes of the twenty-four 'main' countries that constituted the Empire to assist the teaching of economic geography in the school classroom. However, business firms and financial houses began to contact the Board for copies, and Tallents was 'flattered and surprised by the lengthy reviews they [the school booklets] secured in the financial press'.[20] Systemising information about trading conditions soon became a particular strength of the EMB.[21] Tallents explained:

> The producers of many different commodities came to us with enquiries about future trends of supply and demand. The only assembled material, on which answers to these enquiries could be based, was to be found in reports prepared by the Department of Agriculture at Washington – written, naturally, from an American point-of-view – and occasionally work done by the International Institute of Agriculture at Rome. It was clear that surveys of the world position of different products, with some attempts to estimate future trends in their production, would be valuable not only to individual producers but to those responsible for forming the agricultural policies of many Empire governments.[22]

In contrast to working on promotions with high-street stores, organising and informing the activities of producers, wholesalers and distributors was an area where the Board's commercial disinterestedness was a strength rather than a weakness. Indeed, the EMB tapped into a growing demand for commercial information as the belief grew in official circles that 'the highways of British business are choked with the uneconomic litter of bygone traditions'.[23]

The impetus for much of the Empire Marketing Board's work – and for Tallents's theories of publicity – was related to the growing vogue for 'scientific', 'rationalised' business.[24] Though it is questionable how widespread this trend was in practice, the topic of 'rationalisation' dominated the business periodicals of the age. Like public relations, 'rationalisation' was never concisely defined. As with the relationship between British and American public relations practice, British 'rationalisation' bore some comparison to US Taylorist practices even as it positioned itself in critical opposition with it. 'Rationalisation' exhorted mergers and organisational efficiency along with the strategic use of the modern media to create, secure and broaden markets. It was accordingly favoured by business, banking and trade unions and coincided with (if it did not directly inspire) the establishment of quasi-corporatist organisations such as Imperial Airways, the British Broadcasting Company (BBC) and Imperial Chemical Industries (ICI).

Innovations at the Board of Trade were also important prompts to EMB action.[25] By 1922 the Board of Trade had the largest ministerial team in Whitehall as government looked for new ways of stimulating economic activity.[26] Home to free-trade sceptics such as Philip Cunliffe-Lister, the Board of Trade sought to tie together the interests of owners, producers and consumers.[27] The Companies Act of 1929 was passed to encourage better governance. Producers were encouraged to invest in new technologies by legislation such as the Merchandise Marks Act, the Weights and Measures (Amendment) Act and the Preservation of Foodstuffs Act, legislation that both compelled farmers to adopt minimum standards and attempted to reduce price competition.[28] These initiatives were accompanied by the growth of various 'scientific shopping' movements.[29] The ideological raison d'être of these movements was best articulated by Lawrence Neal's *Retailing and the Public*, which argued that economically inefficient 'overlap' must be eliminated by greater co-operation.[30] The EMB's manage-rialist approach was cemented by the appointment of Sidney Webb as Amery's successor at the Colonial Office.[31] As Tallents acknowledged in the Board's first annual report:

> Fundamentally the stimulation of Empire marketing must depend on the private enterprise of producers and traders ... The best service that can be done to the Empire producer is to place freely at his disposal the resources of science and economic investigation – to see that he is made aware of sowing and planting, of tending and harvesting; to show him how his produce should be graded and packed to ensure that it is transported safely and without deterioration: to suggest lastly how its presentation, in the shop window or on the counter, may be fitted to win the housewife's critical eye.[32]

This holistic approach to business practice also reflected a growing interest in the Co-operative Society, which was considered both a model of rational business and a beacon of ethical practice.[33] With five million members, its own factories and a massive procurement budget, the Co-op offered a voluntarist economic model of how the Empire could develop.

As the assistance given to Empire Shopping Weeks was gradually eclipsed by the provision of advice and information to business customers and scientific researchers, the Empire Marketing Board began to focus on correcting the lack of knowledge that British producers had of Empire trading conditions and customs. After all, the public could not be criticised for their failure to shop 'rationally' if the nation's producers, distributors and retailers were unable to organise themselves in such a way as to facilitate 'rational' decisions. 'Ignorance of our own Empire is not complimentary to us', warned a businessman: 'whilst in Mombassa I received two letters: one from one of the leading British advertising agencies, addressed to, "Mombassa, South Africa" and another from a British research association addressed to "Mombassa, India"'.[34]

Having identified a real business need for reliable information, Tallents increasingly used EMB funds to sponsor it. In the long term, the EMB hoped that funding a new post in Imperial Economic Relations at the London School of Economics would lead to a more comprehensive appreciation of the difficulties faced by Empire producers.[35] In the short term, Tallents appointed E. M. H. Lloyd to compile weekly reports on trading conditions. These 'weekly intelligence reports' were collated from Dominion Trade Commissioners, shipping companies, 'UK representatives' at foreign ports and customs officers. The guides were a success, eventually covering everything from the likely orange yield of Brazil to the amount of mutton held in cold storage in the USA, via the estimated arrival time of consignments of South African 'soft fruits' into Britain. Subscriptions were sold to businesses at home, around the Empire and (at a premium) to 'foreign' organisations.

Further analysis of the EMB reports prompted a range of targeted interventions. It was discovered that New Zealand wool was undervalued and the EMB brokered a research collaboration between the New Zealand government and the British Leather Manufacturers Research Organisation to investigate why. Equally, Palestinian grapes, Cypriot hazelnuts and Zanzibaran pineapples were revealed to be commercially viable products (though experiments in growing rice in Harwich and Southend were less successful) and economic resources were subsequently encouraged in their direction.

These modest successes were prompted by a broader engagement with the worldwide crisis in agriculture. The Board's effort to stimulate agricultural production in the Empire had led Lloyd to contrast imperial initiatives with the work of both the US President Herbert Hoover's Federal Farm Board and Soviet collective agriculture.[36] Lloyd emphasised the importance of managerialist intervention – tariffs, quotas and marketing schemes were identified as methods by which Empire producers could escape both the discipline of the market and control by the state.[37] In EMB eyes, technical advances and the growth in productive capacity made the reordering of the world economy inevitable.[38] Collective security would be achieved, they believed, by the organisation of self-governing cartels within a wider economic union. 'Joint tasks of Empire' was the phrase adopted as the Board began to change the terms in which Empire was discussed. Dominions were addressed as partners, while the Board's responsibilities to colonies were couched in a language that borrowed heavily from contemporary issues. 'It is particularly important to build up a balanced economy', the Board briefed *The Times*, 'and not let a Colony, with its superstructure of adminis-trative and social services, become dependent on a single crop whose price is subject to all sorts of extraneous influences'.[39] EMB projects such as sponsoring the introduction of new crops into Mauritius resonated against the discredited 'dustbowl' economics of the Depression era.[40]

As well as educating producers, manufacturers, retailers and government throughout the Empire, the EMB sought to engage with consumer groups. The aim was to build a wider understanding of existing economic, political and social needs that could be used to 'improve' decision-making at every level of society. Perhaps the Board's most significant achievement was that it developed a civic outlook that left space for individual initiative and volunteer activity (as well as national difference) while attempting to co-ordinate state power and the private sector strategically.[41] The EMB recognised that science and commerce might be ever more globalised but government was not. At its most elevated the Board can be conceived as an intellectual clearing house for a range of liberal experimentation, idealising transnational associations over world government.[42] The free flow of advice and education, in Tallents's view, would ensure international harmony and social solidarity.[43]

The influence of Sir William Crawford and the growth of governmental advertising

After the First World War, the daunting tasks of social and economic reconstruction loomed large and the imperative to recapture overseas markets lost during the conflict brought government into the commercial arena.[44] In 1917, the Department of Overseas Trade (DOT) had been created by fusing – and then expanding – the commercial intelligence branches of the Board of Trade and the Foreign Office.[45] The new department was given responsibility for the organisation and promotion of exhibitions such as the British Trade Industries Fair. Its early efforts attracted criticism from leading businessmen who were quick to contrast the exceptional aesthetic and organisational standards set by the Leipzig fair in Germany with the DOT's pedestrian efforts. In comparison with the Italian National Institute for Export, the DOT's promotional plans appeared both strategically reticent and under-funded.[46] This lackadaisical attitude seemed indicative of a wider malaise. British business, it was hypothesised, was recovering slowly because the nation's mastery of the 'new' techniques of sales and marketing lagged behind its long-established manufacturing standards. Hence, by 1927, the importance of advertising had been imprinted on mainstream thinking. Prime Minister Stanley Baldwin wrote:

> We must all work together with a view to the restoration of trade and national prosperity. The problem before us is to produce goods that are required and to let the world know we have them. On the production side I have no fears ... On the selling side we must modernise our methods and make use of the great developments which have taken place recently in the art of advertising.[47]

Advertising was identified as a potential panacea for the nation's economic woes. This analysis assumed the garb of anecdotal wisdom after it was discovered that all the typewriters in the Royal household were manufactured by foreign firms. The ensuing media storm – ended when a contrite King agreed to replace them with British machines – revealed that no British typewriter manufacturers believed it necessary to advertise.[48] As elements of the British establishment begin to question the continued utility of laissez-faire, 'advertising in the national interest' emerged as a major topic of discussion.[49]

Prior to his introduction to Tallents, the successful advertising tycoon Sir William Crawford had been lobbying the political establishment for over a decade. To counter negative perceptions of advertising, Crawford nosily aligned himself with the most progressive and popular social campaigns of the era. The Imperial Economic Conference programme of 1923 contains – in the kind of idiom that the EMB would make its own – a typical entreaty:

> That old communities may be richened; that new communities may leap to life; that the deserts of the world be made gardens – this is our work. Trade is the main spring of progress. Advertising is the herald of trade. The pens in our hands are the makers of the new earth.[50]

Throughout the 1930s Crawford appropriated the many public platforms he occupied to propagate the beneficial effects of advertising on national wealth and to stress its humanitarian function.[51] His work for the Milk Marketing Board, for example, was supplemented by scientific research which Crawford used to highlight the nutritional deprivations of working-class Britain.[52] Crawford's work for the EMB was an important part of this broader personal campaign. Before the EMB, advertising was popularly associated with gross exaggeration and misstatement, while its practitioners were commonly portrayed as debased and vulgar. 'Jokes about advertising', sighed an *Advertising World* editorial, 'are becoming as universal as jokes about Jews, Scotsmen and mothers-in-law'.[53]

The EMB's media activity sat at the convergence between an older practice of commercial showmanship and a newer vogue for business information. Under Crawford's tutelage, EMB publicity became an umbrella for a range of independent advertising initiatives that synthesised these trends. The Buy British campaign of 1931 provided the outstanding example of Crawford's influence. Given less than two months to co-ordinate a campaign to spend Britain out of the slump, Crawford's contacts ensured that some fifty thousand newspaper column inches, one million poster sites and a Great Western Railway train were donated to the EMB's cause.[54] A venture organised along the lines of a bring-and-buy sale had been given the polish of a modernistic advertising campaign. Co-operative selling campaigns were to become fundamental to the EMB's modus operandi as well as Tallents's conception of national projection.

As well as being endorsed by Crawford, co-operative selling

movements appealed to government because it allowed the sharing of costs and responsibility.[55] Indeed, the DOT came to recommend co-operative selling abroad as the most effective way of promoting British industry. Arthur Michael Samuel counselled British business:

> A combined effort, perhaps undertaken by a trade association on behalf of the trade, will often be more effective than effort in small units ... It will be objected that a firm wishes to keep its own name before the public. But the battle is won if you can get the foreign buyer interested in a British supply of a particular kind of goods. Make the buyer aware that British firms can produce the goods he requires and keep him interested. He will soon discover the names of the firms to be approached.[56]

For the Empire Marketing Board co-operative selling had a tactical as well as a practical appeal. Although the EMB had its roots in Baldwin's promise to promote Empire fruits, tobacco and wines at the Imperial Economic Conference of 1923, the actual practice of promoting imperial produce was fraught with hazards. In an era where 'publicity' was invariably understood by the political establishment as buying newspaper advertisements, the House of Commons was uneasy about the prospect of spending a proposed £650,000 a year on publicity. As well as specific complaints that the government was underwriting goods made under poor conditions of labour, home producers complained that their taxes were being used to promote foreign goods.[57] The result was that the Board would spend on publicity no more than a quarter of its budget (which was itself much reduced) and it would later be the area where economies were first sought.[58]

This organisational pressure forced the EMB to become adept at embedding its initiatives in the work of partner organisations. It worked on national initiatives with bodies such as the Food Manufacturers' Federation, National Milk Publicity, the National Food Canning Association and the British Glasshouse Produce Marketing Association. These events covered everything from packing demonstrations to advising salesman how to draw the maximum profit from National Mark schemes, via the awarding of a trophy designed by Charles Holden for the best small trader of Empire goods.[59] These bespoke activities were well publicised regionally with apparently impressive results. An Empire butter drive in the North West, for example, saw the percentage of

shops stocking Empire butter in Lancashire rise from 43.3% to
73.5%.[60] Overall, Tallents estimated that the voluntary preferences
encouraged by the EMB were worth £15,000,000 a year.[61]

Imperial politics had prevented the Board from advertising
particular products leaving the EMB with little choice but to
become partners in more general commercial and governmental
activity. Without Crawford's experience in co-operative selling,
such a crippling limitation might have condemned the EMB's
campaigns to aimless irrelevance.[62]

Sam Black later bemoaned the blurring together of advertising
and public relations practice, arguing that the British failure to
delineate the twin professions had retarded their development.[63]
The lack of focus perhaps delayed the emergence of public
relations as a narrower discipline of management, but the cross-
fertilisation pragmatically engineered by Crawford and Tallents
had immediate political advantages. Tallents eased Crawford's
path into the establishment. Crawford's work for the EMB earned
him a knighthood (the KBE stood for 'Keep Buying Empire', joked
The Times.)[64] and later helped ensure that Crawford's agency kept
the BBC's account until 1975.[65] Crawford's standing was further
secured by his agency's work for the Ministry of Information
during the Second World War.[66] Conversely, Crawford's network
of business contacts made his patronage of the EMB economically decisive.[67] Indeed, Tallents would later attribute Crawford's
appointment to the GPO's Advisory Board in 1933 as responsible
for the upturn in advertising revenue generated by the Telephone
Directory. More personally, in 1935 Tallents received the highest
honour in the British advertising world, the Publicity Cup of
Britain. Crawford, it is worth stating, had founded the Publicity
Club that awarded it.

Nevertheless, beyond necessity and the politics of personnel
advancement, the 'ethical' mix of salesmanship and information
pioneered by Crawford and Tallents at the EMB had profound
implications. LeMahieu has convincingly suggested that over the
course of the interwar period Britain evolved a genuinely national
public culture that, however imperfectly, provided common
reference points. He cites the refusal of significant sections of
the cultural and intellectual elite to retreat when faced with the
radical challenges of new media as crucial to this process. The
intersection of business, government, scientific research and new
media innovations that Crawford and Tallents helped co-ordinate
into a national brand formed an integral constituent part of this

wider public culture. 'The new art of public relations formed part of a complicated mosaic, extending at least back to William Morris and the Arts and Craft Movement', argued LeMahieu, 'which sought to do for sight and sound what John Reith and the BBC hoped to accomplish in sound.'[68]

The Empire Marketing Board: ideals and politics

Self-consciously modelled on medieval guilds, the Board's research stations from Aberdeen to Tanganyika aimed to 'insulate, without driving into a monastic system' the independence of researchers.[69] This stress on preserving researchers' independence was to have interesting political consequences. The ostensible focus of the EMB-funded Plant Breeding Station at Aberystwyth, for example, was to return unproductive pasture throughout the Empire to agricultural use.[70] The Board's funds allowed George Stapledon's expertise (Stapledon was Director of the Plant Breeding Station) to be applied to newly established research facilities such as the Plant Breeding Centre at Palmerston North, New Zealand.

However, during his Board-funded visit to Australasia, Stapledon concluded that the Commonwealth could no longer be the farm of Great Britain, just as Great Britain could no longer be the workshop of the world.[71] Not only did Britain need rebalancing, but its relation with the Empire had to be transformed. Conceptually Stapledon's projects were typically EMB in as much as they were centrifugal rather than centripetal.[72] 'It would be an interesting freak for history to play', Stapledon wrote, 'if instead of a great Empire naturally declining, as is the wont of Empires, this Empire of ours simply changed its centre of gravity'.[73] Tallents's EMB was animated by a similar liberal faith that scientists and businessmen would be able to broker pan-imperial collaboration where governments failed. He believed that the mechanics of high politics had obscured a convergence of expertise and interests.

The EMB's vision could not have been more different from the jingoistic course propagated by Lord Beaverbrook and Lord Rothermere. After the Conservatives' election defeat of 1929, the two press barons used the issue of Empire Free Trade as the focus of their efforts to depose Stanley Baldwin.[74] When the first salvoes of the press barons' campaign were unsuccessful they bankrolled fifty candidates to stand against Conservative MPs on a 'United Empire Party' platform. The press barons used subscriptions from their (mostly Conservative) readers to put up anti-Baldwin 'Empire Free Trade' candidates at strategically selected by-elections. The press barons' 'Empire Crusade' was ruthlessly direct, attracting 170,000 members to the new political party in a fortnight. *The Daily Express* stopped printing the speeches of politicians who did not sign up to its campaign for imperial tariffs, *The Daily Mail*'s leaders attacked the personal life and family background of the Prime Minister Stanley Baldwin, and David Low was asked to direct his *Evening Standard* cartoons at the Conservative leadership.[75] So pervasive was Beaverbrook's campaign that according to his biographers he 'forgot his doctrine that the first duty of a newspaper was to tell the news of the day. Instead it became the duty of his newspapers to tell only the news of the Empire Crusade.'[76]

Although John Grierson described the Empire Marketing Board as 'the only organisation outside Russia that understood and had imagination enough to practise the principles of long-range propaganda', the immediate material results of the press barons' campaign lay in stark opposition to the EMB's record.[77] Despite the fact that 85% of the EMB's time was spent administering scientific grants, substantially more than 15% of the Board's funds was spent on publicity campaigns.[78] During the Board's seven years of existence £1,224,562 was invested in media work, a figure that does not compare too unfavourably with the £1,962,630 the EMB spent on scientific ventures.[79] The Board's lack of effectiveness vis-à-vis its original aims had already attracted criticism in the House of Commons ('charming and beautiful as no doubt many of them [the posters] are, I doubt whether the modern advertising genius ... would be proud of them');[80] the press barons' campaign further brought the EMB into disrepute.

Ridiculed by Lord Beaverbrook as 'dull, academic, without anything fresh', the EMB's publicity had placed emphasis on producing publicity with either educational content or utilitarian value.[81] It had commissioned a total of over ten million leaflets on topics such as *Why Should We Buy from the Empire?* and organised discursive public lectures on themes such as 'The British Empire and what it means to you'. The EMB's generous definition of educational work saw it provide the BBC with research for educational broadcasts, sell cookery books of *Empire Dinners* at *The Daily Mail*'s Ideal Homes Exhibition and display instructional films at Victoria railway station. This work was now curtailed by the press barons' aggressive brand of 'informative' leaflets.[82] In an effort to distance itself from the press barons' aggressive editorials, the EMB began to concentrate more on 'Buying British'. Ultimately, the press barons' campaign resulted in the disbandment of the EMB as Baldwin was forced to adopt imperial tariffs to repel the attack on his leadership.

As well as shifting its rhetoric, the press barons' campaign also highlighted the EMB's ideological awkwardness. While the barons argued that 'Empire Free Trade' would enable the UK to retain its economic and political primacy, the EMB Publicity Committee remained wary of stark economic determinism. As Frank Pick put it:

> I am always just a little suspicious of efficiency mongers. There is much to be said for all the waste you can afford. I admit just now that we cannot afford much but we must try. Out of waste comes originality and progress, art and science, all that's really good. America goes in for efficiency, and so it misses most of these good things.[83]

Projects such as the purchase, and shipping, of a tinning machine to the Cayman Islands demonstrated the unique position that the Board occupied. Modern business definitions of marketing emphasise the relentless effort to integrate research, production, advertising, selling and distribution in pursuit of a given market sector: the EMB believed that the 'logic' of the market could (and on occasion should) be ignored.[84] In this instance, it was unconvinced that the Cayman Islanders' plan to export turtle soup would prove popular, but believed it had a duty to assist their efforts regardless.

Moreover, while the Empire was absent from the press barons' campaign, the EMB was critical of the poor standards of living found throughout the Empire. It sponsored medical research projects in nineteen different Dominions and Colonies that revealed, for instance, that 80% of the Indian population was living with hookworm. Although it was self-serving, Tallents's retrospective claim that 'the biological needs of the Commonwealth seemed to the EMB more insistent and more important than the political problems which held the spotlights in public debate' has a truthful ring to it.[85] The EMB's activities were united by an authentically independent-minded and humanitarian streak. The Board's language was unmistakably moral:

> I read an eyewitness account of a thousand men with six-wheel lorries, camels and flame guns feverishly digging trenches in

the desert of Sinai on the lines of advance of a locust invasion. The insects bore into the trenches 'as a continuous greenish-yellow cascade', and every ten minutes the trenches, a mile in length, were swept with petrol flames. The picture gave sharp meaning to the prophet Joel's magical phrase – 'the years which the locust hath eaten.'[86]

It seems likely that the EMB's findings had an influence on the drafting of the Colonial Development Act of 1929.[87] This bill, sponsored by Leo Amery, was, in the words of his most sympathetic biographer, 'the first example of western economic assistance to the non-developed world ever to be enshrined in legislation'.[88]

However, the idea that the British state should fund new imperial educational projects, road-building ventures, hydro-electric plants and agricultural research programmes during a period of domestic hardship, and the rise of national independence movements, won few converts outside of Amery's close circle.[89] Even Empire enthusiasts realised that the vision of the Commonwealth being developed by the EMB was – at best – an ideal.[90] The EMB had been created to promote the Empire uncomplicatedly, but its freedom from political control and Civil Service norms saw it propagate an independent line that stressed the necessity of imperial development. As the EMB collated previously lacking knowledge of economic and social conditions across the Empire, Tallents's conviction that conditions in the Empire were 'backward' grew.[91] 'Human life and health', Tallents reflected, 'were being wasted on a gigantic scale'.[92]

The vulnerability of EMB schemes in the maelstrom of 'high politics' hinted at the extent to which Tallents's benevolent attempts to increase the amount of information in the public sphere left him a hostage to political fortune. His imaginative ventures at the EMB struggled to compete in the commercial mainstream and yet they were not unobtrusive or politically calculating enough to earn their keep in government. Additionally, while Tallents's enlightened administration failed to convince politicians decisively, it also attracted a degree of disapproval from intellectuals and radicals. Unaccountable to the electorate and free from commercial pressures, the Board was apt to appear a mechanism by which a bureaucratic elite could evade democratic control. By stressing the depoliticised 'rational' underpinnings of co-operative imperial development (such as shared languages, political customs, shipping and units of weight and measurement) the Board's vision could also be interpreted as a plan for smuggling continued British pre-eminence through the back door of common sense. Indeed, Tallents and his collaborators spoke of the Empire as a prototype of the world economic unit of the future in a way that appealed to high imperialists.[93] 'The Empire is not superimposed on nations', as Leo Amery had it, 'but, like the Kingdom of Heaven, something within each of them'.[94]

By the time Aldous Huxley began writing a series of critical articles on the EMB, he had already become established as an important cultural commentator. Suspicious of popular culture ('for the people, but not by the people') and the direction of applied science, Huxley believed that the work of the EMB plugged directly into the era's least edifying intellectual currents. 'In itself, Sir Stephen's project is excellent' wrote Huxley, before arguing that the EMB had created a precedent which would encourage political economists of the future 'to train up a race, not of perfect human beings, but of perfect mass producers and mass consumers'.[95] Huxley worried that intelligent discernment would be discouraged on the basis that it was economically 'inefficient', while the new promotional techniques pioneered by Tallents would eventually reduce the mass of the population to a somnambulant state. Or, as *The Daily Telegraph* more glibly reported, 'it has been estimated that 50 per cent of women's conversation is concerned with clothes and 25 per cent with films'.[96]

Aspects of the work of the Board (for which Huxley's cousin, Gervas, worked as a press officer) were simplified, literalised and exaggerated into *Brave New World* (1932). Retrospectively an element of *Brave New World* is apparent in the Empire Marketing Board's research programme. Huxley's dystopian novel has the Alphas of the London hatching centre administering the Epsilons of Mombasa, while Tallents hoped that funding pioneering research on animal glands would enable steers to mature 50% faster than normal and boost the lifetime production of milk by a cow from 200 gallons to 2,000 gallons.[97] He further claimed that the EMB's poultry research had reduced excessive embryonic mortality by funding studies that monitored the relationship between genetics, body weight, feed consumption, hatchability, egg production and egg weight.[98] There is even a link between 6LL3, aka Dolly the Sheep, and the Chair in Animal Genetics created by the EMB at Edinburgh University in 1927. Dolly the Sheep (1996–2003) was the first mammal to be cloned using the process of somatic cell nuclear transfer.

Without substantial political patronage, public popularity or easy intellectual appeal the EMB's 'far-sighted' approach was apt to be labelled incompetent, irrelevant or dreamily misguided by contemporary critics attuned to more immediate social, economic and political crises.[99] Tallents boasted that the EMB was 'happily free from the entanglements of statute or precedent or party', but this could seem like a euphemism for an absence of clear purpose.[100] 'The public in those days was not much interested in the Empire', recalled Tallents; 'home problems were many and urgent. Europe and its post war troubles loomed large and near. The Empire seemed in comparison remote, dim and dull.'[101]

Stephen Tallents and the development of public relations at the EMB

Inadvertently created by the Prime Minister Stanley Baldwin in lieu of Imperial tariffs, the initial political rationale responsible for establishing the EMB ('forty millions of people had to be induced to change their habits') did not provide Tallents with a practical idea of what the Board's day-to-day role was to be.[102] When the EMB was established, Amery handed Tallents the last two reports produced by the Imperial Economic Committee and then left Britain to tour the Empire.[103] Tallents recalled, 'I read most of the two reports; but, as I had little knowledge of the Empire and no acquaintance with publicity I did not suck much advantage from reading.'[104] Tallents's ignorance ensured that, while the EMB was the first governmental marketing organisation, it – quite incredibly – made no effort to define what marketing actually was. The modern understanding of marketing is that it is an organisational philosophy that was developed as an alternative to, and critique of, product-orientated businesses that 'sell what they produce rather than what the market wants'.[105] It is a philosophy that holds that businesses should increase efficiency by tailoring their output to particular target markets rather than chasing extra profits through over-production and aggressive selling. By publishing market information Tallents's EMB inadvertently produced some useful marketing tools, but this was not the focus of its work.

Instead Tallents addressed the problem of 'marketing' in a manner which reflected his Civil Service training: he consulted a range of 'experts' while dismissing the exclusive claims of any specialist. Intuition was afforded a particularly privileged position. When asked to explain the nature of his work at the

EMB, Tallents quoted Cromwell ('He goes furthest who knows not where he is going') and enigmatically explained, 'it may be that "another commonplace model to paint" was all that Raphael thought as he began the Sistine Madonna'.[106] Tallents may have spoken of the creation of 'the world economic unit of the future', but in articles and speeches he expressed a marked dislike of planned capitalism and 'the government of the expert'. He argued:

> The enormous advances made during the last century in mechanical science have led recent generations to force mechanical conceptions upon subjects to which they are at best only partly applicable ... In reality government is nearer to an art than a science, and it is well, if we would understand the quality of the supreme faculty of government, to stress the analogy of the arts.[107]

Accordingly, the EMB's cultural initiatives would allot imagination and personal discretion a privileged position. Unable to form lasting working relationships with either Rudyard Kipling (this is discussed in more detail in the next chapter) or Henry Tonks of the Slade School, Tallents eventually brokered a series of socially, politically and professionally acceptable compromises with William Crawford.[108]

Sir William Crawford was a perfect mentor for the EMB because he had been instrumental in driving the professionalisation of British advertising practice. He had written guidelines and statements of best practice and facilitated the creation of regulatory bodies such as the Audit Bureau of Circulation. During the course of his professional life Crawford would found 'the highly systemised modern agency' and consign the 'generalist clerk' of early advertising practice to history.[109] Yet, despite his self-proclaimed role as a moderniser, Crawford was also perfect for the EMB because his personality was grounded in the pre-scientific management age. He adopted market research but distrusted and frequently overruled his analysts' findings. Tallents remembered Crawford as a *homme excessif* fond of provocative bon mots such as 'I know nothing about advertising', 'you are not proposing to spend enough money' and 'I warn you that you won't like what I am now going to show you!' He was, said Tallents, a brash showman who 'possessed remarkable, in some degree mysterious, qualities'.[110] For Tallents, these methodological idiosyncrasies were evidence of the ability to broker creative compromises. 'Scent is all important to the huntsman,' as Tallents had it, 'and it is not less important to the governor, whose assets are in his sub-conscious as well as conscious qualities'.[111]

These semi-official collaborations were indicative of the social glue that held together many of the EMB's initiatives. Indeed, the suspiciously personal nature of many of the EMB's projects suggest that Tallents was keen to bring 'the Empire Alive' to himself as much as to the general public.[112] After noting that Empire wines seemed to induce 'unwonted abstemiousness on the part of guests invited to enjoy them', Tallents set up a sub-committee to deal with the 'problem'.[113] The Board was eventually persuaded to fund an enquiry that saw Sir David Chadwick chair a 'preliminary investigation into the problems of the maturation on wine', the East Malling research station produce a memorandum on vitacultural research, and Paul Rotha complete a short promotional film.[114]

Such indulgences do not detract from the EMB's strategic importance as an association of like-minded professionals. At the Ministry of Food Tallents had consulted with a consumer council, businessmen and local officials. The Board's contribution to imperial scientific, commercial and cultural life was constituted from a similarly broad base of sources. At the EMB, Tallents continued to stress the need for larger organisational and professional co-operation to be built upon good personal relations. Tallents idealised the example of the Kew botanists who had unobtrusively (as he believed) enabled the further development of Indian forestry and played a key role in the expansion of the Malayan rubber industry. The Imperial Bureau of Entomology established at Farnham was thus revered for its informality as well as its expertise. Tallents recalled:

> An English Country House can seldom have been turned to such strange purposes – its drawing room filled with insect cages, and guinea pigs pasturing on its tennis court. Its fame brought enquiries from strange quarters. The story went that an old lady drove up one day to its gates in a car and her chauffer led up the drive on a string a fine specimen of one of the large Hawk caterpillars.[115]

Such an approach was consistent with Tallents's argument that the best way to emulate the achievements of Commonwealth scientists such as Dr Frederick Grant Banting and Sir Chandrasekhara Venkata Raman was to create and encourage pan-imperial social and professional networks.[116] Hence, the EMB built libraries, sponsored forums for the sharing of scientific expertise, distributed statistical and market information, and paid for science students to be seconded to Uganda, Nigeria, the Gold Coast, Sudan, Ceylon, Barbados, Antigua and British Guiana. 'The EMB had among its advisors not only the best scientists of the day but manufacturers and merchants, artists and designers and filmmakers, fruiterers and grocers and bakers', boasted Tallents, 'and by them the outlook and the sympathies of the EMB were enlarged beyond the normal confines of a government department'.[117]

Business historians have claimed that the 'marketing paradigm' of applied research and market information came to prominence in the USA during the 1950s, a shift made possible by postwar affluence and the increasing importance of consumer choice. The competitive advantage American firms held over British businesses in the first half of the twentieth century, it is argued, can partly be explained by the closer integration of producers, distributors and retailers that existed in the USA.[118] If it is true that marketing philosophies did not exert a significant influence in Britain until the 1960s the EMB's approach was entirely rational.[119] By a political quirk, the Empire Marketing Board had been created in advance of the wider commercial and organisational ability to comprehend or systemise its services.[120] Established before the founding of corporate research departments, and before the integration of those research departments into the production process had reached a critical mass, the EMB could do little more than fund university lectureships and amateur scientific collaborations. Equally, the disproportionate attention that the EMB's publicity paid to small, regional businesses was inevitable in an age where even the largest multiple, Debenhams, was recognised as a phenomenon of the new manufacturing towns of the Midlands and South East.[121]

The interwar period saw free traders and protectionists clash over a series of political, social and economic battlegrounds. The EMB represented a practical attempt to negotiate constructive 'democratic' compromises between these two ideological poles of opinion. Tallents's work at the EMB led him to conclude that future peace and prosperity could be secured only by the establishment of a far-reaching system of communications able to co-ordinate together pockets of innovative practice. His, still barely articulated, notion of public relations was born of the EMB's effort to consolidate the era's most progressive elements of organisational practice.

Notes

1 Institute of Commonwealth Studies, Tallents papers, File 1, S. Tallents, 'The Problem of Economic Development', 3 September 1926.

2 More generally, interwar distaste for nationalism and militarism resulted in enthusiasm for the Empire being couched in internationalist terms. See B. Porter, *The Absent-minded Imperialists: Empire, Society and Culture in Britain* (Oxford, 2004).

3 Many EMB collaborators would become involved in the establishment of United Nations organisations. See M. Mazower, *No Enchanted Palace: The End of Empire and the Ideological Origins of the United Nations* (Princeton, New Jersey, 2009), and F. Trentmann, 'After the Nation State: Citizenship, Empire and Global Coordination in the New Internationalism, 1914–1930', in K. Grant, P. Levine and F. Trentmann (eds) *Beyond Sovereignty: Britain, Empire and Transnationalism c.1880–1950* (Basingstoke, 2007), pp. 34–53.

4 'Greece and Rome and Macedon, Spain and Portugal, France and Holland all in their time threw long shadows; and when England by her sea power won her place in the sun, her shadow was the longest of them all. To-day that morning of the world is past, and the sun, standing higher in the heavens, is nearer to filling its traditional role of shining alike on the just and the unjust. The shadows of the peoples are more equal and the long shadows have grown less.' S. Tallents, *The Projection of England*, p. 11.

5 *One Family* cast British aristocrats as human representatives of the Colonies and Dominions, a conceit which mimicked the wartime practice of inviting society women to serve behind the tills of famous department stores on special charity days.

6 Up from 30% at the beginning of the period. W. Teignmouth Shore, 'The Empire and the Housekeeper', in *Daily Mail Ideal Home Exhibition Catalogue* (London, 1927), p. 219.

7 'It was never very convincing', as Stephen Constantine put it, 'to argue that imperial enthusiasms entered their long goodnight during or shortly after the First World War'. S. Constantine, '"Bringing the Empire Alive": The Empire Marketing Board and Imperial Propaganda, 1926–1933', in J. M. MacKenzie (ed.) *Imperialism and Popular Culture* (Manchester, 1986), p. 192.

8 Outlined, for example, in V. Ward, 'Marketing Convenience Foods between the Wars', in G. Jones and R. Tedlow (eds)

Adding Value: Brands, and Marketing in Food and Drink (London, 1994), pp. 259–288.

9 The Lord Chancellor's Committee's endorsement of Resale Price Maintenance in 1930 resulted in department stores using ever more extravagant shopping spectacles to attract custom. See W. Lancaster, *The Department Store: A Social History* (Leicester, 1995).

10 Gervas Huxley, *Both Hands* (London, 1970), p. 128.

11 For more on Harrods' interwar displays see T. Dale, *Harrods: The Store, the Legend* (London, 1981), and T. Dale, *Harrods: A Palace in Knightsbridge* (London, 1995).

12 HAT, Selfridge archive, press cuttings, 'Housewives Insist on the Empire Loaf', *The Daily Express*, 13 May 1930.

13 'If the Empire Marketing Board campaign continues at this rate', jibed the *Aberdeen Press and Journal*, 'Britain will have no alternative but to annex the world'. Tallents papers, File 31, 'Marketing Notes for Amendments', 'Penalty of Empire', *Aberdeen Press and Journal*, 26 May 1932.

14 It is possible that they were perceived as heirs to Victorian spectaculars such as the Japanese exhibition at Knightsbridge that famously inspired *The Mikado*. See J. Flanders, *Consuming Passions: Leisure and Pleasure in Victorian Britain* (London, 2006).

15 See S. Tallents, 'Advertising and Public Relations To-day', *The Journal of the Royal Society of Arts*, Vol. CIV, No. 4967, 23 December 1955, pp. 94–107.

16 See S. Constantine (ed.) *Buy and Build: The Advertising Posters of the EMB* (London, 1986).

17 This observation was made by George Pilcher, the Unionist MP for Penryn and Falmouth and future secretary to the Royal Empire Society. He continued, 'Another advertisement was one recommending people to drink more milk. I noticed some small capitals printed on the picture, and I crossed the road to read them. They consisted of a Latin motto. I was educated at a classical university but I could not translate those Latin words.' See *Hansard*, 12 November 1928, vol. 222, cols 626–629.

18 Frederick Marquis of Lewis of Liverpool qtd in Lancaster, *The Department Store*, p. 103.

19 The general trend for patriotic advertising is noted in R. Graves and A. Hodge, *The Long Week-end: A Social History of Great Britain 1918–1939* (London, 1941).

20 Tallents papers, File 30, 'Marketing'.

21 An EMB colleague later assessed the significance of their work, 'Our market research derived from the Consumer's Research studies that were already being carried out by advertising and consumer research firms before the EMB came into existence. [However] the world surveys which we produced dealing comprehensively with a particular kind of product, eg. oranges, cocoa, wool were models of their kind and it is perhaps here that later influence of the EMB might be traced. Both the International Institute of Agriculture and the US Department of Agriculture issued subsequently surveys of the same kind, and in my opinion the EMB studies had no small influence on those two much larger organisations.' Tallents papers, File 31, 'Marketing: Notes for Amendments', 'Letter from Dykes', 17 May 1944.

22 Tallents papers, File 30, 'Marketing'.

23 Viscount Leverhulme, 'The Real Remedy for Trade Depression', *Advertising World*, Vol. XLIX, No. 1, October 1925, p. 30. Or as Lawrence Neal put it, 'The new generation ... With minds trained in accurate thought, they have looked on the world of business and found it sadly confusing – and from the confusion they have seen economic waste springing up'. L. E. Neal, *Retailing and the Public* (London, 1932), p. vii.

24 This was a vogue created by the Harvard academic A. W. Shaw. See A. W. Shaw, *Simplification* (Chicago & New York, 1927).

25 The establishment of a marketing board was first proposed by the Board of Trade although ironically both the Board of Trade and the Department of Overseas Trade were hostile to the EMB as it threatened to challenge their control over expanding policy areas.

26 The President of the Board of Trade was supplemented by a Parliamentary Secretary, as well as a junior minister responsible for heading the Department of Overseas Trade (which also answered to the Foreign Office) and a further Secretary in charge of the Mines Department. See J. A. Cross, *Lord Swinton* (Oxford, 1982), pp. 43–91.

27 The Board of Trade was run by the practical minded economist, and future Chief Economic Adviser, Sir Sydney Chapman. As a university lecturer in Manchester Chapman had appointed successful businessmen as part-time lecturers and emphasised the importance of developing applied solutions. Chapman correspondingly invited businessmen such as Gordon Selfridge, Sir William Lever, the Underground's Lord Ashfield and Cunard's Alfred Allen Booth on to advisory committees.

28 Cunliffe-Lister's department attempted to insulate the British economy from the shocks of an unfavourable macro-economic climate through proposing (usually unsuccessfully) safeguarding legislation. The quota-setting Cinematograph Act of 1927 provided Cunliffe-Lister with a rare victory over the free traders.

29 Selfridge, for example, marked the new era of 'scientific shopping' by distributing 'enthusiasm pills' to staff and dropping 'inspiring mottoes' in their pay packets. Harrods' newly marbled 'hygienic' food store was a similar cause of media celebration and the subject of much cheap imitation. See G. Crossick and S. Jaumain, 'The World of the Department Store: Distribution, Culture and Social Change', in G. Crossick and S. Jaumain (eds) *Cathedrals of Consumption: The European Department Store, 1850–1939* (Aldershot, 1999), pp. 1–45.

30 Alongside Neal, H. E. Morgan was another important business 'moderniser'. Morgan's much-discussed 1914 work, *The Dignity of Business*, argued that British business needed to attract more intellectual talent to survive the dawning era of internationalism. He also believed, *à la The Projection of England*, that more needed to be done to protect and promote 'goodwill' towards Britain and its products. See H. E. Morgan, *The Dignity of Business. Thoughts & Theories on Business & Training for Business* (London, 1914), pp. 21–32, and the four volumes of H. E. Morgan and E. H. Butcher, *The Retailers' Compendium: A Complete and Practical Guide to Successful Shopkeeping Enterprise* (London, 1924).

31 Webb assured Amery 'the new Government would be no less interested in the work of the Empire Marketing Board that their predecessors in office had been'. NA, CO760/12, 'Minutes of 37th Meeting of the Board', 17 July 1929.

32 NA, CO323/982/3, 'The Empire Marketing Board – A Year's Progress'.

33 The Co-op had a representative on the EMB Publicity Committee. The interwar years are often identified as marking a high point in the fortunes of the Co-op, with success of flagship stores (like Army & Navy) allowing it to expand into regional city centres. Like the EMB, the Co-op also employed interesting architects such as L. G. Elkins. For a celebratory outline see J. Birchall, *Co-op: The People's Business* (Manchester, 1994), pp. 108–135.

34 E. Morison, 'Why Britain Is Losing Its Dominion Markets', *Advertising World*, Vol. 50, No. 7, October 1926, p. 538. Or alternatively: 'I have before me as I write an excellent

advertisement produced by a firm of high standing, offering ladies bicycles in a country where no woman is allowed to be in the streets uncovered, to say nothing of being allowed on a bicycle.' R. T. Lang, 'Empire Advertising', *Advertising World*, Vol. XLIX, No. 4, February 1926, p. 482.

35 The post was filled by John Coatman, previously Professor of Political Science at Delhi University. Coatman's reputation had been established by a series of reports he had drafted on the economic potential of India. Though his post was scrapped after the dissolution of the Board, Coatman remained a liberal enthusiast for Empire. In books such as *Magna Britannia* (1936) and *The British Family of Nations* (1950) he argued that the Commonwealth offered the first practicable model of international co-operation. Coatman followed Tallents to the BBC in 1937.

36 For more on Lloyd's meeting with (and assessment of) Hoover see LSE Archive, Lloyd papers, 4/7, 'Lloyd to Tallents', 6 August 1930.

37 See V. S. Patvardhan, *British Agricultural Marketing: A Study in Government Policy* (London, 1965).

38 It is arguable that Walter Elliot developed his quasi-corporatist vision of agriculture at the EMB. Elliot's Conservative planning would heavily influence Macmillan's National Industry Council. See A. F. Cooper, *British Agricultural Policy, 1912–1936. A Study in Conservative Politics* (Manchester and New York, 1989), pp. 160–183, and 'Mr Walter Elliot', *The Times*, 19 January 1958, p. 14.

39 Institute of Commonwealth Studies, Tallents papers, File 12, 'Joint Tasks of Empire', *The Times*, 5 July 1933.

40 Indeed, revisionist post-colonial theorists, such as Joe Powell, suggest that EMB attempts to develop and manage the imperial environment represented a (limited) Commonwealth equivalent of Roosevelt's New Deal. J. M. Powell, 'The Empire Meets the New Deal', *Geographical Research: Journal of the Institute of Australian Geographers*, Vol. 43, No. 4, December 2005, pp. 337–360.

41 James Vernon has argued that official efforts to manage hunger necessitated the development of a hybrid political form that existed somewhere between liberalism and social democracy. It is significant that John Boyd Orr's Rowett Institute, the focus of much of Vernon's work, was funded by the EMB. See J. Vernon, *Hunger: A Modern History* (Cambridge, MA, & London, 2007).

42 This point exemplifies a broader phenomenon described by Frank Trentmann. F. Trentmann, *Free Trade Nation: Commerce, Consumption, and Civil Society in Modern Britain* (Oxford, 2008).

43 For a related expansion on this see F. Trentmann, 'Coping with Shortage: the Problem of Food Security and Global Visions of Coordination, c.1890s–1950', in F. Trentmann and F. Just (eds) *Food and Conflict in the Age of the Two World Wars* (Basingstoke, 2006), pp. 13–48.

44 Britain's precarious trading position was inevitably explained in sporting analogies. 'Trade is like sport. There was a time when British sport was predominant; when other nations competed vainly; when a French rugby team was hardly taken seriously; when in boxing, rowing, cricket, running, wrestling, in practically every branch of sport the Britisher was supreme. Now the French have beaten as in the rugby international; America holds the boxing ring; we are outplayed in golf and tennis, and in every direction our competitors have become formidable rivals. So it is with trade.' L. Cooke, 'The Voice of the Brand: the Value of the Mark of Identity in Overseas Trade', *Advertising World*, No. 12, October 1927, p. 811.

45 As early as 1885, increased international competition had resulted in a Royal Commission berating the quality and scope of the state's commercial intelligence services. However, its recommendations only belatedly led to the creation of the Board of Trade's Commercial Intelligence Branch in 1900.

46 The resources of the Italian National Institute for Export draw frequent admiring glances in the trade literature of the period. See, for example, L. C. Blennerhassett, 'Cutting out the Guesswork in Overseas Marketing', *Advertising World*, No. 3, January 1927, pp. 417–422.

47 S. Baldwin, 'Letter from Stanley Baldwin', *Advertising World*, No. 3, January 1927, p. 347.

48 See for example 'Sales of British Typewriters', *The Times*, 13 April 1926, p. 12, and B. Cable, 'Advertise British Goods', *Advertising World*, No. 8, June 1926, p. 206.

49 As Sir William Clark, DOT's Controller General, put it, 'Looking back we may, I think, legitimately conclude, without in any sense undervaluing the service done to commercial enterprise by the removal of all restrictions on its liberty, that the extremer manifestations of the laissez-faire doctrine were a reflection of abnormal prosperity rather than its cause.'

W. Clark, 'Government and the Promotion of Trade', *Public Administration*, Vol. 1, No. 1, 1923, p. 28.

50 Qtd in G. H. Saxon-Mills, *There Is a Tide … The Life and Work of Sir William Crawford, Embodying an Historical Study of Modern British Advertising* (London, 1954), p. 128.

51 He had organised the International Advertising Exhibition of 1920 at White City and was crucial to the staging of the Empire Exhibition at Wembley. From 1923 he also acted as publicity adviser to the Imperial Economic Committee and the Ministry of Health. S. Anthony, 'Crawford, Sir William Smith (1878–1950)', *Dictionary of National Biography*, Oxford University Press, 2004 (http://www.oxforddnb.com/view/printable/40828, accessed 9 October 2008).

52 Here Crawford was following in the footsteps of other Tallents collaborators, such as John Boyd Orr, *Food, Health and Income* (London, 1936), and Julian Huxley, *Scientific Research and Social Needs* (London, 1934). See H. Broadley and W. Crawford, *The People's Food* (London, 1938).

53 'What the Public Thinks about Advertising', *Advertising World*, No. 1, October 1925, p. 120. Literary works of the period invariably satirised the profession: see for example, Walter Hackett and Roi Cooper Megrue, *It Pays to Advertise*; Sinclair Lewis, *Babbit*; John North, *Girl or Boy* and H. G. Wells, *Tono-Bungay*.

54 For Crawford's influence on the Buy British campaign, see Tallents papers, File 14, 'The Buy British Campaign'. Tellingly, the practice of commercial firms donating space to government advertisers was resurrected during the Second World War when, for example, another Crawford client, the Brewers Society, gave its booked advertising space over to the 'What do I do if …' series of government announcements.

55 Other government departments, anxious to secure the co-operation of the wider business community, were quick to imitate the Board's methods. Crawford's Milk Marketing Board campaign for the Ministry of Agriculture, for instance, apparently induced Cadbury's to adopt its famous glasses-pouring-milk logo.

56 A. M. Samuel, 'Goods Do Not Sell Themselves', *Advertising World*, No. 3, January 1927, p. 351.

57 See *Hansard*, 31 March 1926, cols 2027–2029. Perhaps at a historical remove we can see that Board was in sympathy with the more fundamental patterns of imperial economic movement

outlined by Cain and Hopkins. The outward flow of EMB's scientific and promotional activities worked against domestic manufacturing industry even as they increased national mastery over emerging specialisms. P. J. Cain and A. G. Hopkins, *British Imperialism 1688–2000* (Harlow, 2001).

58 The Treasury was implacably opposed to the Board. R. Self, 'Treasury Control and the Empire Marketing Board', *Twentieth Century British History*, Vol. 5, No. 2, 1994, pp. 153–181.

59 A market stall in Fulham and W. Pardoe of Peckham Rye were among the first winners. Tallents Papers, File 28, 'Supporting papers', 'Hythe to Tallents', 22 June 1944.

60 NA, CO760/7/655.

61 Tallents papers, File 43, 'EMB Epilogue'.

62 Co-operative selling appears to have been an early initiative of Sir Francis Goodenough at the Gas, Light and Coke Company (GLC). Goodenough had persuaded GLC's competitors of the need for the gas industry to sell its services to the public collectively. The success of this innovation had created something of a vogue for co-operative advertising. Grocers, for instance, were inspired to create a 'Retailers Propaganda Organisation' which conducted a highly successful 'Eat More Fruit' campaign that spawned among other unlikely merchandise a best-selling record, 'The Eat More Fruit Foxtrot'. See G. Boggon, '"Eat More Fruit" Campaign', *Advertising World*, No. X, July 1926, pp. 242–243.

63 Black, *Public Relations*, p. 9.

64 'Advertising Empire Goods', *The Times*, 28 June 1927, p. 9 qtd in J. Freeman, 'The Publicity of the Empire Marketing Board 1926–1933', *Journal of Advertising History*, No. 1, December 1977, pp. 12–14.

65 See BBC Archive, R43, 'Internal Memo: Advertising Publicity Account', 27 October 1938, 'Jones to Crawford', 13 March 1941 and 'GMP to CA', 13 March 1941.

66 Crawford's agency was behind famous campaigns such as 'Dig for Victory', 'Make Do and Mend', 'Careless Talk Costs Lives' and 'Salute to Russia' as well as all the recruitment drives organised through the Ministry of Labour for the Army, Navy and Royal Air Force.

67 The weight of Sir William Crawford's influence over the advertising profession is difficult to overstate. Rival newspapers – including *The News of the World* and *The Sunday Dispatch* – would quote his approval in their trade advertising. These

full-page advertisements place a quarter-page picture of Crawford towering above a testimonial. The fact that Crawford's name would often be followed by the tagline 'Advisor to the Empire Marketing Board' suggests the EMB's media work was more prestigious than many historians have allowed.

68 LeMahieu, *A Culture for Democracy*, p. 170.

69 Tallents, *Projection of England*, p. 40.

70 See R. J. Moore-Colyer, *Man's Proper Study: A History of Agricultural Science Education in Aberystwyth, 1878–1978* (Llandysul, 1982), and R. J.Moore-Colyer, *Sir George Stapledon and the Landscape of Britain* (Aberystwyth, 1997).

71 For more on Stapledon's visit see R. Waller, *Prophet of the New Age: The Life and Thought of Sir George Stapledon* (London, 1962).

72 For example, Stapledon appropriated EMB funds to employ William Davies as an Empire Grassland Investigator. Davies travelled peripatetically around the Empire (he took in everywhere from the Falkland Islands to Rhodesia) collecting and disseminating ideas and information.

73 Qtd in Waller, *Prophet*, p. 151. See also G. Stapledon, *The Way of the Land* (London, 1942).

74 See A. Chisholm and M. Davie, *Beaverbrook: A Life* (London, 1993), pp. 280–293.

75 See S. J. Taylor, *The Great Outsiders: Northcliffe, Rothermere and The Daily Mail* (London, 1996).

76 A. J. P. Taylor, *Beaverbrook* (London, 1972), p. 273.

77 J. Grierson, 'The EMB Film Unit', in F. Hardy (ed.) *Grierson on Documentary* (London, 1946), p. 98.

78 As Leo Amery regretfully admitted, 'the conspicuous success of our [the EMB's] publicity schemes tended to impress the general public that they were the main part of our work'. L. Amery, *My Political Life. Vol. 2* (London, 1953), p. 348.

79 However, this is slightly misleading as the EMB rarely covered the entire cost of a particular scientific research programme. Instead, EMB funding was used as a primer to attract funding from other sources. The financial impact of the EMB's spending was thus considerably more significant than this figure suggests.

80 Grant, *Propaganda and the Role of the State*, p. 52.

81 Chisholm and Davie, *Beaverbrook: A Life*, p. 284. Amery further expanded his 'dull' vision in L. Amery, *Empire and Prosperity* (London, 1929).

82 Beaverbrook's appropriation of the EMB's rhetoric led William

Beveridge to publish (and broadcast) an anti-imperial preference tract: see Sir William Beveridge, *Empire Free Trade: A Reply to Lord Beaverbrook* (London, 1931).

83 Tallents papers, File 26, 'The Start'.

84 For example see M. Baker, *Marketing Strategy and Management* (Basingstoke, 1992), P. Korder, *Marketing Management* (London, 1997) and D. Jobber, *Principles and Practices of Marketing* (New York & London, 2004).

85 Tallents papers, File 25, 'Prologue'.

86 Tallents papers, File 27, 'The Task'.

87 See S. Constantine, *The Making of British Colonial Development Policy, 1914–1940* (London, 1984).

88 R. Lewis, *In the Name of God Go!: Leo Amery and the British Empire in the Age of Churchill* (London, 1992), p. 26.

89 Amery's enthusiasm for funding ambitious imperial development schemes apparently earned him the Cabinet nickname the 'Mad Mullah'. After the establishment of a national government, the Labour free-trader Philip Snowden was appointed Chancellor and apparently asked Baldwin to banish Amery from the Cabinet altogether. See C. Barnett, *The Collapse of British Power* (London, 1972), p. 129.

90 Austen Chamberlain remembered, 'Leo irritated the Dominion Prime Ministers as much as he worried his colleagues'. D. Faber, *Speaking for England: Leo, Julian and John Amery, The Tragedy of a Political Family* (London, 2005), p. 208.

91 For example, the EMB had hoped to persuade the procurement offices of local authorities and large commercial organisations to adopt a policy of imperial preference. However, the only major organisation that could be persuaded to adopt such a policy was London County Council, whose decision to adopt an 'Empire woods only' purchasing policy proved a triumph of patriotism over prudence. The Board's shame was such that Tallents was induced to thank the LCC publicly for persevering, 'in spite of a rather disheartening experience with the poor manufacture and poor grading' of the products they received. See Tallents papers, File 40, 'Empire Timber'.

92 Tallents papers, File 27, 'The Task'.

93 Internally, Tallents's vision was strongly contested, and often ridiculed. Sir Walter Elliot pithily rebuked Tallents's political vision for the Empire: 'arranging marriages for children in their infancy is terribly fallacious'. Tallents papers, File 26, 'The Start'.

94 Qtd in Faber, *Speaking for England*, p. 213.

95 Huxley developed his critique of the EMB in A. Huxley, 'Science and Civilisation', *BBC Radio*, 13 January 1932; A. Huxley, 'Notes on the Way', *Time and Tide*, 7 May 1932, pp. 514–516; and A. Huxley, 'Ballyhoo for Nations', *Nash's Pall Mall Magazine*, Vol. XCV, July 1935, pp. 18–21. See also D. Bradshaw (ed.) *The Hidden Huxley* (London, 1994).

96 HAT, Selfridge archive, press cuttings, 'British Films as Model', *Daily Telegraph*, 2 April 1932.

97 Tallents's faith in unspecified research into 'glands' perhaps reflects popular enthusiasm for Dr Serge Voronoff's experiments on monkey glands, which promised to add years to an average human lifespan. Many public figures, including businessmen like Gordon Selfridge, as well as playwrights such as George Bernard Shaw and artists like Augustus John, expressed an interest in Voronoff's work. See D. Hamilton, *The Monkey Gland Affair* (London, 1986).

98 Tallents subsequently admitted he did not wholly understand what it was he had been so enthusiastic about, but joked that this was because 'poultry research evidently had the bit between its teeth in 1930'. Tallents papers, File 29, 'Scientific Research'.

99 The flimsy character of the Board's supporters can be glimpsed from the protesting letters written to *The Times* by people of good character when it was announced that the EMB was to be closed. See also J. M. Lee, 'The Dissolution of the EMB: Reflections in a Diary', *Journal of Imperial and Cultural History*, Vol. 1, No. 1 (1972).

100 NA, CO323/982/3, 'A Years Progress'.

101 Tallents papers, File 43, 'EMB Epilogue'.

102 NA, CAB 3/26/11, 3 February 1926.

103 In addition to climbing the two mountains that bore his name, Amery became the first minister to visit all of the Dominions in a single year. In 1927/8, for instance, he covered 55,000 miles and made three hundred speeches. Amery's prolonged absences make it difficult to sustain the argument – often made – that he was the Board's ideological 'author'. In addition to his physical absence, Amery appears to have been managerially lax. When composing his memoirs in 1951 he wrote to Tallents asking for guidance, admitting he had 'very little idea of the amount of work we did or even began'. Ironically, the key role Tallents played in the running the EMB is best reflected in Amery's personal memoirs, the content of which, and sentiments contained in, are elaborations upon Tallents's own unpublished

assessment. See Tallents papers, File 45, 'L. S. Amery's Chapter on the EMB in "*My Political Life*" Vol. 2', 'Amery to Tallents', 9 July 1951.

104 Tallents papers, File 26, 'The Start'.

105 R. Church, 'New Perspectives on the History of Products, Firms, Marketing, and Consumers in Britain and the United States since the Mid-nineteenth Century', *The Economic History Review*, New Series, Vol. 52, No. 3, August 1999, p. 408.

106 Tallents was paraphrasing Samuel Alexander's – another Balliol Liberal – *Art and the Material* (Manchester, 1925).

107 Tallents papers, File 28, 'Plan or Man'.

108 Tonks suggested that the EMB's maps of the new Empire should take inspiration from the maps in the Vatican library. Tonks was possibly also useful in that he provided the EMB with a link to the exceptional band of young British modernists formerly under his tutelage such as Paul Nash and Paul Rotha.

109 'With his passing, an era also passed away – an era which he perhaps more than any other man had helped to found. In thirty years the place in advertising of the specialist artist and writer had been established beyond cavil and for ever ... There was no need after this time to preach the use of advertising. The day of the "torch-bearer" was accordingly all but gone. Around the creative element has grown the highly systemised modern agency. The big organisation has grown so big, its departments so numerous, its interlocked activities so complex, that is beyond the power of one man to be its sole executive, in intimate contact with every client and every detail.' G. H. Saxon-Mills, *There Is a Tide ... The Life and Work of Sir William Crawford, Embodying an Historical Study of Modern British Advertising* (London, 1954), p. 177.

110 See S. Tallents, 'Sir William Crawford', *The Times*, 30 November 1950, p. 8, and Saxon-Mills, *There Is a Tide*, p. 128 and p. 175.

111 Tallents papers, File 28, 'Plan or Man'. Tallents's thoughts seem to have been inspired by an exchange between H. G. Wells and Stalin that provoked further contributions from Bernard Shaw, Ernst Toller and J. M. Keynes. See *New Statesman & Nation*, 27 October 1934.

112 Through Tallents's work at the EMB he 'got to know most of the leading agricultural research workers in the Kingdom, and today I have but to look around my own house and garden to recall them. There grow the willows which, on the advice of Dr Patton, I sought from the Long Ashton Research Station. There

grow the fruit trees and bushes which I acquired from the East Malling Fruit Station ... there grow the Balsam Poplars and the maples which Sir Arthur Hill advised me to set in a row by our front gate.' Tallents papers, File 43, 'EMB Epilogue'.

113 Tallents papers, File 38, 'Empire Wines'.

114 'I found the work fascinating by reason of its novelty and of the zest and high quality of the brains which guided it ... I remember lunch at which Andre Simon served the guests with pink champagne flown over from France that morning; a day which I was invited to a wine samplers' exercise of their art, and a delightful dinner party in Francis Perry's Wimbledon house, at which he decanted for us two pre-phylloxera clarets – of '65 and '70 – and a claret of '99 with which to compare them'. Tallents papers, File 38, 'Empire Wines'.

115 Tallents papers, File 29, 'Scientific Research'.

116 Dr Frederick Grant Banting pioneered the treatment of diabetes at the University of Toronto. Sir Chandrasekhara Venkata Raman was knighted for his discovery of the Raman Effect. For more on Tallents's enthusiastic scientism see S. Tallents, 'The Progress of Empire Research', *Discovery*, July 1932, pp. 207–211.

117 Tallents papers, File 43, 'EMB Epilogue'.

118 See I. Ansoff, *Corporate Strategy* (London, 1986), and G. Tweedale, 'English Versus American Hardware: British Marketing Techniques and Business Performance in the USA in the Nineteenth and early-Twentieth Centuries', in R. T. Davenport-Hines (ed.) *Markets and Bagmen: Studies in the History of Marketing and British Industrial Performance 1830–1939* (Aldershot, 1986), pp. 57–81.

119 ICI and Unilever are frequently named as the only two British companies of the interwar period that display the characteristics of 'modern' businesses. Of course, the idea that vertically integrated organisations are 'modern' is now rather old-fashioned.

120 This is another factor which explains why even sympathetic contemporaries found the Board's example looming ever larger as time passed. See, for example, L. S. Amery, *The Forward View* (London, 1935), p. 195.

121 Sir Ernest Debenham was invited to develop the EMB's ideas for marketing milk in 1932. See E. Debenham, *A National Milk Marketing Scheme for Great Britain* (London, 1932).

3

The Projection of England and documentary cinema

The pioneers of public relations in Britain imaginatively utilised a range of new technologies to illuminate and interpret the nation's approach to the commercial, bureaucratic and scientific challenges of the age. The EMB Film Unit established in 1928 was crucial to the development of this radical function of public relations. Working with a young technology encouraged Tallents to indulge in, and experiment with, new approaches to both the method and manner of communication. Specific insights provided by the EMB's film-making experiments were extrapolated by Tallents into a more general understanding of new media technologies. Tallents's educational and patriotic conception of public relations was in turn shaped by the successes of the Film Unit.

The publication of *The Projection of England* in 1932 marked an important milestone in the development of Tallents's approach to public relations as it focused a series of overlapping debates about the impact of new technology on the relationship between the state and its citizens. Tallents's pamphlet argued that a new type of national personality was emerging as the geography of the globe was reshaped by new developments in transport and media communications.

The Projection of England details a dawning age where a nation's image is made up of many component parts. For instance, Tallents begins by listing typical icons of Britain (he uses England and Britain interchangeably) such as Big Ben, *Punch*, the London Underground and the FA Cup Final. The national presence described by Tallents was at the same time more modest and much larger than 'traditional' forms of national expression. This was because Tallents believed that the cumulative impact of a nation's traditions and popular rituals, along with the things it produced, and the art and science it patronised, were intensified by powerful new internationalist media.

Much of *The Projection of England* focuses on the dangers of ignoring the need for the new kind of cultural diplomacy entailed by these 'democratising' technological changes. According to Tallents, the projection of Britain was essential to maintaining healthy relationships with the Empire, to improving the quality and value of the nation's exports, and to securing a steady flow of essential imports such as food. Or as he loquaciously writes:

> In the age of shadows, countries were mainly self-contained, and derived from outside prestige little save power, pride and luxury, to-day they depend upon each other alike for their bread and for their peace. No civilised country can to-day afford either to neglect the projection of its national personality or to resign its projection to others.[1]

However, the practical recommendations of Tallents's pamphlet are few and far between. 'What is needed to secure this projection? he asks rhetorically: 'the fashionable answer leaps out in demand for the better co-ordination of existing agencies [but] I dread that familiar prescription, which is for ever upon the lips of a generation thinking always in terms of mechanical engineering and never of biology or art'. Rather than laying out a scheme, the central propagandist point of *The Projection of England* is that governmental work in the media sphere needed to become more proactive. As the pamphlet's title suggests, Tallents was particularly concerned with the impact of film. He argued – perhaps conscious of Bernays's description of 'the American picture as the greatest unconscious carrier of propaganda in the world today' – that US dominance of a new global industry had 'turned every cinema in the world into the equivalent of an American consulate'.[2] Here *The Projection of England* sought to tap into well-worn establishment anxieties.

In 1916, the National Council of Public Morals had sponsored Sir James Marchant to investigate 'the physical, social, moral, and educational influence of the cinema', and Marchant's concern about the undesirable effects of 'alien' influence on national morale resonated throughout the period.[3] Over the course of the interwar years the British Board of Film Censors (BBFC) also became steadily more influential. 'The success of our government of subject races', argued Sir Hesketh Bell of the British Empire Film Institute, 'depends almost entirely on the degree of respect which we can inspire'. Bell took exception to exposing 'primitive people' to 'demoralising films, representing criminal and immodest actions by white men and women'.[4] The impact of this chorus of political anxiety was exemplified by Philip Cunliffe-Lister's Cinematograph Protection Act of 1927. The act sought to limit American influence on British film theatres by outlawing the practice of 'blind-booking', limiting the similarly restrictive practice of 'block-buying' and introducing a minimum 'quota' of British films to be screened.

These ad hoc protectionist measures were not conspicuously successful. The BBFC's credibility was undermined by its reliance on box-office receipts, which made it reluctant to censor Hollywood product but incentivised the restriction of British, European or 'art' releases.[5] Equally, BBFC Presidents such as Edward Shortt and William Tyrrell were veteran Civil Servants who appeared to dislike, and were often contemptuous of, cinema and cinemagoers.[6] Meanwhile Cunliffe-Lister's legislation was diluted to ensure that it was revenue-neutral. Although the Cinematograph Act stimulated domestic production, the short-term effect of the legislation led to American-owned subsidiaries mass-producing low-budget 'quota-quickies' that were perceived to damage further the status of Britain and British film.[7] No wonder that in *The Projection of England* Tallents observes that that government policy towards cinema remained focused on 'preventing the bad', to paraphrase Wallas again, rather than 'promoting the good'. 'It is probable that more has been said and written during the last year about the connexion between British films and the British Empire than ever before', noted *The Times*: 'countless people write and talk about it, but no one does anything'.[8]

The creation of the Empire Marketing Board Film Unit

The Projection of England was written as the Board run by Tallents was effectively being wound up; it served both as an application for his next job (Tallents wanted to join the BBC) and as a defence of the Board's record. Not only are the frustrations of Tallents's aborted work at the EMB central to the pamphlet's specific insights, but the broader diplomatic vision expressed in *The Projection of England* is in reflective dialogue with the work of the Board. Specifically, Tallents was attempting to justify the continued existence of the Film Unit established by the EMB and to assert the value of the distinctive aesthetic it had developed.

When the EMB Film Unit was created, the British state had yet to define its proper relationship with cinema. In 1924 the British government had appointed the first Cinematograph Officer, Edward Foxon-Cooper. Foxon-Cooper's role was split between Customs and Excise (where he administered duties) and cataloguing and administering the film collection of the Imperial War Museum.[9] Eventually the popularity of the government's war films (for screening and sampling by the commercial film industry) led to Foxon-Cooper's full-time appointment – an appointment approved by the Treasury on the grounds that it was self-financing.[10]

The EMB Film Unit was little more than a handful of novice freelance film-makers, but in the eyes of the interwar Civil Service it represented a costly and controversial initiative. Understandably, the Unit's first film attempted to address the anxieties of imperial-minded Conservatives. Having taken the revolutionary step of establishing a film unit, Tallents's proceeded with extreme caution. In fact, the EMB's first production had its roots in a social meeting between Tallents and Rudyard Kipling.[11] Kipling suggested that the EMB should not only commission posters but reproduce them in easily accessible formats such as jigsaw puzzles, playing cards and postcards. He also instructed Tallents to monitor the development of television. However, Kipling was most excited about the idea of an official Empire film. He began:

> Reeling off a series of scenes depicting Empire trade, eg. The Phoenicians landing on the coast of Britain, the farmer at work while Cavaliers and Roundheads rode irrelevantly by; the first days of trade in India; and so on. The Empire had grown, he said, simply because we gave protection wherever we went, the English saying they'd be damned if they were going to have trouble in this district, as it interfered with their trade. The range of protection used to be the 14 yards range of their Brown Bess and now –.[12]

On Kipling's urging, Tallents commissioned Walter Creighton to direct *One Family*. Creighton was experienced in the staging of military tattoos but a novice film director, and it is tempting to mock the technical incompetence of the exceedingly bad film he produced at Kipling's behest.[13] Four years in the making, the film had been conceived as a cinematic equivalent of an imperial exhibition. George V's personal determination to counter the 'Americanisation' of British cinema led him to invite the EMB to shoot the film inside Buckingham Palace. The crassness of its concept, which saw a little boy dream of touring the Empire to collect the ingredients needed to make the King's Christmas pudding, was exacerbated by the presence of 'six magnificently attired' society beauties who appear as symbolic representations of the United Kingdom and the Dominions. Such details lent the picture the air of, at best, an upper-class vanity project. 'We have waited for a march past of the British Empire on screen', wrote Alastair Cooke, 'and now we get it, we find it allied to a Christmas shopping tour conducted by a little boy with ungracious manners and a squeaky voice'.[14]

Nevertheless, aspects of *One Family*'s exhibition would become influential. *One Family* occupied the central point of an extravagant media happening in much the same way that the screening of Hollywood westerns such as *The Covered Wagon* were preceded by 'Arapahos' dancing around the cinema in war paint.[15] As Tallents remembered:

> Well-heralded by photographs in the daily press, the film [*One Family*] had an elaborate first night at the Palace Theatre on July 7th 1930. The Programme opened with stirring music from the band of Irish Guards, and included also The Daily Dozen at the Zoo, Mickey Mouse in his Barnyard Concert, some solos by a tenor and an introduction by Mr J. H. Thomas.[16]

The EMB would further refine the techniques used to promote *One Family* in the 'Buy British' campaign. The 1931 campaign audaciously utilised tannoys at greyhound stadiums and the aviation skills of Amy Johnson, while its centrepiece was a Tallents-scripted newsreel address by the Prince of Wales that was watched by an estimated 17.5 million people. The speech was intended to enlist the co-operation of community groups and social organisations from lord provosts and lord mayors to the Trade Union Congress via the RAC and the Girl Guides.[17] In the same manner that *One Family* looked like an aristocratic home video, the 'Buy British' campaign might be taken to represent a multi-media village fete.

Financially, *One Family* was not a success. Its budget totalled £15,740, but the film secured bookings of only £334 and its dismal box-office returns led to questions in the House.[18] The failure of *One Family* similarly led the EMB to abandon the bombastic idiom of First World War era films and instead evolve a cinematic language that was first utilitarian, and then anthropological, and eventually socially democratic. For the rest of his career, Tallents's multimedia extravagances would became ever more assured, unforced and sophisticated.

The EMB's contribution to scientific and educational films

One Family's failure encouraged the Board to concentrate on professional and educational films aimed at non-commercial audiences.[19] This was a pragmatic intervention. 'If the Civil Service, or any other public service must have its illegitimate children', Tallents approvingly quoted Grierson, 'it is best to see that they are small ones'.[20]

The EMB began administrating scientific grants at a point in time when interest in the science film had begun to grow.[21] British Instructional's *Secrets of Nature* (from 1934, *Secrets of Life*) series of wildlife shorts, for example, quickly garnered an enthusiastic following after their launch in 1922. This popular series bridged the divide between education and entertainment by replacing their educational titles (*How Plants Feed*) with snappier names (*Queer Diet!*) when they were commercially released.[22] The *Secrets of Nature* films both attracted the attention of Hollywood and were praised by the British establishment.

Co-existing alongside this commercially-orientated expertise was a more utilitarian series of science films. In 1927, the British radiologist Ronald Canti presented to the Xth International Congress of Zoology in Budapest a series of amateur films that caused a worldwide sensation. Canti had pioneered the use of stop-motion photography to demonstrate the effect of radium on cancerous cells.[23] *The Times* noted the ability of Canti's pioneering work to 'leave spectators gasping in astonishment', while his peers described him simply as a genius.[24] Canti came to Tallents's notice via his prominent role in the British Empire Cancer Campaign. They became friends, and this friendship probably encouraged Tallents to fund the film-making activities of other scientific acquaintances.[25] Critics had noted that 'the limited field of nature study micro-photography' was the only area where Britain had achieved international pre-eminence.[26] The EMB's focus on scientific and educational film had a basis in national expertise and sprang from an informed understanding of what type of audiences its Film Unit could realistically reach.

Arthur Elton's *An Experiment on the Welsh Hills* is illustrative of the EMB's broad approach to the scientific film. Ostensibly made to illustrate aspects of George Stapledon's research at the Welsh Plant Breeding Station, Elton's film was designed to pique the interest of educational and culturally informed audiences as well as scientists. It made a strong aesthetic appeal, abstracting startling shots of idle mining equipment against the bleak backdrop of the Welsh Black Mountains in a manner that aped the modernist idiom of Alexander Dovzhenko.[27] The EMB hoped that Elton's film would, like Canti's, attract interest, attention and funding. Equally, following the template established by the *Secrets of Nature* series, *An Experiment on the Welsh Hills* was commercially exhibited (in re-edited form) as *Shadow on the Mountain*. Furthermore, *An Experiment on the Welsh Hills* fused these two pre-existing traditions of scientific film with a wartime strand of government film production. During the War, the armed forces had commissioned films to demonstrate training methods and disseminate engineering skills. Wright's film positioned itself as an in-house production able to efficiently demonstrate the EMB's research programme to an audience dispersed throughout the Empire.

An Experiment on the Welsh Hills served an additional propagandist purpose by focusing on the kind of modernising co-operative development that imperialists such as Leo Amery identified as central to the future of the Empire. Stapledon's attempts to breed grasses capable of restoring the pastures of Australia, New Zealand and South Africa vindicated the EMB's developmental mission.[28] The film's approach was similar to the line taken by the Commission on Cultural and Educational Film who argued, 'film can as well display the ancient dignity of The Mahabharata as teach the Indian peasant the elements of hygiene and sanitation. In Africa it can aid the missionary, the trader and the administrator.'[29]

As the EMB Film Unit owed its existence to a donation of stock footage by the Canadian Motion Picture Bureau, it is unsurprising that its films stressed the co-operative nature of the Empire.[30] While the Canadian Motion Picture Bureau library apparently reached 25 million North Americans a year, the Board's film makers worked with basic equipment. They used a dentist's drill as a film winder, bits of found timber as tripods and the lavatory wall of their Wardour Street offices for screenings. Here was irrefutable evidence that the EMB Film Unit could not approach the Dominions 'with the conviction of chosen people, elected to lighten the Gentiles'.[31] This lack of technical capacity was also another important determining factor in the decision to specialise in scientific and educational films. 'Educational films' were all that it could be consistently produced from the donated Canadian footage. Early shorts such as *Furry Folk* (about beavers) or *Lumber* (on lumberjacks) were re-edits of the donated stock footage. Edgar Anstey remembered that the EMB:

> Used to give us some very old films belonging to the Canadian Motion Picture Bureau, and we would have to re-edit them; make new pictures from them. This really was editing experience, taking material photographed for one purpose and making a different film from it. That is what the Russians had to do at the time. In fact, Grierson pinched the idea from them ... You attempt to attach a story line from within all kinds of material. I had pictures of penguins, penguins courting, penguins playing, hunting, slipping on ice, and from this mass of stuff I had to devise a story.[32]

The 'schools film' *Conquest* (1930) provides an example of the simplistic didacticism of the EMB's early work. 'Man', reads an early title, and we are shown a primitive man, 'faced by natural barriers of mountain ranges' which we are again shown. Such literalism betrayed *Conquest*'s genesis in old film footage.[33] Bombastic 'educational' title cards merely provided the means to bridge the gap between fundamentally unrelated sequences pilfered from a range of sources. Educational films did not have to be technically impressive (the advent of sound was beginning to compromise seriously the commercial viability of silent pictures) and could be edited together at little cost.[34] Not-for-profit educational distribution also exempted the EMB from royalty payments. By distributing *Conquest* as an educational film, the EMB successfully deflected attention from its aesthetic shortcomings. The film critic C. E. Lejeune even praised *Conquest* for telling 'the story of colonisation in a language, comprehensible and acceptable to the schoolchildren of the Empire'.[35]

The EMB's central focus on scientific and educational films has encouraged historians to argue that the EMB Film Unit displayed a superior, class-determined attitude to mass entertainment. The analogy between the educational efforts of the EMB Film Unit and the output of the BBC is commonly made and not entirely misplaced. The EMB certainly expressed a public dislike of 'self-expression and other beautiful whatnots of a youthful and simply vague existence'.[36] However, overemphasising the ideological determination of the EMB to 'uplift' public taste obscures both the real demand for scientific and educational films that existed and the pragmatics of the Board's situation.

Although they were technically primitive, the EMB's commitment to educational films represented a bold and radical intervention. By 1932, Tallents's organisation was producing over forty titles a year in a sector that only maverick public school-teachers such as Ronald Gow and W. H. George had previously pursued with any vigour.[37] Radical councils in Glasgow, Battersea and Bermondsey (where films were made from the leftover X-ray stock of a tuberculosis testing programme) had also established limited educational film-making programmes, but the national audience which the EMB's educational films had created was unprecedented.[38] In the first year of its operation, the Empire Film Library supplied films to an estimated audience of 517,000 school-children. As it was not until 1933 that an affordable and reliable 16mm sound film projector became available, if we accept the EMB's figures as accurate, this was an exceptional achievement. Five years after the EMB created the Empire Film Library it had become the largest distributor of educational films in the country. Charles Cleland – an influential Scottish educationalist and future head of the British Film Institute – wrote in 1933 that the possible loss of the EMB film library was 'from a schools point of view, a national disaster'.[39]

John Grierson and the development of documentary film

Fundamental to the organisation, aesthetic and relative success of the Empire Marketing Board Film Unit was John Grierson. Grierson had been recruited from the University of Chicago where, studying under Walter Lippmann, he had become interested in the challenges of mass democracy.[40] Lippmann was a lapsed liberal concerned that the rise of emotive new mass-media technologies would undermine the rational democracy of the printed word.[41] 'He saw the average citizen as a tired little man in a going-home bus, with neither the leisure nor the will for anything so intellectual as rational judgement', as Grierson later surmised it: 'on the whole, Lippmann did not appear to believe in the dream of the universal educationalist that more and more education would smooth the path for democracy, but more likely that it would bore democracy to death'.[42]

It is significant that Grierson's own education had been

interrupted by the Great War, and like many of his generation he felt a degree of estrangement from the civilian society he returned to. His evangelism for documentary cinema was directly related to his antipathy for what he perceived as a complacent educational establishment. However, while accepting Lippmann's analysis, Grierson rejected his pessimism.[43] According to Gervas Huxley, Tallents was soon to fall completely under Grierson's dynamic spell as the pair rapidly developed a common rhetoric.[44] The intellectual overlap was widely acknowledged by contemporaries.[45] Echoing Grierson, Tallents came to conceive of film as a development which had the potential to be 'an instrument of untold good', but which was being perverted into 'an instrument of incalculable and irreparable harm'.[46] Where Grierson preached 'facts with faith', Tallents espoused truth expressed as 'a living principle of action'. Where Grierson claimed that the development of a new form of mass education was 'as important in man's history as the Copernican revolution', Tallents posited 'film, radio, poster and exhibition as the sextant and compass which would manoeuvre citizenship over the new (democratic) distances'.[47] The notion of documentary cinema ('the creative treatment of actuality') developed by Grierson at the EMB appears best understood as an attempt to bolster a progressive sense of imaginative cohesion able to embrace every aspect of the nation. According to Grierson, documentary cinema should shun melodramatic tales of aristocrats and entrepreneurs and instead celebrate everyday heroism.[48]

Over the past three decades the 'Grierson tradition' has become a byword for uninspired worthiness, but Grierson's early work at the EMB could as easily be defined by a boyish and undogmatic enthusiasm.[49] In Chicago Grierson had written film reviews rather than completing academic work. Directed by Walter Lippmann to study the psychodynamics of popular cinema, Grierson instead travelled to Hollywood where he nurtured an appreciation for figures such as Josef von Sternberg, Charlie Chaplin, Erich von Stroheim, Harry Langdon and King Vidor. Of future importance to the EMB was his friendship with Robert Flaherty, whose study of Eskimo life, *Nanook of the North* (1922) – funded, owing to lack of Hollywood interest, by a fur coat manufacturer – became a worldwide phenomenon. It was in his review of Flaherty's third film, *Moana*, that Grierson first coined the term 'documentary'.[50]

Equally, Grierson's importance at the EMB was arguably developing his position as researcher and theoriser into the role of a producer. Historical legend places substantial weight on the immediate critical success of Grierson's *Drifters* (1928). Aesthetically, *Drifters* borrowed heavily from Sergei Eisenstein's *Battleship Potemkin*. While the latter was effectively banned in Britain, Grierson had made a shot-by-shot record of Eisenstein's masterpiece when studying in America. Screened before the premiere of Eisenstein's film at the London Film Society, *Drifters* apparently made the ageing *Potemkin* appear more like watered-down Grierson than a trail-blazing child of the Revolution.[51] *The Evening Standard* instantly acclaimed Grierson as a cinematic pioneer who stood alongside Eisenstein, Pudovkin, Lubitsch and Hitchcock. Tallents recalled that the *succès d'estime Drifters* enjoyed was the greatest relief in his career 'since the day in February 1918 which had shown that rationing would cure the food queues'.[52] Eisenstein was left to complain to Ivor Montagu that *Drifters* had stolen 'all the best parts of *Potemkin*'.[53]

John Grierson assiduously cultivated the *Drifters* myth as the EMB's documentary star began to rise. It is a myth that can be straightforwardly unpicked. *Drifters*, subject matter was apparently determined to appease the EMB's Financial Secretary at the Treasury, Arthur Michael Samuel, author of *The Herring: Its Effect on the History of Britain*. Equally, *Drifters* could not have been made without the input of the British Trawler Foundation's 'Eat More Fish!' campaign. Sir Gordon Craig judged it 'completely over the head of the man in the street'.[54] Arthur Elton remembered that 'renters thought so badly of *Drifters* it was block-booked with *The Co-Optimists*, an exceedingly poor musical'.[55]

However, there is something to be said for Grierson's argument that *Drifters* attempted to move the documentary film forward from Flaherty's more straightforwardly anthropological approach.[56] The *Drifters* myth has also, more importantly, obscured what a personal film it is. Grierson had served on a minesweeper during the War, and the high number of casualties suffered by the conscripted Scottish fishermen had made a deep impression. Grierson wrote:

> Men at their labour are the salt of the earth; the sea is a bigger actor than Jannings or Nikitin; and if you can tell me a story more plainly dramatic than the gathering of the ships of the herring season, the going out, the shooting at evening, the long drift of the night, the hauling of nets by infinite agony of shoulder muscles in the teeth of a storm, the drive home against a head sea, and (for finale) the frenzy of a market in

which the said agonies are sold at ten shillings a thousand, and iced, salted and barrelled for an unwitting world – if you can tell me a story with better crescendo in energies, images, atmospherics and all that make up the sum and substance of cinema, I promise you I shall make a film of it when I can.[57]

Despite Grierson's reputation as a puritanical curmudgeon and the involved nature of this theorising, the EMB's documentary output disproportionately romanticises Scotland and the sea.[58] This idealism manifested itself in Film Unit productions such as *Salmon Leap!*, *Granton Trawler*, *Liner Cruising South*, as well as his abandoned follow-up to *Drifters*, a sprawling epic that was to detail the workings of the Port of London Authority. In the same way Tallents's fondness for willow cricket bats, rat-skin leather, squirrel pie and innumerable other presumably anachronistic practices of British life were reflected by the EMB Film Unit's equally disproportionate output of rustic shorts such as *Plums that Please*, *Modern Apple and O'er Hill and Dale*.[59] The documentary cinema developed at the EMB Film Unit was a documentary cinema of optimism, affection and enthusiasm. It informs the broader mid-twentieth-century 'redistribution of esteem' described by Ross McKibbin.[60] Film theorists who emphasise the lack of ideological rigour, or systematic social criticism, are largely missing the point. 'The thrill of documentary', recalled one member of the Film Unit, 'was putting the people of Britain on the screen, recorded for all time'.[61]

The organisation of the EMB Film Unit

When Tallents was attempting to protect the EMB Film Unit from dissolution, he warned potential allies, 'you will not confuse, any more than I confuse in my own mind, limited actual achievements with actual possibilities'.[62] Contemporary film critics agree that the majority of EMB films are not of lasting aesthetic interest but have paid less attention to the importance of the human infrastructure built by the EMB.

Tallents's Civil Service career was punctuated by a genuine, and rather mischievous, enthusiasm for the arts.[63] As well as befriending the poets Walter de la Mare and Humbert Wolfe, he encouraged William Beveridge to publish *John and Irene*, pursued correspondence with the curators Sydney Cockerell and John Summerson, and became a patron and collector of the artists

Graham Sutherland and Eric Ravilious.[64] Tallents also developed his own creative outlets, publishing two short-story collections (his first collection, *The Starry Pool*, was well reviewed by *The Times Literary Supplement*) as well as producing regular articles and sketches for *Punch*, *The Manchester Guardian* and *The Sunday Times*.[65] Grierson, it is worth stating, was recruited to the EMB on the recommendation of the poet Robert Nichols rather than for his expertise in the social sciences.[66] Tallents was fond of stockpiling talent ('nominally under my control but really working on their own initiative') and he encouraged his prodigy to do likewise.[67] He advised Grierson:

> We should aim at building up a school of young producers, selecting carefully for the purpose young men (or women) of first-class ability and intelligence but without requiring of them previous film experience ... I remember being confirmed in my support of the idea of a school on these lines by the encouragement of Charles Morgan, then dramatic critic of *The Times*, who quoted to me what had been done in something of the same style by M. St. Denis and his Compagnie de Quinze.[68]

Basil Wright, Arthur Elton, Paul Rotha and Edgar Anstey formed the core of young film-makers attracted by Grierson. They were put to work alongside sculptors, graphic artists, painters, writers and poets on the EMB's neo-renaissance project. 'The time has come', Grierson paraphrased Tallents, 'to bring the artist once more into effective contact with contemporary life, and by bringing him and the Cinema together, to release a cultural force of unrivalled possibilities'.[69] Here Tallents had possibly also learned much from William Crawford, whose employment of Ashley Havindin – a Bauhaus enthusiast – had brought important artists and designers such as Herbert Bayer, Jean Cocteau, Eric Gill, Boutet de Monvel, Maholy-Nagy and Edward McKnight Kauffer into his firm's orbit.[70]

As well as building up a cadre of creative staff, Tallents and Grierson created a network of patrons. Tallents's peers and protégés at the Ceylon Tea Propaganda Board (for whom Gervas Huxley had left the EMB), Shell (Jack Beddington), Imperial Airways (Snowden Gamble), the Gas, Light and Coke Company (Clem Leslie) and the Orient Line (Tommy Tallents) were crucial to the development of the EMB's documentary ethos. Winning the patronage of corporate interwar Britain had the secondary benefit of plugging the EMB Film Unit into the orbit of emerging hi-tech industries and thus serving Tallents's broader interest in national projection. Tallents believed that 'projection' should combine elements of British life (like the monarchy) of general interest to foreign nationals, with less publicised national characteristics better fitted to the new world of mass communication.[71] There will be those who are interested in seeing England as an up to date and efficient industrial workshop', he argued, 'and there will be others to whom she will appeal as a homely country of small fields'.[72]

Securing the sponsorship of modern business also naturally led the EMB, in advance of intellectuals such as George Orwell and J. B. Priestley, to emphasise the importance of an emerging Britain run by a new class of technicians.[73] As well as updating the image of Britain 'projected' abroad at international exhibitions, the films allowed the EMB to develop a network of patrons among the intelligentsia that included H. G. Wells, Julian Huxley and J. B. S. Haldane.[74] Indeed, the Film Unit allowed activist intellectuals an important platform for refining their appeals to the public. 'I am a public enemy', as J. B. S. Haldane memorably intones in *The Smoke Menace*, 'I live in a house with several open coal fires, but I am not sufficiently ashamed'.

Informal but pervasive, the workings of the EMB Film Unit tied together socially conscious film-makers, progressive organisations and civil society. Distributed via co-operative networks of schools, colleges, YMCAs, churches, men's clubs, women's organisations and educational associations (as well as commercial chains), the EMB's brand of documentary cinema, like so much of British public relations activity during the interwar period, drew its legitimacy from its basis in associational and voluntary culture.[75] The EMB had the endorsement of the Federation of British Industry, but the TUC also considered its films to be 'extraordinarily good'. The Film Unit's successes illustrated that while the Board had been created by flag-waving politicians it became a conduit for a variety of non-political links within a technocratic middle class.[76] Its films imbued a moral and emotional sense of togetherness with representations of social and technological interconnectedness.

Song of Ceylon and the projection of Empire

Appointed in 1928, Grierson spent his first year at the Board writing reports on scientific and factual films. Tallents had bemoaned the lack of spending on science and agriculture throughout the Empire ('Money devoted to research is not a luxury; it is not an entirely sound investment; it is rather a condition of survival'). Grierson built this insight into the EMB's film policy, contrasting slovenly imperial practice with the newest developments from around the globe.[77] Taking his cue from Soviet cinema, Grierson propagated the need for a new kind of cinema that both fulfilled an educative function and displayed aesthetic and technical virtuosity.[78] He had arrived at the EMB as the film critic who claimed to have popularised Eisenstein in the English-speaking world, Grierson was to become the film officer who brought dialectical montage to Whitehall.[79]

Strengthened by the failure of *One Family*, Grierson directed Tallents towards the work of early Soviet film-makers such as Sergei Eisenstein, Vsevolod Pudovkin and Dziga Vertov.[80] The bold glorification of 'progress' in these films, according to Grierson, could provide the EMB Film Unit with a template which they could appropriate and amend. 'Let them see the Commonwealth, not in terms of old imperial slogans', counselled Grierson, 'but in the mechanical and scientific terms of tomorrow'.[81]

Victor Turin's *Turk–Sib* was a particular favourite of the EMB Film Unit.[82] A paean to progress that details the construction of the Turkmenistan–Siberia railway, *Turk–Sib* was revered by Grierson and the Film Unit because it used the tropes of Hollywood's 'frontier' pictures (Turin had worked in Hollywood) to tell the story of the opening up of a geographically remote area of the USSR. The fact that the Turk–Sib railway directly linked Turkmenistan and Siberia, rather than running through an established urban centre, was taken to prove that the USSR was a distinctive organisation of Socialist Republics free from the centrifugal exploitation characteristic of existing empires.[83] The Civil Servants were impressed.[84] Tallents wrote:

> We have ready to our hand all the material to outmatch *Storm Over Asia* by a film that should be entitled *Dawn Over Africa*. The history of our imperial development is rich in themes not less great than that of the Turkestan–Siberian Railway. The story of the Hudson Bay Company alone would provide a theme, which, incidentally, would not be dependent, as is that of *Turk–Sib*, upon an illusionary representation of successful achievement. In the countryside and country life, which have inspired so noble a body of English poetry and

painting, we have themes not less beautiful than *Earth*, and
we are under no necessity, as was Dovjenko, to disguise them
under the appearance of political propaganda.[85]

Tallents's visit to the Barcelona exhibition of 1929 marked a
defining moment in his conception of 'national projection'. Beside
the dynamism of Mies van der Rohe's German stand, Tallents
was struck by the tired complacency of the British pavilion. For
Tallents, the failings of the British display at Barcelona emphasised
the necessity of 'projecting' a contemporary picture of Britain and
the British Empire. The production of *The Song of Ceylon* marked
the culmination of a sustained attempt to 'project' an up-to-date
picture of Britain's relationship with its colonies. 'The injunction
"know thyself" applied as much to an Empire as to an individual,
mused Tallents: 'without that knowledge the Empire travelled
blindfolded'.[86]

Basil Wright's 1933 film *The Song of Ceylon* could not stand in
greater contrast to *One Family*. Utilising a symphonic structure
apparently borrowed from Walter Ruttman's *Berlin: Symphony of
a City*, *The Song of Ceylon* is knowingly modernist. The assertively
experimental soundtrack blends extracts from a seventeenth-
century travelogue, read by the Burgher (Eurasian Sri Lankan)
pianist Lionel Wendt, with snippets of Sinhalese-inspired music
and an array of found sounds.[87]

The Song of Ceylon also stands in challenging counterpoint
to the mainstream cinema of the era. During the interwar period
Alexander Korda freely raided the British Empire's pantheon of
Boy's Own heroes. Figures such as Gordon of Khartoum, Dr David
Livingstone and Lawrence of Arabia were held aloft as exceptional
illustrations of the national character.[88] Films such as *Sanders of
the River* (1935), *Rhodes of Africa* (1936) and *The Four Feathers*
(1939) almost unreflectively depicted the apostles of Empire as
spreaders of law and order who had sacrificed themselves to free
indigenous people from superstition and witchcraft.[89] Wright's
film, instead, approaches its subject with an icy anthropological
earnestness.

Despite the idiosyncratic vision expressed in Wright's film,
discussions of *The Song of Ceylon* still often revolve uneasily
around the degree to which Basil Wright can be implicated in, or
absolved from, the moral charge of 'imperialism'.[90] Occasionally,
Wright's focus on the physical rituals of Ceylonese society is
taken to be indicative of a subversive (homosexual) interest in the

Sinhalese people's primeval nature.[91] But beyond recognising that Wright's film can be understood in the context of the modernist fascination with the 'primitive', these critical writings blunt Wright's subtleties. The lack of synchronisation between image and soundtrack, for example, is often richly suggestive. When snippets of plum-voiced gentlemen dictating letters ('your obedient servant') are used to overlay a sequence showing native labourers picking tea, for example, the film is encouraging the audience to make imaginative equivalences that are relativist rather than 'imperialist'.[92] *The Song of Ceylon* apparently illustrates Tallents' observation that each of the Dominions and Colonies 'wanted to project their own distinctive manner of living, and in each case a very different manner of living from our own'.[93] Indeed, Graham Greene congratulated Wright for shunning the temptation to 'pretend to know' Ceylon and for attempting to treat its culture with sympathy and respect.[94] The film subsequently won the Prix du Gouvernement Belge and arguably became Britain's first art-house success.[95] Tallents later boasted, 'the film bears about the same relation to ordinary travelogues that Keats' "Ode to a Grecian Urn" bears to a cheap pottery catalogue'.[96] *The Song of Ceylon* remains the fullest (and most artistically successful) expression of the odd educational ethos developed by Tallents and Grierson at the EMB.[97]

The EMB Film Unit and the development of public relations

The idea of documentary cinema developed at the EMB Film Unit has exerted a disproportionate influence on British cinema.[98] It offered apprenticeships to important and interesting film-makers, made films that bought international recognition to a previously maligned domestic industry and nurtured a generation of administrators, intellectuals and lecturers that set up archives, libraries and cultural institutions that propagated the importance of film to national life. The disproportionate influence of 'the *Drifters* tradition' is now also profoundly distrusted by many contemporary film historians, who rightly point out that a large amount of early film history was written by Grierson's prodigies.[99] During the Thatcherite period the EMB's influence was attacked on the grounds both that it had turned British cinema away from the commercial sector and that it had unimaginatively tethered ideas of 'quality' to a realist aesthetic.[100] Its hunger for 'a new type entertainment' and distaste 'for the sex and crime material of which two-thirds of our present [film] programmes consists' made it appear prudish, middlebrow and paternalistic.[101]

Furthermore, the EMB Film Unit was seen to have neutered the individual political freedom of documentary film-makers. Produced with corporate or government money and lacking in sustained systematic social criticism, its films have been accused of 'squaring the circle of right-wing money and left-wing kudos'.[102] Because the EMB Film Unit was an exercise in public relations, film historians have felt comfortable reducing the EMB's work to corporate (and imperial) propaganda.[103] Increasingly, government suspicion of the Film Unit in the 1920s has been attributed to its lackadaisical bureaucratic practices rather than the content of its films.[104]

Much of this criticism appears guilty of transposing its own anxieties back into the past. Lacking a sound historical footing, it makes a literal equivalence between the practice and politics of present-day public relations and 'public relations' during the interwar period. The form of 'public relations' practiced by the EMB Film Unit was directly related to the growth of inter-war forums for fostering, as Arthur Marwick termed it, 'middle opinion'.[105] It was an educational cinema watched by, and sometimes starring, intellectuals who believed in the primacy of scientific and technological solutions over party politics. It served the technocrats, philanthropists and bureaucrats who were to staff the policy-making committees of the Welfare State, together with the voluntary, professional and commercial organisations which were to advise it into the 1950s. At the close of the Second World War, *The Manchester Guardian* even identified documentary cinema 'as the main highway of future social progress'.[106] The Butskellite solidity of the documentary movement so apparent in retrospect (to contemporaries the EMB film-makers took a hungry-eyed approach to an unusual range of aesthetic and intellectual influences) perhaps explains the subsequent hostility of new right and new left critics.[107] Retrospectively, the documentary cinema created by Tallents and Grierson looks like a cultural appendage of the hated postwar settlement.

The development of documentary cinema at the EMB illustrates something of the trajectory of the wider practice of public relations throughout the 1930s. Early EMB films like *The Song of Ceylon* and *Industrial Britain* were essentially expositional 'closed' texts. *Industrial Britain*'s commentary posited steel-workers as the skilled successors to the Egyptian empire and compared potters in Stoke with their forebears in ancient Greece.[108] After the Film Unit transferred to the GPO with Tallents in 1933, however, the documentarists were able to address their subject matter in less mediated terms. Most EMB films had been silent, but the purchase of portable sound equipment enabled the Film Unit to record authentic speech (first heard in Harry Watts's *Six-Thirty Collection*) more easily and film on location (most movingly in *Housing Problems*, where East Enders speak directly to camera).[109] Talking generally about public relations we can see how the EMB's early efforts to present predetermined ideas were gradually abandoned. Projection, it was concluded, could work only if it built upon a profound understanding of the intended audience. Moreover, understanding this true nature meant adopting a more open, and less hierarchical, relationship between Britain and the Empire. The radical crux of the argument in *The Projection of England*, then, was not the argument that Britain needed to master the new media arts but the recognition that mastering these arts entailed a profound reorganisation of government, industry, science and society.

Notes

1 Tallents, *The Projection of England*, p. 11.
2 Bernays, *Propaganda*, p. 156, and Tallents, *The Projection of England*, p. 29.
3 J. Marchant, *The Cinema in Education* (London, 1925).
4 Qtd in R. Smyth, 'The Development of British Colonial Film Policy, 1927–1939, with Special Reference to East and Central Africa', *Journal of African History*, Vol. 20, No. 3, 1979, p. 438.
5 George Dulac's abstract *Le Coquille et Le Clergyman* was banned on the grounds that 'this film is so cryptic as to be meaningless. If there is meaning it is doubtless objectionable.' Qtd in T. D. Mathews, *Censored: What They Didn't Allow You to See, and Why – The Story of Film Censorship in Britain* (London, 1994), p. 61.
6 Grierson wrote: 'Poor dear censor Wilkinson, with his Blake's poetry and his beloved pre-Raphaelites, has, in the jungle of Wardour Street, the strength of ten ... created by the Trade as an image of gratuitous fright, it is not surprising that his slogan "no controversy" – which to philosophy and all the world is "no reality" – is abjectly obeyed'. J. Grierson, 'On the Course

of Realism' in C. Davey (ed.), *Footnotes to the Film* (London, 1937), p. 141.

7 G. Perry, *The Great British Picture Show* (London, 1985). It can be argued that the Act radically stimulated Britain's film output, making the UK the second largest film-producing nation in the world and laying the long-term foundations for the popular British industry's postwar success. See M. Sweet, *Shepperton Babylon: The Lost Worlds of British Cinema* (London, 2005).

8 *The Times*, 24 May 1926, p. 14.

9 NA, STAT 14/438, 'Cinematograph Section. Establishments and Functions'.

10 The government instructed its departments to co-operate with film companies only for large fees. See NA, STAT 14/438, 'Cinematograph Section. Establishments and Functions', 'Official Film Profits', *The Morning Post*, 1 February 1927.

11 Tallents had served alongside Kipling's son in the First World War and takes a role in Kipling's account of the Battle of Festubert. See R. Kipling (ed.), *The Irish Guards in the Great War: The First Battalion* (London, 1923), pp. 95–98.

12 Tallents papers, File 28, 'Supporting Papers', 'Notes of a Talk with Mr Rudyard Kipling'.

13 In fairness to Creighton, the first fruit of *One Family*, a short extract entitled *Southern April* ('a study of a day in a South African spring') was praised by Paul Rotha and *The Observer*. The review claimed that the short displayed 'what lovely things can be done with a camera and a microphone by a man of both sensibility and idea'. Tallents papers, 'A Southern April', *Observer*, 30 June 1930.

14 Qtd in A. Cooke (ed.) *Garbo and the Night Watchmen: A Selection from the Writings of British and American Film Critics* (London, 1937), pp. 49–50.

15 'Live natives' were commonly used to promote films with 'exotic' subject matter. See P. H. Hansen, 'The Dancing Lamas of Everest: Cinema, Orientalism, and Anglo-Tibetan Relations in the 1920s', *The American Historical Review*, Vol. 101, No. 3, June, 1996, pp. 712–747.

16 S. Tallets, 'The Birth of the British Documentary (Part I)', *Journal of the University Film Association*, Vol. 20, No. 1, 1968, p. 21.

17 See Tallents papers, File 6, 'The Buy British Campaign', Draft of HRH The Prince of Wales' address on 16 November.

18 *One Family* was perceived to follow in a governmental tradition of wasteful and over-ambitious cultural patronage. The commissioning of D. W. Griffith to create *Hearts of the World*, 'a (First World War) drama of humanity, photographed in the battle area' was the most celebrated cinematic example of this. See K. Brownlow, *The War, the West and the Wilderness* (New York, 1979).

19 Tallents remembered watching films such as '*Solid Sunshine*, a New Zealand film on butter production, perhaps the brightest of the many films made by overseas governments at that time in praise of particular products. We ran over a series of advertising films made by Kodak and Kia Ora. In *Electricity on the Farm* we saw an interesting attempt by Jean Benoit-Levy to bring home to farmers what the introduction of electric power might mean to them. In *Influenza* we noted a useful German health propaganda film.' Tallents, 'The Birth of the British Documentary (Part I)', p. 18.

20 S. Tallents, 'The Documentary Film', *The Journal of the Royal Society of Arts*, Vol. XCV, No. 4733, 20 December 1946, p. 76.

21 There is an argument that the development of the non-fiction film is intertwined with the beginnings of a mass education programme to increase the public understanding of science. See T. Boon, *Films of Fact: A History of Science in Documentary Films and Television* (London, 2008).

22 See M. Field and P. Smith, *Secrets of Nature* (London, 1934).

23 Canti devised a way of preventing the light needed to expose film from stunting the growth of the cells. It is a testament to the voracity of Canti's intellect that what began as a series of experiments in part constructed from his son's Meccano finished with Canti adapting the first 1,000,000 volt Deep X-Ray machine for use at St Bartholemew's Hospital just before his death in 1936. See G. Foxon, 'Early Biological Film: The Work of R. G. Canti', *University Vision*, No. 15, December 1976, pp. 5–13.

24 'Dr Canti. A Pioneer in Films for Research', *The Times*, 9 January 1936, p. 12.

25 It might also be relevant that Arthur Elton, Stuart Legg, Humphrey Jennings, Stuart Legg and Basil Wright were all recruited to the Film Unit from Canti's base in Cambridge. See I. Aitken (ed.) *The Documentary Film Movement: An Anthology* (Edinburgh, 1998), pp. 2–10.

26 The Commission on Cultural and Educational Film, *The Film*

in National Life: Being the Report of an Enquiry Conducted by the Commission on Educational and Cultural Films into the Service which the Cinematograph may Render to Education and Social Progress (London, 1932), p. 12.

27 Tallents was a Dovzhenko enthusiast. He wrote of *Earth*: 'Who, that has ever seen it could ever forget his moving shots of rain falling upon apples.' Tallents, 'The Birth of the British Documentary (Part I)', p. 19.

28 It must be stressed that Stapledon conceived of people's responsibility to the environment in a spiritual as well as political way. See G. Stapledon, *The Land Now and To-morrow* (London, 1935), and R. Waller, *Prophet of the New Age: The Life and Thought of Sir George Stapledon* (London, 1962).

29 Commission on Cultural and Educational Film, *The Film in National Life*, p. 137.

30 NA, CO 760/37, 'EMB Film Committee. Minutes and Papers', F. C. Badgeley, 'Report on the Activities of the Canadian Motion Picture Bureau', 24 August 1928.

31 Tallents, *Projection*, p. 37.

32 Edgar Anstey qtd in C. Belfrage (ed.) *All Is Grist* (London, 1988), p. 80.

33 See R. Low, *The History of the British Film, 1929–1939: Documentary and Educational Films of the 1930s* (London, 1997), p. 61.

34 Britain's exhibitors adopted sound with a rapidity unmatched on the continent. In 1929, 22% of cinemas were wired for 'talkies', this number had reached 63% by 1932. See D. Cook, *A History of Narrative Film* (New York & London, 1990).

35 C. Lejeune, 'This Week's Films', *The Observer*, 14 September 1930. Seemingly only one regional critic questioned Grierson's bluff: 'Grierson calls his film, a film for schools. Whom did he consult in making it with a knowledge of schools? I personally deplore any praise given to his work at the present time, however imaginative and enterprising it may be, as I think that both administratively and artistically, it is along entirely wrong lines and is likely to remain there until he and the EMB come down to real life and consult people with knowledge about schools.' 'Review', *Newcastle Evening Chronicle*, 25 November 1935, p. 31.

36 This was a phrase of Grierson remembered by Tallents. BBC Archive, Stephen Tallents, 'The Factual Film', *BBC Radio*, 5 February 1947.

37 Grierson later wrote the foreword to W. H. George's *The Cinema in School* (London, 1935).

38 Under the direction of Charles Cleland a series of education films were commissioned by Glasgow council, some of which were directed by Grierson's sister. For more on local government film, see E. Lebas, '"When Every Street Became a Cinema": The Film Work of Bermondsey Borough Council's Public Health Department, 1923–1953', *History Workshop Journal*, 39, 1995, pp. 42–66.

39 C. Cleland, 'Displaying the Empire', *The Times*, 17 August 1933, p. 6.

40 The young Grierson made the acquaintance of Robert M. Hutchins and studied alongside Harold Lasswell, two figures whose life and work was to have important ramifications in what was to become Grierson's field of expertise. See Harry S. Ashmore, *Unseasonable Truths: The Life of Robert Maynard Hutchins* (Boston & London, 1989), and Dwaine Marvick, 'The Work of Harold D. Lasswell: His Approach, Concerns and Influence', *Political Behaviour*, 1980, pp. 219–229. It should be noted that Grierson never wrote an essay or sat an exam during his period of 'study' in America. See Jack C. Ellis, 'The Young Grierson in America, 1924–1927', *Cinema Journal*, 1968, pp. 12–21.

41 In three books, *Public Opinion* (1922), *The Phantom Public* (1925) and *A Preface to Morals* (1929), Lippmann threw off his early radicalism to argue that the distortions of mass democracy endangered civilisation. For a thorough analysis of Lippmann's thinking see Ronald Steel, *Walter Lippmann and the American Century* (Boston, 1980).

42 Grierson archive, G4/19/17, 'Searchlight on Democracy', written for an adult education conference in England, Summer 1939.

43 See Jack C. Ellis, 'Grierson at University', *Cinema Journal*, 1973, pp. 39–47. At Glasgow, Grierson had studied under A. D. Lindsay, 'the Balliol philosopher' and staunch supporter of the Worker's education movement. Grierson also said his familiarity with Burns, Macaulay and Mill enabled him to reject Lippmann's pessimistic conclusions. See I. Aitken, *Film & Reform: John Grierson and the Documentary Film Movement* (London & New York, 1990).

44 Huxley described Grierson as 'a Scot with the air of a tough little terrier'. Huxley, *Both Hands*, p. 128.

45 A cartoon in *Punch* published alongside a review of Tallents's

The Projection of England pictured Grierson alongside Tallents, navigating their way across said distances. 16 August 1933. Grierson archive, G6A.8.6, 'cartoon of Grierson and Tallents steering a ship entitled "Protection of Britain"'.

46 Tallents, *The Projection of England*, p. 30.

47 John Grierson, 'On the Course of Realism', in C. Davey (ed.) *Footnotes to the Film* (London, 1937), p. 144.

48 British film was suspected of prizing 'aristocratic' tastes. See K. Bamford, *Distorted Images: British National Identity and Film in the 1920s* (London & New York, 1999).

49 For a searching debate about this see A. Higson, '"Britain's Outstanding Contribution to Film": The Documentary-realist Tradition', in C. Barr (ed.) *All Our Yesterdays: 90 Years of British Cinema* (London, 1986), pp. 72–97.

50 To begin with, Grierson used 'documentary' as an adjective – a corruption of the French – rather than a noun: '*Moana* ... has documentary value'.

51 Grierson re-edited *Drifters* again for a TV documentary to further strengthen the comparison. BBC Archive, A. Elton, 'Projection of Britain', *BBC Television*, 23 November 1954.

52 Tallents, 'The Birth of the British Documentary (Part II)', p. 28.

53 I. Montagu, *With Eisenstein in Hollywood: A Chapter of Autobiography* (Berlin, 1968), p. 31.

54 NA, CO 760/37, 'EMB Film Committee. Minutes and Papers', 'Craig to Tallents', 28 February 1929.

55 Tallents papers, File 36, 'Cinema. Supporting Papers', Letter from Arthur Elton, 13 September 1944.

56 Or as Tallents put it, '*Drifters* was a real pioneer and more. It rejected the escapism of the ordinary box-office film. It did not seek to spirit its audience away from real every-day life to dream. It had no snob appeal, making falsely glamorous and desirable to humble people the fundamentally commonplace and vulgar luxuries of the rich. It took as its raw material the everyday life of ordinary men and from that neglected vein won interest, dignity and beauty ... It differed from Robert Flaherty's work in that it did not go to the far North or the South Seas in search of the remote of the exotic. It differed from the work of the Soviets in that it was harnessed to no political theme. Owing much to those two sources, it yet enjoyed a greater liberty and struck a more universal note than *Nanook* or *Turksib*.' Tallents, 'The Birth of the British Documentary (Part II)', p. 28.

57 J. Grierson, 'Making a Film of the Actual', *Close-Up*, Vol. V, No. 5, November 1929, p. 403.

58 Harry Watt claimed that he had been given a job at the Film Unit only because he was Scottish and served at sea. H. Watt, *Don't Look at the Camera* (London, 1974), pp. 35–36.

59 Tallents wrote a column on country living for *The Observer*; a selection of these were later published as *Green Thoughts* in 1952. Paul Rotha was dismissed after failing to film some tulips which Tallents liked. P. Rotha, *Documentary Diary: An Informal History of the British Documentary Film, 1928–1939* (London, 1973), pp. 40–41.

60 See R. McKibbin, *Classes and Cultures: England 1918–1951* (Oxford, 1998; 2000).

61 P. Jackson, *A Retake Please! From Night Mail to Western Approaches* (Liverpool, 1999), p. 25.

62 Tallents papers, File 11, 'Letters about EMB, 1933', 'Letter to B. Bruce', 2 February 1933.

63 Tallents regretted that the Board of Trade he had joined in 1909 was not the 'academy of belles lettres' denounced by Edmund Burke, where 'every department of literature, the solid and the entertaining, the instructive and amazing, had its separate Professor'. Tallents, *Man and Boy*, p. 161.

64 For more on Tallents's correspondence with Cockerell see British Library, Sydney Cockerell letters, Add. 52755 ff. 1–5. Tallents's correspondence with John Summerson is at the Victoria and Albert Museum, John Summerson papers, SUJ/3/3, SUJ/3/4 and SUJ/3/6. Tallents's friendship with Sutherland and the extent of his collection of Ravilious paintings were revealed to me by personal interview with his daughter. 'Interview with Miranda Pemberton-Piggot', 11 February 2007.

65 On *The Starry Pool* see H. Child, 'Home from the War', *Times Literary Supplement*, 8 January 1918, p. 358. By contrast, the *TLS* wrote that *The Dancer* displays 'a passion for the dainty, and, in the dialogue, an artificiality that is almost an affectation' that results in 'passages that make one wince'. It is difficult not to agree with this verdict. G. W. Bullett, 'The Dancer and Other Tales', *Times Literary Supplement*, 21 September 1922, p. 598.

66 It appears likely that Grierson approached Nichols after reading his fellow countryman's attack on governmental attitudes to film in *The Times*. See 'Films and False Values', *The Times*, 20 January 1927, p. 8.

67 LSE Archive, Lloyd papers, 'Tallents to Lloyd', 28 March 1935.

68 Tallents, 'The Birth of the British Documentary (Part II)', p. 29.

69 Modern Records Centre, TUC Archive, MSS. 292/675.63/2, 'The Power of the Cinema as a Cultural and Propagandist Force – Talk by John Skeaping, John Grierson and Robert Flaherty', 21 January 1935.

70 Crawford's innovations were not uniformly popular ('the advertiser is being led up the garden path by young men and women from Chelsea who cannot draw, but who, nevertheless, must live') but they were much discussed. See P. Belloc, 'What Use Is All This Impressionist Stuff?', *Advertising World*, Vol. 52, No. 6, May 1927, p. 21.

71 From their rebranding as 'The Windsors' to the birth of a popular honours list and the publication of best-selling books such as *The King's Dogs*, the Royal Family were actually amongst the most skilful users of the media. This argument was strikingly put by Sian Nicholas in a paper at a 'Media and History' conference at London University in 2005. S. Nicholas, '"Kings or Fellow Human Beings": The Monarchy and the Media in Inter-war Britain', 30 June 2005. See also F. Prochaska, *Royal Bounty, The Making of a Welfare Monarchy* (New Haven and London, 1995).

72 Tallents, *Projection*, p. 37.

73 J. B. Priestley was famously intrigued by the 'new' England of suburbs and Woolworths. See J. B. Priestley, *English Journey* (New York & London, 1934). George Orwell reasoned that among the new indeterminate class of light industry and new technology that lived in Barnet, Dagenham, Hayes and Slough 'belong the people who are most at home in and most definitely of the modern world'. G. Orwell, 'The Lion and the Unicorn', in B. Crick (ed.) *George Orwell: Essays* (London, 2000), p. 158.

74 See H. G. Wells, *The Work, Wealth and Happiness of Mankind* (London, 1932).

75 J. Grierson, 'Films in the Public Service', *Public Administration*, Vol. XIV, No. 4, October 1936, p. 368.

76 It has been argued that the exhibitions which EMB films were exhibited in were crucial to this social network. P. Greenhalgh, *Ephemeral Vistas: The Expositions Universelles, Great Exhibitions and World's Fairs, 1851–1939* (Manchester, 1988).

77 Tallents papers, File 26, 'The Start'.

78 The Imperial Economic Committee had already discussed the Empire's weak position in the field. See 'Films and the Empire',

The Nineteenth Century, Vol. 19, No. 596, 1926, London, pp. 497–510.

79 F. Hardy, *John Grierson: A Documentary Biography* (London, 1979), p. 41 At the time Soviet films were effectively suppressed. See Mathews, *Censored*.

80 On seeing *One Family*, Grierson is reported to have said to Wright, 'Ha Ha, Wright, that's O.K. From now on Creighton's out and we're in.' Tallents papers, File 36, 'Cinema. Supporting Papers', 'Letter from B. Wright', 22 August 1944.

81 Leo Amery Papers, AMEL 2/1/25, J. Grierson, 'National Film Service in the Dominions'. Grierson later reflected that the principal effect of the EMB Film Unit was to 'change the connotations of the word "Empire". Our original command of peoples was becoming slowly a co-operative effort in the tilling of soil, the reaping of harvest, and the organisation of a world economy. For the old flags of exploitation it substituted the new flags of common labour; for the old frontiers of conquest it substituted the new frontiers of research and world wide organisation. Whatever's one's politics, and however cynical one might be about the factors destructive of a world economy, this change of emphasis had an ultimate historical importance. History is determined by just such building on new sentiments.' The volume from which this quotation is taken is dedicated to Stephen Tallents. J. Grierson, 'The EMB Film Unit', in F. Hardy (ed.) *Grierson on Documentary*, pp. 48–49.

82 It later inspired *Night Mail*, the (GPO) Film Unit's most fondly remembered work. Basil Wright wrote, '*Turksib* dramatically bought to life an economic, social and geographical problem ... [but this became] in Turin's hands an exciting and inspiring film. His images, in terms of communities seen largely through individual and personal needs, were built up through crosscutting, not merely shot by shot but also sequence by sequence, to a point when a sudden shout of a locomotive starting off in a cloud of hissing steam seemed not just a solution but a veritable god from heaven.' B. Wright, *The Long View: An International History of Cinema* (London, 1974), p. 117.

83 Recently the post-colonial theorists Lindsay Proudfoot and Michael Roche have argued that twentieth-century imperial development was neither solely centrifugal nor centripetal, but diversely discursive. The EMB Film Unit's dependence on the Canadian Motion Picture Board and films imported from New Zealand is a good example of the complicated nature of imperial

development. See L. Proudfoot and M. Roche, 'Place, Network, and the Geographies of Empire', in L. Proudfoot and M. Roche (eds) *(Dis)Placing Empire: Renegotiating British Colonial Geographies* (Aldershot, 2005), pp. 1–15.

84 See C. Ellis and B. A. McLane, *A New History of Documentary Film* (New York & London, 2005), pp. 57–76.

85 Tallents, *The Projection of England*, pp. 31–32.

86 Tallents papers, File 32, 'Prelude to Publicity'.

87 In 1937 Wendt abandoned classical music to concentrate on a career in photography. Wendt's photographs of Ceylon make a suggestive counterpoint to Wright's film. L. Wendt, *Ceylon* (London, 1950).

88 Jeffrey Richards has argued that these films displayed an image of 'The operation of British character at its best, a character that was a cross between evangelical commitment, strength of purpose and hard work and chivalric ideals of leadership, service and sacrifice … The great heroes of the empire were heroic individualists who embodied the national character in its noblest form – stoicism, service, duty. Almost all of them died, making the ultimate sacrifice and becoming effectively the gods and martyr saints of an Imperial religion, representing a potent fusion of Protestant Christianity and British imperialism.' J. Richards, *Films and British National Identity* (Manchester, 1997), p. 41.

89 Ironically, Korda's films followed Hollywood trends which, in films such as *The Lives of a Bengal Lancer*, had appropriated the British Empire as a suitable setting for generic cross-cultural romances and 'women in peril' pictures. Gore Vidal wrote, 'there were ubiquitous newsreels of the King and Queen on coronation day, as well as feature films of gallant little England menaced by Spain's Armada and Napoleon's armies. There were also biographical films of Chatham and Pitt, of Clive and Disraeli, of Wellington and Nelson. It was not until 1939 that we [Americans] got part of our story, *Gone With the Wind*. But by then a whole generation of US filmmakers had defended the frontiers of the Raj and charged with the light brigade at Balaklava. We served neither Lincoln nor Jefferson Davies; we served the Crown.' Qtd in T. D. Mathews, *Censored*, p. 97.

90 See, for example, M. Stollery, *Alternative Empires: European Modernist Cinemas and the Culture of Imperialism* (Exeter, 2000).

91 J. Donald, 'Introduction', in J. Donald, A. Freidberg and

L. Marcus (eds), *Close-Up 1927–1933: Cinema and Modernism* (London, 1998), pp. 28–35.

92 There has been some debate about how far 'progressive' images of Empire during the interwar period rested upon covert assumptions of racial hierarchy. While it is true that the EMB's films and posters do not preclude 'imperialist' readings, the EMB's research and the films it made about the research undermine any kind of universal 'imperialist' judgement. See D. Simonelli, '"Laughing nations of happy children who have never grown up": Race, the Concept of Commonwealth and the 1924–25 British Empire Exhibition', *Journal of Colonialism and Colonial History*, Vol. 10, No. 1, Spring 2009.

93 Tallents, *The Projection of England*, p. 37.

94 G. Greene, *Mornings in the Dark* (London, 1995), p. 93.

95 The contrast between the international prize-winning 'sophistication' of *Song of Ceylon* also makes an interesting comparison with, for example, French attempts to promote imperial achievements in film such as *Harmonieux Ombrages d'Indochine* and *Collines Parfumées des Plateaux Moïs*.

96 S. Tallents, 'The Documentary Film', *The Journal of the Royal Society of Arts*, Vol. XCV, No. 4733, 20 December 1946, p. 80.

97 Unlike Greene, who characterised Korda's epics as preposterous spectacles, Grierson and Wright attacked the popular imperialist films of the age for their racism and unreality. Later, Wright acclaimed Harry Watt's Australian western, *The Overlanders*, as the true heir of EMB idealism. The 'sweep, range and essential humanity' of Watt's tale of ranchers in the Outback proved 'that there are more Commonwealth nations stories able to fire people's imagination than Hollywood ever imagined.' B. Wright, 'The Cinema', *The Spectator*, Vol. 177, No. 6172, 11 October 1946, p. 364.

98 For a searching debate about this see A. Higson, '"Britain's Outstanding Contribution to Film": The Documentary-realist Tradition', in C. Barr (ed.) *All Our Yesterdays: 90 Years of British Cinema* (London, 1986), pp. 72–97.

99 Paul Rotha's *The Film till Now* (1930) was the first 'serious' film book published in Britain. The dust jacket of Andrew Buchanan's contemporaneous *Films: The Way of the Cinema* (London, 1932) was a still from *Drifters*.

100 See P. Wollen, 'The Last New Wave: Modernism in the British Films of the Thatcher Era', in L. Friedman (ed.) *British Cinema and Thatcherism: Fires Were Started* (London, 1993), pp. 35–51.

101 Tallents, *The Projection of England*, p. 32. *The Film in National Life* was equally insistent: 'we do not want to spoil good entertainment, but, by adding a new ingredient, to give richness to the mixture'. *The Film in National Life*, p. 13.

102 B. Winston, *Claiming the Real: The Documentary Film Revisited* (London, 1995), p. 60.

103 The EMB's film-makers determinedly, almost defensively, stressed their reformist credentials to Elizabeth Sussex. See E. Sussex, *The Rise and Fall of British Documentary* (Berkeley, 1975).

104 Nicholas Pronay, who worked unhappily with Grierson, argued that his boss's unpopularity was a simple matter of office politics. 'Cooking figures, loading arguments, bringing discreet pressure by leaks to the press were perfectly alright by Civil Service conventions – provided it was aimed at the politicians. But to do that to your fellow Civil Servants broke the rules of the club.' N. Pronay, 'John Grierson and the Documentary – 60 Years On', *Historical Journal of Film, Radio and Television*, Vol. 9, No. 3, 1989, p. 235. For the most convincing iteration of this thesis, see P. Swann, *The British Documentary Movement, 1926–1946* (Cambridge, 1989).

105 Marwick, 'Middle Opinion in the Thirties: Planning, Progress and Political "Agreement"', *The English Historical Review*, Vol. LXXIX, No. CCXI, 1964, pp. 285–298.

106 'Editorial', *The Manchester Guardian*, 31 March 1944.

107 See Patrick Russell and James Taylor (eds) *Shadows of Progress: Britain's Forgotten Post-war Documentaries* (London, 2010).

108 As the director Harry Watt explained it, 'Every film we made had this in it, that we were trying to give an image of the workingman away from the Edwardian, Victorian, capitalist attitudes.' Harry Watt qtd in E. Barnouw, *Documentary: A History of the Non-fiction Film* (New York & Oxford, 1974), p. 90.

109 *Housing Problems* was made by the GPO Film Unit trainees Edgar Anstey and Arthur Elton, although financed by the gas industry.

1 Tallents's elopement with Bridget Hole, the wealthy heir of Samuel
Hugh Franklin Hole, prompted a society scandal. The marriage proved
advantageous to Tallents but it was not a happy union.

2 & 3   In one of the EMB's early campaigns Tallents used photographs
of his own family to promote the benefits of drinking milk. Such images,
along with the decision to house the Board's posters in museum-like
display cases, imbued the Board's promotional work with a character of
polite formality.

4 & 5 In the EMB's posters, shop displays and films, an Arts and Crafts-esque devotion to ensuring that everyday objects were finished to the highest aesthetic standards fused with an intuitive understanding of the new multi-media landscape. Mark Gertler's posters, for example, were designed to resonate with shop window displays.

6 & 7 Although John Grierson's *Drifters* was part of a campaign to increase sales of fish, its everyday subject matter, skilful use of Soviet montage, and sets by the sculptor John Skeaping, helped redefine the idea of sponsored film and by doing so broadened the aesthetic and intellectual parameters of British cinema. 'It may be that', as Tallents put it, '"another commonplace model to paint", was all that Raphael thought as he began the Sistine Madonna.'

THERE'S ALL THE HEALTH OF THE SEA IN FISH

8 The publication of *The Projection of England* secured Tallents and Grierson an international reputation. Tallents posited 'film, radio, poster and exhibition as the sextant and compass which would manoeuvre citizenship over the new (democratic) distances.'

[*The Protection of Britain*

Mr. John Grierson and Sir Stephen Tallents

9 & 10 As Britain's biggest employer of scientists, the GPO was well placed to sponsor projects that fused new technology, applied engineering and modern aesthetics. Hi-tech exhibition pavilions and eye-catching innovations (such as streamlined air mail vans) represent only the most visible tip of the GPO's innovations.

THE DENBIES THAT THOMAS CUBITT PULLED DOWN

THE DENBIES THAT THOMAS CUBITT PUT UP

NEW TOWN: HARLOW

Contoured model constructed for the Development Corporation to the design of FREDERICK GIBBERD

Scale: 1/2,500 *Dimensions*: 10 ft. × 7 ft.

PROPOSED TOWN CENTRE—WESTON-SUPER-MARE

Model made for the Corporation to the design of CLOUGH WILLIAMS-ELLIS and LIONEL BRETT

Scale: 1/500 *Dimensions*: 7 ft. 6 in. × 6 ft.

11 & 12 & 13 Despite his attachment to the rural idyll of St John's Jerusalem in Kent, Tallents was also an advocate of 'appropriate' modernist development. His well-publicised familial relationship to the 'progressive' architect Thomas Cubbit underpinned a catholic interest in architecture that was to prove useful in negotiating between the conflicting aims of architects, planners, politicians and people at the Ministry of Town and Country Planning.

EXHIBITION STAND

Two views of the stand designed by RICHARD GUYATT for
Messrs Josiah Wedgwood & Sons Limited (B.I.F. 1949)

Dimensions: 27 ft. × 22 ft. 6 in.

14 & 15 Not only did working on The Lion and Unicorn pavilion at The Festival of Britain enable Tallents to flesh out ideas first expressed in *The Projection of England*, but it gave Cockade (Tallents' model-making company), the impetus to establish itself as one of the leading exhibition design consultancies of the immediate post-war period.

4

A triumph of public relations:
The GPO, 1933–1935

Sir Kingsley Wood pulled Tallents and his Film Unit from the wreckage of the EMB in August 1933. Wood, who served as Post Master General (PMG) from November 1931 to June 1935, had been given responsibility for reorganising the Post Office (GPO) in the wake of the criticisms made by the Bridgeman Committee of 1932. The national government wanted the GPO to operate along 'modern' principles similar to organisations such as the Central Electricity Board. It was a modernisation project that had two strands. Firstly, it sought to free the GPO from direct political control. The Treasury had previously used GPO revenues to cross-subsidise deficits elsewhere, taking an annually determined sum out of Post Office revenues to help balance the national finances. As a result of the national government's reforms, the Treasury would receive a fixed-dividend while the PMG would delegate more of his powers to newly appointed independent business administrators. Freed from short-term political interference, the Post Office would – in theory – be able to concentrate on developing its services and, in particular, the national telephone network. The second, psycho-logical, strand of Wood's modernisation project saw 'Controllers' with external expertise appointed in place of the 'Secretaries' that had risen through the Post Office ranks. Stephen Tallents's appointment to the Post Office Board in the newly created role of Controller of Public Relations represented an attempt to mentally embed Wood's modernisation project. More specifically, Tallents was tasked with developing a programme of public diplomacy that was able to stave off public disquiet and political criticism.

The development of public relations at the Post Office

As early as 1922 a House of Commons Select Committee on the Telephone Service made an unfavourable comparison between British take-up of the telephone (about 2% of the population) with American (around 12%). Consequently, Liberals placed the expansion of the telephone service at the heart of their 1929 election manifesto. In *We Can Conquer Unemployment*, and the subsequent *How to Tackle Unemployment*, they argued that the telephone network should be expanded through a programme of public works.[1] Conservatives such as Viscount Wolmer, by contrast, believed that the GPO's failure to invest adequately in the telephone service variously suggested the wisdom of 'Americanisation' and part-privatisation.[2] 'I have no prejudice against nationalisation, but I am bound to say that while the Post Office monopoly gives us obvious advantages in point of economy', as *The Observer* had it, 'no private business could survive if conducted as dully and simply as the Post Office'.[3]

Tallents had first been appointed to the GPO's Publicity Committee by Clement Attlee in 1931. Ideologically committed to nationalisation, Attlee was embarrassed by the widespread accusation that the Post Office was stifling technological innovation.[4] After undertaking a course in new business administration at Imperial Chemical Industries (ICI), he vowed to restore the GPO's standing as 'the outstanding example of collective capitalism'.[5] The advice of the newspaper magnate Lord Iliffe (who was also an adviser to the EMB) led Attlee to further consult with Sir William Crawford, who in turn recommended Tallents.[6]

Advised by Chancellor Neville Chamberlain that the GPO would not be split up or part-privatised, Kingsley Wood appointed Tallents to the Board in a bid to neutralise a politically divisive issue.[7] Here he looked across the Atlantic to the example of the American Telephone and Telegraph Company (AT&T). Under the leadership of Theodore Newton Vail, AT&T had developed an expansive attitude to publicity and public relations that reflected both Vail's idealism and the company's near-monopoly power.[8] AT&T portrayed itself as a benevolent organisation whose huge resources enabled the individual to communicate freely. 'When you lift the Bell receiver', the company claimed, 'you are in contact with the world'.[9] By appropriating the rhetoric of enlightened internationalism, AT&T pre-empted growing political criticism of its private ownership of a public technology. Tallents was to do likewise. His role 'was to be wider and of a higher status than that of a sales and publicity officer' and, like the head of public information at AT&T, Tallents was given a seat on the board.[10]

The GPO's lack of enthusiasm for telephony reflected the financial fact that £4.7 million of the GPO's £6.7 million loss in 1921 had been generated by the telephone service. The costs of expanding the telephone network, once a small but profitable luxury sideline (in conjunction with a fall in telephone charges) transformed it into a financial burden. The telephone was already an important business tool – Tallents's task was to domesticate it.

March 1934 saw the launch of 'Telephone Week', the Post Office's equivalent of the EMB's 'Buy British' campaign: 270,000 posters, 500,000 postcards, newsreels and shop furniture formed the basis of an extensive integrated marketing campaign.[11] With considerable resources at his disposal even last-minute ideas could be successfully incorporated into the sales drive. Tallents explained:

> To pick a small example, a few weeks ago it was noted that a public library advertised its willingness to answer enquiries by telephone. We have pursued this idea with the Library Association and expect shortly with their advice to approach every public library in the country, individually, pointing out the revised uses of the telephone to libraries, at the same time keeping our local sales staff in touch with what is being done.[12]

The spotting of the newspaper advertisement mentioned above, for example, quickly led to the printing of a series of customisable adhesive labels (bearing the words 'Telephone your orders') for distribution among small businesses. Such initiatives made Telephone Week an immediate success. The GPO's temporary shop in the Strand attracted 400,000 visitors. Regional outlets in Nottingham (148,666), Plymouth (108,710), Scarborough (109,108) and Ipswich (50,709) proved equally popular.

Telephone Week borrowed from the psychology as well as the methodology of the EMB's 'Buy British' campaign. Though noticeably more directive than the EMB's campaigns, the GPO's Telephone Week nevertheless conceptualised itself as a sales drive organised in the national interest. Tallents directed the GPO towards 'the awakening of a national "telephone mindedness"' rather than simply 'selling the telephone service to the individual'.[13] The encouragement of 'telephone mindedness' determined the development of new GPO services such as Directory Enquiries, the Speaking Clock and '999'.[14] These initiatives reinforced Tallents's attempt to position the telephone as an informal, everyday technology. Telephone Week, for instance, saw the GPO sponsor telephone chess matches between British regions.

Although they were presented as innovations in the idealistic vein of Rowland Hill's introduction of the national penny post in 1840, Telephone Week's success arguably rested upon incessantly advertised cuts in line rental charges and the sweeping away of extraneous deposits and surcharges. Previously, the Post Office had preferred to employ canvassers rather than advertise heavily. Indeed, the role of the GPO's first publicity officer – A. G. Highet, appointed in 1929 – had been to write leaflets for canvassers. However, Telephone Week's directness proved untypical. Instead, Tallents's used the initiative's success as the pretext for bringing existing sales and publicity staff under his control.[15] Rather than refining sales techniques, Tallents was to spend his time at the GPO broadening the idea of 'salesmanship'.

The development of background publicity

Background publicity was the term given by Tallents to the broad range of media and cultural activity that the GPO sponsored in an effort to raise its public profile rather than to achieve specific economic outcomes. In March 1933, Tallents commissioned MacDonald Gill to produce 'a single dignified design' that could be used throughout the GPO's publicity 'in the same way we use our emblem of the Crown and the initials at the EMB'.[16] Gill's new brand became central to the practice of background publicity: it was the psychological conceit by which a range of otherwise disparate activities were connected together to 'bring the post office alive'.[17] As Tallents had it:

> Any big undertaking, which succeeds in creating in the public mind an interest in its work, a conviction that it is actively trying to serve the public, a belief that it is more likely to be right than to be wrong, and a desire on the part of the public to co-operate with it, is saving friction in the working of the machine, discouragement among its staff and waste of time and effort in dealing with groundless or trivial complaints and suspicions.[18]

Taking Tallents's cue, the Post Office's early publicity initiatives sought to imbue the new GPO brand with positive associations. In 1934, the cable ship HTMS *Monarch* was sailed up the

Thames for the public to board. Speakers were erected outside the GPO's Strand shop to blare out a concert performed by Jack Hylton's jazz band as they were flown over London in an Imperial Airways plane. The extraordinary team of modernist musicians collected at the GPO Film Unit produced an avant-garde selection of 'novel GPO sounds' for broadcast by the BBC, and the Film Unit produced *Pett and Pott*.[19] Alberto Cavalcanti's short, which contrasted the sensible phone-owning Petts with the snobbish servant-keeping Potts, was the Film Unit's first full-scale venture into sound, and arguably the first slice of mass-appeal Surrealism ever committed to celluloid.[20] These attention-grabbing stunts punctuated the GPO's frequent displays at consumer events, such as the *Ideal Homes* show, at which the Post Office positioned itself as a patron of popular modern design.[21] Models of 'mutton chopped whiskered sub-postmasters' were used to illustrate 'the quaint old days of dusty inefficiency' that proceeded the GPO's stark, Edward McKnight Kauffer-designed, present.[22] The GPO even supplied actresses, such as Ursula Jeans, with custom telephone sets, and placed GPO receivers in the popular musicals of British film director Victor Saville.[23] 'Background publicity' entailed maintaining a constant low-level presence that would occasionally be thrown into sharp relief by targeted campaigns.

At the first remove the Post Office campaigns can simply be considered as better-funded iterations of EMB initiatives. Under Tallents the GPO produced a range of educational materials, supplying schools with educational posters, toy telephone sets, model post offices and instructional pamphlets on the history of communication written by Balliol scholars such as J. D. Beazley.[24] The GPO even collaborated on a children's book, *Peter and the Post Office*, which saw a magic dolphin give a small boy an explanatory tour – in a manner eerily similar to *One Family* – of GPO processes. 'I think you have seen a good deal of the Post Office and what it does', concludes the dolphin, 'It works day and night for you and if it were ever to stop for only one day the consequences would be disastrous'.[25] However, whereas the EMB was a collection of politicians, businessmen, scientists and artists held together by a small cadre of Civil Servants, the GPO was a massive organisation – until 1922 the largest employer in Britain – and in constant contact with the public. This close contact with the public enabled Tallents to let his initiatives-from-the-middle evolve an afterlife of their own. For instance, the decision to equip every Post Office in the United Kingdom with new high-quality pens not only attracted a deluge of publicity (some 2,500 column inches) but transformed into 'The Brighter Post Office' movement, a series of locally organised voluntary events that rejuvenated ageing post offices.

Tallents's determination to influence the design of postal workers' uniforms, the development of the air mail label and the layout of new post offices demonstrated an equally instinctive grasp of the need to build an emotional as well as official relationship with the public. He instructed colleagues that public relations had become a social necessity because the problems of distribution were beginning to displace the problems of production.[26] As scarcity receded, prospering in a world which gave citizens 'choice' demanded the provision of thoughtfully administered public services able to interact more casually with the public.[27] 'In one instance a lady from Wimbledon deplored the proposal to change her number 3015 as she said her family were tennis enthusiasts', went one well-practised anecdote; 'fortunately it was possible to offer 4030, and this number was at once accepted'.[28] As well as educating customers, Tallents was also believed in the necessity of educating staff. The dissemination of writing kits to local post offices was representative of the thinking behind Tallents's attempt to encourage a more personable approach.[29] His Head of Correspondence argued:

> Great masters of prose can no doubt master the official style, just as great poets welcome the restriction of the sonnet; but the ordinary man, compelled to avoid the first person active, has to use barbarous phrases like 'It is feared that' ... Our letters should help to bridge the gap between the Civil Service and the public; and our archaic formulae, which give the impression that our speech and our thought are different from those of the ordinary man, make that gulf wider.[30]

Tallents's strategy was praised by magazines like *Advertising World* and imitated by the likes of Shell, ICI, the Gas, Light and Coke Company, the Underground and Imperial Airways.[31] Indeed, the myriad social connections between these companies' public relations departments were an important constituent part of 'background publicity'.[32] Variously benevolent and spectacular, philanthropic and self-indulgent, 'background publicity' demonstrated not only how small improvements in presentation or service could yield a larger cumulative psychological effect but how massive organisations could personalise their public image.

The GPO's adoption of 'background publicity' also reflected the peculiarities of the political climate in an era of national government.[33] Previously, public relations at the Post Office had been associated with personal boosting. After the Select Committee on the Telephone Service had accused the GPO of believing that 'the public was made for the Post Office, and not the Post Office for the public', the then PMG Sir Laming Worthing-Evans had appointed H. Chapman as an Intelligence Officer.[34] The exact function of this ex-Ministry of Food Civil Servant is vague, but, by drafting an anonymous newspaper article in praise of 'Worthy', Chapman became the focus of a Parliamentary scandal.[35] Because of previous mistakes, Tallents's practice of public relations at the GPO took care to be consensual and self-effacing because previous practices had been so controversial.[36]

One advantage of the Post Office's background publicity campaigns is that they entailed a degree of diplomatic negotiation, and thus the actual process of organising the GPO's background publicity ventures became part of Tallents's public relations programme. So Wood, for instance, wrote to MPs of all parties to encourage public declarations of support for Telephone Week.[37] Here was evidence of the effectiveness of Tallents's entreaty that background publicity ought to 'enlist the willingness, indeed the active desire, of private citizens to do something in the public interest'.[38]

Working through chambers of commerce and trade unions, as well as organisations as unlikely as the National Association of Master Bakers, Confectioners and Caterers, increased the GPO's reach. By courting the patronage of politicians, and co-opting private and voluntary organisations into GPO campaigns, Tallents aggregated public opinion and blunted or marginalised both political and public criticism.

The internal politics of background publicity

Under the leadership of Evelyn Murray, the last Secretary of the GPO, senior management had thwarted several previous attempts to 'modernise' the Post Office. Indeed, Murray was scathing of what he saw as the capriciousness of politicians who demanded change, 'simply because it was conceived on grandiose and revolutionary lines and furnishes an opportunity for "constructive thought"'.[39] Murray's opposition to 'modernisation' protected the patch of a tier of senior management that objected to any curtailment of promotion by seniority, but it also stemmed from a genuine determination to project the service from cuts and defend the conditions of the lower ranks of staff. The brazenly commercial suggestions of both the Lever Committee of 1927 and the Simon Committee of 1929 (staffed by senior figures from Dunlop Rubber, ICI and the Underground) confirmed the general prejudice of Civil Servants that the adoption of modern business methods entailed the betrayal of public service ideals.[40] Although Wood dispensed with Murray and leaned heavily on external expertise, he still needed to reach an accommodation with the Murrayites who remained in the upper echelons of the Post Office's management.

Before Tallents's appointment, the initiatives of sales staff were dismissed on the grounds that 'the general atmosphere of exhortion, assertion, asseveration and "boost" in which publicity staff more or less generally live is a handicap in forming judgements'.[41] Received management scepticism had it that 'unless a particular service was widely useful on its merits advertisement had little or no effect [while] if it did possess these merits it developed without advertisement'.[42] It is worth stressing that what looks like uninspired inertia on the part of senior management also had a moral basis. The instrumental function of advertising, in particular, sat uneasily on the conscience of classically trained public servants. One official complained about the proposal to advertise the telegraph service:

> It may be taken for granted that nobody, broadly speaking, fails to send a telegram which it would pay him to send because it does not occur to him that he can send a telegram … Hence the objective of advertisement would be, broadly speaking, to persuade people to send telegrams which it was not worth their while to send. We are to use the art of psychological suggestion for the inducing of people to waste money in a particular way. The way itself is a blameless one, and is no doubt much better than many ways in which people waste their money, whether with or without the stimulus of advertisement. But a government service may be expected to have regard to other considerations than that of diverting as much money as possible into its own pockets.[43]

By contrast, background publicity proved more acceptable to opponents of 'modernisation' then previous initiatives because its aims were broader than mere salesmanship. The GPO had been monitoring the Canadian Post Office's 'educational' use of lectures, broadcasts and exhibitions since 1924, and while the managerial majority remained sceptical the Canadian approach did have its adherents.[44] Tallents's work could be seen as following the Canadian approach to public relations. He used modern communication methods to stretch simple forms of public instruction into a more sophisticated notion of customer service. Indeed, the use of modest contemporary posters and artful films encouraging the public to address envelopes carefully and post early could even be defended as contemporary iterations of nineteenth-century practices.[45] Simply put, 'background publicity' challenged the notion that promotional work represented an abuse of the GPO's monopoly power. 'It is the goodwill based on respect and regard that is most in keeping with our way of life in this country', reflected one Civil Servant, 'and it appears that it is with this democratic conception that Sir Stephen Tallents concerned himself while at the Post Office'.[46]

While GPO management remained agnostic to Tallents's innovations, postal workers became enthusiastic converts. Wages had fallen by 3% during the interwar years, as postal workers, like teachers and those in the armed forces, saw their incomes fall in the aftermath of the slump.[47] The Trades Disputes Act of 1927 had weakened and isolated Civil Service unions, while growing political and press criticism of the GPO further affected morale.[48] In this context, Tallents's schemes were welcomed by the GPO's dominant union, the Union of Postal Workers (UPW), as a mechanism for putting the Post Office's critics on to the back foot.

There was an interesting additional philosophical basis to postal union enthusiasm for 'public relations'. The UPW was heavily influenced by the Guild Socialism movement. This quintessentially British mixture of anti-state expansionism, medievalism and syndicalism had been fed through the union leadership by the teachings of G. D. H. Cole at Ruskin College, Oxford.[49] Postal workers had been among the first unions to align themselves with Cole's National Guild League, and had been campaigning for greater involvement in the running of the GPO since the publication of *Workers Control of the Post Office* in 1919. Worker participation was conceptualised as a corrective to bureaucracy, red tape and incompetent Civil Service management; the UPW hoped Tallents's appointment would lead to a greater appreciation of staff initiatives. The GPO's Whitley Committee had been

arguing since 1926 that management failure to adopt a strong
policy of public relations was undermining the Post Office's
viability.[50] The UPW accordingly idealised public relations as a
way in which 'the old and short-sighted take-it-or-leave-it attitude
would be entirely discredited and a new make-the-fullest-use-of-
me policy encouraged'.[51]

The development of internal publicity

With nearly a quarter of a million staff working in 23,000
offices, the interwar Post Office was a complex organisation that
encompassed strikingly different roles. The GPO's size led to an
inevitable amount of disconnection between, for instance, workers
on the GPO's underground railway and operators on the international telephone exchange. Thus, in addition to projecting facets
of GPO activity to the public, Tallents began to promote the Post
Office to its workers. He argued that staff should no longer be
left, 'as though they were trained zoologists, to deduce a complete
skeleton from the evidence of a single bone'.[52] Morale and organisational efficiency demanded that the workings of the GPO should
be more widely understood.

Launched in 1934, *The Post Office Magazine* was created
to give 'the individual Post Office servant a sense of the larger
activities of which his personal work was a part'.[53] Modelled
on the London Transport magazine, *Pennyfare, The Post Office
Magazine* contained regionalised reports and listings of the
cultural and sporting activities of GPO staff. Unlike its more
formal predecessors, *St Martins-le-Grand* and *Telephone and
Telegraph Journal,* it also utilised modern fonts, experimented
with new photographic techniques and was staffed by former
newspaper journalists. A consequence of bringing in external staff
was that, while some regular features, such as 'Our Working Day',
were obviously premeditated to expound particular processes
of the GPO, the editorial line is strikingly independent-minded.
The admission of a secretary that 'The work of a typist is on the
whole, monotonous' hastened the scrapping of 'Our Working
Day', and other overtly pedagogical items quickly suffered the
same fate.[54] Instead, *The Post Office Magazine* reflected Tallents's
apparently genuine enthusiasm for the GPO. The content of the
magazine alternated between 'real-life' stories, miscellany sourced
from GPO history (such as how Henry Turner posted himself, the
first person to do so) and some entertainingly unlikely items such

as the belief of staff at Popesgrove that they had been cursed by
the evil eye.[55] The magazine was dominated by visual material,
especially cartoons and large photo stories such as 'Bonny Banks
of Loch Lomond – A Red Van amid scenes of Scottish Romance
and History', 'Climbing a million steps to deliver to South
Stack Lighthouse, Anglesea [sic]' and 'Picturesque Post Offices in
Chettle and Shaftesbury, Dorset'. Both thematically and in tone
it could even be argued that The Post Office Magazine bears
striking resemblance to Tallents's own writing, especially as the
pronounced neo-Romanticism is invariably balanced by detailed
articles about the GPO's engineering and scientific research –
including a bizarre piece on how 'correctly selected furniture'
could reduce harmful sound vibrations.[56]

Overt GPO propaganda in The Post Office Magazine was
surprisingly slight, and official pronouncements were often treated
rather sceptically. For instance, perhaps reflecting Union unease
about the impact of motorisation, a story about telegraph delivery
boys receiving motorbikes was both guarded in its praise and
nostalgic for 'the olden days'.[57] The public are also often portrayed
with an amused cynicism. 'If he [a potential male customer] is
henpecked it will be futile to picture the joys of listening to his
wife's voice when absent from home', wrote a frustrated telephone
salesman, 'similarly, if house and furniture are over-insured he
will not consider it an advantage to be able to communicate
quickly with the fire station'.[58] The promotional value of The Post
Office Magazine stemmed from its self-confidence. The publication's editorial freedom, combined with its high production values,
encapsulated a pride and confidence in the postal service which
did not require tight policing. 'Of course there's drudgery as well
as interest, in Post Office work', Tallents wrote, 'so there is in all
departments and all businesses. But the balance of interest in Post
Office work seems to me unusually high.'[59] Implicit in the pages
of The Post Office Magazine is Tallents's conviction that the GPO
and its works are genuinely important. The generosity of this
approach to internal public relations bought further benefits. As
the Editor observed:

> The boycott of the Postal Office by the local press is well
> known yet the fact remains that The Post Office Magazine
> is continually being 'lifted' by such newspapers. The reasons
> of course are obvious. The local editor will put an embargo
> on 'dope' supplied by the Post Office, but as all editors have

a craving for a good 'story' their professional feelings get the better of them when they see first class stuff by Mr Briant in a copy of *The Post Office Magazine* ... I believe more could be done in this rather subtle way of getting the Post Office across through that very local press which is officially boycotting us.[60]

Not only were *The Post Office Magazine*'s stories 'lifted' by the press but it rapidly established itself as a commercial success. Early circulation estimates budgeted for sales of 40,000 but the first issue sold out and had to be reprinted and by May 1935 sales had climbed to 172,619.[61] Tallents reflected proudly that only *The Strand Magazine* outsold the GPO's publication, an astonishing achievement for what had been primarily intended as a staff publication.[62]

The public window which Tallents's reinvigorated magazine opened on to the internal activities of the Post Office was supplemented by the work of the GPO Film Unit. The 1936 documentary *Night Mail*, which began life as a series of articles in *The Post Office Magazine*, is the most celebrated example of this.[63] Commissioned by Tallents in partnership with the London, Midland and Scottish (LMS) railway, the film documents a typical shift on the Travelling Post Office, laying particular stress on how the everyday feats of railwaymen and postal workers combine into an extraordinary feat of collective organisation.[64] The narrative theme is mirrored by the artistic execution, as after a Spartan beginning the film climaxes in a cacophony of Soviet-style montage and W. H. Auden's poetry.[65]

The film's dramatic heart is provided by an extended middle sequence in which a trainee is instructed how to bound mail into leather pouches and then – at an exact point determined by counting the number of beats between bridges – deliver them safely via a mechanical arm into gibbet-like GPO collecting apparatus. By foregrounding the unusual and previously obscured skills needed to work at the Post Office, *Night Mail* proved extremely popular with both postal and railway workers.[66] The film also exemplifies Grierson's belief that his film-makers should emphasise the debt which society owed to postal workers, 'the milkman, the engine driver, coal miner, the lot of them'.[67]

Night Mail was a modest commercial triumph that was roundly acclaimed by all sections of the press. *The Times* praised *Night Mail* for illustrating 'the marvellous exactitude with which His

Majesty's mails are distributed and delivered', while *The Daily Worker* remarked that 'the cool, competent way in which the men go about their job awakens pride and admiration in those who appreciate the dignity of labour'.[68] Media acclaim for the Travelling Post Office workers who 'have their own vernacular and lead a sailor's life except that their ship is the train' was further observed to impact positively on morale. 'Publicity helps to give the staff of the post office a sense that their work is properly understood and appreciated by the public', acknowledged Tallents, 'an effect of publicity of which the importance is only now emerging'.[69]

Night Mail is also illustrative of the wider principles of Tallents's conception of public relations as outlined in *The Projection of England*. Much like the Soviet film *Turk–Sib*, *Night Mail* posits the train as an industrial enabler and social integrator, the path of its tracks marking out a newly democratised space.[70] The train is characterised as a medium for connecting physical and social spaces, linking an everyday post box in Bletchley with the mines of Wigan, the steel works of Warrington and the machine shops of Preston. The film is about the social and cultural infrastructure that binds together Britain as much as the organisation of the GPO. *Night Mail* might have borrowed much from early Soviet cinema, but the film is shot through with characteristically British humour. It is difficult to imagine the proletarian exclamation, 'Take it away sonny boy!' being answered with a chirpy 'right-ho, handsome!' in Dziga-Vertov. Accordingly, *Night Mail* became a fixture of British Council exhibits and was exhibited at the New York Exhibition of 1939 as an illustration of the 'new Britain'.

The GPO and the projection of Britain

As well as promoting the GPO, much of Tallents's public relations activity at the post office consciously serviced the patriotic function outlined in *The Projection of England*. Tallents argued:

> We need to build up, piece by piece, a picture for our own people, and also for others, of what this country has done, is doing and seeks to do in its endeavour to equip itself, without the revolutionary changes which most of the great nations of the world have deemed necessary to the magnitude of the task, to meet a wholly new range of modern conditions.[71]

Operationally, the Post Office was well suited to fulfil Tallents's wider ambitions, as the GPO provided the infrastructure through which the nation communicated. The GPO's role in the provision of mail, radio and telephonic communications assigned it an important structural role in the production, distribution and consumption of media information.[72]

During the interwar years the FA Cup Final at Wembley became a distinctive national occasion. Heavily promoted by the BBC and by *The Daily Express*, 'The Road to Wembley' focused previously dominant regional rivalries into an all-encompassing and internationally recognised form. It was a development that reflected patterns of migration from the footballing heartlands of the depressed northern cities to the prospering Midlands and South-East, as well as the impact of powerful new media technologies.[73] *The Post Office Magazine*'s coverage of the Jubilee FA Cup Final detailed everything from the role of the GPO's radio masts at Rugby – which earned imaginative comparison with St Paul's Cathedral – to how its pictures-by-wires service enabled evening newspapers to rush action photographs into their first editions.[74] By publicising the role played by the Post Office in the staging of the FA Cup Final – as well as other fixtures of the national sporting calendar such as Test Matches at Lords and the Derby – *The Post Office Magazine* attempted to enthuse staff, impress the public and implant the importance of the GPO into the national psyche.

Martin Weiner famously argued that Britain's industrial vitality was sapped by the emergence of a pseudo-gentrified bureaucratic culture which disparaged commerce and elevated Arcadian interests.[75] The propaganda work of the Post Office, like the work of the EMB before it, is a firm refutation of Weiner's thesis. Even at its most conservative, the GPO's brand of muted modernity appears to be a reassuring sheen floating knowingly on the surface of an organisation in the midst of radical transformation. Indeed, the mix of cutting-edge nostalgia, rustic sci-fi and neo-Soviet bombast give an almost postmodern quality to the material culture of Tallents public relations programme.[76] *The Post Office Magazine*, like so much of the GPO's internal publicity, ultimately reassembled GPO triumphs past and present into a celebratory multimedia march past. As one contributor wryly had it:

> The trooping of the colour in front of Buckingham Palace draws thousands of appreciative spectators: why not the trooping of the mail bags in front of Mount Pleasant? Something to really

stir the blood and brighten the eyes; a return to the old days
when the Trade Guilds held their masques and displays and
England was merry indeed.[77]

This comparison between Tallents's publicity methods and the
'masques and displays' of olden days is not as absurd, or uninten-
tional, as it now appears. Tallents's public relations activity
sponsored everything from the British Industries Fair to local
carnival floats in an attempt to bind together schools, businesses,
sporting events, state institutions and local communities. Drawing
in national newspapers, the Victoria and Albert Museum and
the GPO Film Unit to launch one thousand million celebratory
stamps, for example, Tallents turned the release of the King's
jubilee stamps into a kind of national exhibition.[78] Here was an
example of the kind of social-cohesion-through-cultural-activity
that Eustace Percy later saw as crucial to laying the groundwork
of the 'Blitz spirit'. He reflected on his early work at the British
Council:

> One could do little, in Sir Stephen Tallents' phrase, to 'project'
> British official policy acceptably to foreign eyes and ears
> but it was beginning to be possible to 'project' the British
> people. That had hardly been possible before. The nation
> whom Baldwin, in his own words, had set out to heal nearly
> fifteen years before had been a patchwork of resentments and
> disappointments ... The new national unity so surprisingly
> revealed in the Silver Jubilee of 1935 had been shaken out of
> its carelessness and seemed to be rediscovering its capacity for
> enthusiasm.[79]

In *The Projection of England* Tallents had suggested an
iconography of Britain (the countryside – the Underground – the
FA Cup Final) that could be used as a kind of cultural shorthand
for communicating modern British values to the world. At the Post
Office a similar effect was achieved through developments such
as the introduction of Sir Giles Gilbert Scott's cast-iron telephone
kiosks and the introduction of the staggeringly successful Speaking
Clock.[80] Tallents's public relations programme, especially his
internal publicity methods, represented a corporate contribution
to this wellspring of national life and self-consciously associated
the GPO with the defining economic, social and cultural markers
of the period.

Stephen Tallents and the GPO

The establishment of public relations at the GPO accompanied a period of corporate reform. During his tenure Tallents had broadened the GPO's conception of publicity so that a sub-section of five people, with a limited remit to increase telephone sales, had become a department of thirty-six. This was a risky long-term strategy because it broke the correlation between the size of the publicity department and the material business benefit it generated. Tallents's idealistic innovations were tolerated by Kingsley Wood on the grounds that they projected innovation while reassuring senior Post Office management. When the Treasury complained, that Tallents's public relations department had expanded too rapidly 'ad hoc and without a clearly thought-out organisation', Woods simply ignored them and his departure in 1935 sincerely weakened Tallents's position.[81] Several months before Tallents's tenure at the GPO came to an end in 1935, the new PMG, Major G. C. Tryon, suggested his department should rein in its activities.[82] He wrote:

> It seems to me that the time has now come to take stock of the position and to consider whether each and every one of the many activities which the public relations department has embarked, or has in mind to embark, is, to put it bluntly, worthwhile and, assuming that it is, whether its development might not be slowed down with advantage ... Staff have hitherto been enthusiastic in their support of the publicity movement. But signs of wariness are not lacking, and there is also, I think, the danger of the staff becoming a little surfeited with the good things that are spread before them. My conclusion – based, it is true, on rather limited evidence – is that the time has arrived to slow things up and consolidate.[83]

This surfeit of good things had delayed the submission of Tallents's first annual report until November 1934, and, though it did make some statistical attempt to quantify his department's work (inches of editorial coverage had risen from 36,000 in 1933 to 56,000 in 1934), it concluded by conceptualising the department's work in metaphorical terms. Tallents claimed that the department's efforts 'can be best compared to a boat which has been rowed out to shore; in which some sail had been set that is beginning to catch the wind; but which will require a good deal more hard rowing'.[84] Such idiosyncrasies led Tryon to become more sceptical of Tallents, who was apparently unable to appreciate that the advantages of his prestige publicity schemes might become apparent only in the long term.[85] As the political imperative to modernise the GPO dissipated, Tallents's eccentricities were more frequently exposed. Tryon found that Tallents could be both infuriatingly vague as well as pedantically exact. Asked to define a GPO publicity expert, Tallents admitted that 'the qualities of a "good mixer" are probably more important for this appointment than a wide knowledge of Post Office operations'.[86] Conversely, the unsolicited series of recommendations he sent to Sir Giles Gilbert Scott detailing the types of glass most suitable for the Jubilee Kiosks upset and annoyed the architect.[87] It appeared to Tryon that Tallents's cultural ambitions ran ahead of his Post Office responsibilities. The GPO's high-powered Poster Advisory Group, for example, which included Jack Beddington, Clive Bell and Kenneth Clark, encouraged the GPO to experiment with everything from the commissioning of 'Negro art' to the employment of Malcolm Campbell's streamlining expert to design an Airmail van.[88] Although it was indulged, the Poster Group was born of Tallents's democratic convictions. He argued:

> Government in the past, at least among the English speaking peoples, has occasionally employed the art of oratory but has neglected the other arts, including the art of writing. This is why, I suggest, even the greatest and weightiest of our government reports have perished, whereas certain speeches made in the cause of government have survived and still appeal to us today ... Publicity of the kind that we want is not to be ordered like a ready-made plaster from the chemist or commissioned in the way that Persian love-letters may be procured from professional letter-writers. Government publicity ... must enlist the services of the artist.[89]

The Poster Advisory Group attempted to realise Tallents's ambitions by associating the GPO with interesting artists such as Edward Bawden, Clive Gardiner, Duncan Grant, Tristram Hillier and Stanley Spencer. Unfortunately, the Poster Advisory Group was also liable to treat the GPO's more prosaic ambitions with disdain. They devised many ideas – such as mounting art on the 'interesting diptych' of a postal van's boot doors – that proved technically unworkable.[90] Moreover, their judgement was not infallible. They had, for example, opposed Tallents's introduction of the Valentine telegram design by Rex Whistler ('the sentiment is completely pagan') which subsequently became extremely popular.[91]

Tallents's successor, E. T. Crutchley, was not drawn from
Tallents's network of public relations specialists. Crutchley's chief
qualification for the Controller of Public Relations post, aside
from his friendship with Major Tryon, was the recommendation
of the GPO secretary Evelyn Murray.[92] Indeed, his appointment
marked the beginnings of what might be described as the revenge
of the Murrayites. Wood's external experts were on their way out.
'Whatever their virtues from the artistic point of view, on which I
do not claim to more authority than that of an ordinary man on
the street', Crutchley wrote of the Poster Group's suggestions, 'I
consider most of them unusable'.[93] The disbandment of the Poster
Advisory Group was quickly followed by Grierson's departure in
1936, as Crutchley abandoned Tallents's high-minded ideals and
sought to install a new sense of discipline.[94] More fundamentally,
he despaired of Tallents's inability to curb expenditure – *The Post
Office Magazine* budget had, for example, 'slid out of the scheme
of control' – and the unequal distribution of work loads.[95]

While Crutchley praised Tallents for developing GPO expertise
in public relations, he would tolerate little further experimentation. There were some valid reasons for this, not least the fact
that the shortcomings of Tallents's initiatives took several years
to emerge. For instance, the implications of turning the search
for the 'voice' of the Speaking Clock into a mass participation
multimedia competition were not immediately apparent. The
'voice' of the Clock had been selected by virtue of an internal
'Golden Voice' competition that attracted 15,000 entrants.[96]
The winner, Ethel Cain, was judged by the Poet Laureate John
Masefield to have 'the voice of a nightingale', but engineers
subsequently found that the intonation of her voice was unsuited
to recording.[97] Cain's celebrity status – the Speaking Clock
received over two hundred thousand calls a week – was resented
by colleagues and eventually allowed her to leave the GPO to
pursue a film career. Cain's acting career was not a success and
her rags-to-riches-to-rags story became a tabloid fixture that cast
the GPO as negligent and uncaring. Issues that had previously
been obscured by Tallents's constant whirl of activity began to
loom large and reinforced management prejudices about public
relations. Managerial fear of failure and an awareness of the
dangers of public exposure began to return. Tallents had helped
the GPO acquire a competent level of public relations expertise
and Crutchley saw no need to extend it further.

Ironically, while Tallents's immediate legacy was appraised

rather ambiguously by the Post Office, his public reputation continued to grow. A previously hostile press commented, 'the praise of the Post Office is nowadays in everybody's mouth, its enterprise, its alertness and responsiveness, its courtesy and humanity.'[98] In 1935, Tallents was awarded the Publicity Cup of Great Britain, the profession's highest accolade. The phenomenal success of the Valentine's Day telegram, followed by the release of *Night Mail*, saw Tallents's stock soar even higher in 1936.[99] At the very moment his successor at the Post Office was compiling a critical report on the workings of the GPO's public relations department, Tallents was joining the BBC with his personal and professional reputation at a new zenith.

Notes

1 See L. George, *How to Tackle Unemployment: The Liberal Plans as Laid before the Government and the Nation* (London, 1930).

2 In October 1931, Viscount Wolmer submitted a petition to the House demanding an inquiry into the running of the Post Office. Although Wolmer had nepotistic reasons for making such a complaint – his father was the owner of a prominent telegraph company – his petition was signed by 320 MPs. See also his later publication, Viscount Wolmer, *Post Office Reform: Its Importance and Practicability* (London, 1932).

3 Postal Archive, POST 33/4308, 'Publicity: Post Office Services, Posters, Signs', Bayliss, 'Question of Advertising Post Office Services', 28 January 1925.

4 The Telephone Development Association (TDA) had been formed by manufacturers in an attempt to stimulate public interest and provoke GPO investment. In 1930 the TDA had published an incendiary pamphlet, *The Strangle-hold on Our Telephones*, which accused the Post Office of retarding national development.

5 See C. R. Attlee, 'Post Office Reform', *New Statesman and Nation*, Vol. II, No. 37, 7 November 1931, pp. 565–566. The Liberal MP Clement Davies arranged Attlee's short internship at ICI. With its peculiar conglomeration of business ambition and public service ('we are not merely a body of people carrying on industry in order to make dividends'), its pioneering of a new management–worker relationship (through the creation of a consultative 'industrial parliament') and its artistic patronage

(through the commissioning of its grand Millbank HQ lit by 'artificial sunlight'), ICI was often identified as the business of the future. See C. Kennedy, *ICI: The Company that Changed Our Lives* (London, 1986), and W. J. Reader, *Imperial Chemical Industries: A History. Volume 1: The Forerunners 1870–1926* (London, 1970). Another source of Attlee's determination to 'raise the status' of public sector salesmanship possibly stems from his involvement, as Chancellor of the Duchy of Lancaster, with driving Christopher Addison's Agricultural Marketing Bill through the House of Commons. See K. and J. Morgan, *Portrait of a Progressive: The Political Career of Viscount Addison* (Oxford, 1980), pp. 191–200.

6 The GLC's publicity chief, Sir Francis Goodenough, had also advised Attlee of Tallents's suitability. As well as poaching Patrick Ryan from the EMB, the GLC would become willing sponsors of Grierson's documentary movement – bankrolling films such as *Enough to Eat?* – and founder members of the Institute of Public Relations. The GLC had developed expertise in this area after the government criticised the electricity and gas industries for failing to accord commercial activities the same status as technical competency. See S. Everard, *The History of The Gas Light and Coke Co. 1812–1949* (London, 1949), and T. I. Williams, *A History of the British Gas Industry* (Oxford, 1981).

7 Surprisingly, there is no biography of Kingsley Wood, so his motivations for shying away from the more radical commercial solutions to the GPO's ills have yet to be definitively unravelled. However, it has been convincingly argued that Wood's caution was born out of the political necessity of appeasing Chamberlain and the considerable economic and organisational difficulties of splitting the GPO into separate postal, telegraph and telephone companies. A. Clinton, *Post Office Workers: A Trade Union and Social History* (London, 1984), p. 289.

8 See Theodore Newton Vail, *Views on Public Questions: A Collection of Papers and Addresses, 1907–1917* (New York, 1917) and Theodore Newton Vail, *In One Man's Life* (New York, 1921).

9 Qtd in S. Ewen, *PR! A Social History of Spin* (New York, 1996), p. 93.

10 Postal Archive, POST121/431, 'Tallents, Sir Stephen; PRO: Appointment Papers', K. Wood, 'Sir Stephen Tallents', 30 August 1933.

11 'I found that he was quite right', noted Attlee, 'a small expenditure yielding good results'. This experience perhaps suggests another reason why Attlee was later to authorise the Royal Commission into the press in 1946. C. Attlee, *As It Happened* (London, 1954), p. 71.

12 Postal Archive, POST 33/5699, 'Public Relations: Committee Notes from the Reviews of the Tallents (1935) and Crutchley (1936) Meetings', S. Tallents, 'Report of Committee of Enquiry into Post Office Publicity, 1935'.

13 Postal Archive, POST 108/5, 'Telephone Publicity Committee Minutes of Meetings 1931–1933', 1st meeting, 25 July 1931.

14 An early version of Directory Enquiries was established in 1929, the Speaking Clock was launched in 1936 and '999' was rolled out on a limited scale in 1937.

15 Interestingly, both of the GPO's existing publicity officers, A. G. Highet and G. H. Taylor, were Scottish. The Glaswegian Highet was moved down to London on account of his spectacular successes as a canvasser. G. H. Taylor had previously been District Manager in Edinburgh. Tighter regulations in Scotland apparently made for a more proselytising sales culture. See Postal Archive, POST 33/3576, 'Public Relations Department: Formation, Part 1'.

16 Postal Archive, POST122/388, 'Training: Use of English in Letter Writing', 'Tallents to Taylor', 16 March 1933.

17 See D. Muir, 'The First GPO Logo', *British Philatelic Bulletin*, Vol. 44, September 2006, pp. 11–14.

18 Postal Archive, POST 33/5699, 'Public Relations: Committee Notes from the Review of Tallents (1935) and Crutchley (1936)', S. Tallents, 'Report of Committee of Enquiry into Post Office Publicity, 1935'.

19 Tallents longed to breed 'a genius of the Walt Disney type' and this ambition led to the commissioning of a range of cartoons for the magazine as well as playful shorts such as *Pett and Pott*, *The Fairy on the Phone* and *A Colour Box* by the Film Unit. He believed that the public sector needed to produce more 'good humoured' publicity. S. Tallents, *Post Office Publicity* (London, 1934), p. 12.

20 *Pett and Pott* is a veritable treasure chest of Surrealist quotations. It was distributed to commercial cinemas in 1934 – a full two years before the much celebrated International Surrealist Exhibition in London.

21 There is much about the GPO's 'low' modernism that resonates

with the account given by Alison Light. See A. Light, *Forever England: Feminity, Literature and Conservatism between the Wars* (London & New York, 1991).

22 Postal Archive, *Post Office Magazine*, 'The Post Office at Jubilee City', May 1935, pp. 160–161. See also *Post Office Magazine*, A. G. Highet, 'Post Office Exhibitions', June 1934, pp. 260–261, and 'Nottingham and Sheffield: Post Office Exhibitions', July 1934, pp. 306–307.

23 National Archives, CO758/93/5, 'Post Office Advisory Publicity Committee: Publicity Work Undertaken by Empire Marketing Board', S. Tallents, 'Report on Telephone Publicity', 17 June 1932.

24 Beazley was a personal friend of Tallents. See *Man and Boy*, p. 127.

25 R. Robinow, *Peter and the Post Office* (London, 1934), pp. 30–31.

26 S. Tallents, *Post Office Publicity*, p. 5.

27 This was a cause pursued by Tallents's friend Julian Huxley. See J. Huxley, 'The State and the Consumer', *Public Administration*, Vol. XIV, No. 3, July 1936, pp. 247–255.

28 E. T. Crutchley, *GPO* (Cambridge, 1938), p. 115.

29 Kipling had complained to Tallents about the poor quality of letters which the GPO 'considered good enough for the taxpayer.' Syracuse University, Kipling Papers, Box 13, 'Kipling to Tallents', 12 July 1935.

30 W. D. Sharp, 'Correspondence with the Public', *Public Administration*, Vol. XIV, No. 3, July 1936, p. 44.

31 The GPO's influence could later be observed at the MOI where, for example, as Head of Film, Kenneth Clark of the GPO's Poster Advisory Committee oversaw its Secretary, A. G. Highet, who was tasked with managing a coterie of ex-GPO staff such as the *Night Mail* director Harry Watt. However, Watt rather unjustly dismissed Highet: 'the whole film effort of Britain at war, both instructional and propaganda, was controlled by someone whose total creative problems had been bounded by whether to paint the Post Office at Nether Wallop white or pink!' H. Watt, *Don't Look at the Camera*, p. 127.

32 Although Le Mahieu tends to analyse the effect of discrete elements of reformist publicity activity rather than its cumulative effect, he does note that one of the most striking features of 'progressive' interwar culture 'was the web of personal relationships and professional favours which linked individuals

from disparate fields'. D. L. LeMahieu, *A Culture for Democracy* (Oxford, 1988), p. 158.

33 For more on the problems of writing about the national government and coalition governments in general see N. Smart, *The National Government, 1931–1940* (Basingstoke, 1999).

34 *Report from the Select Committee on the Telephone Service, 1922* (20 March 1922), paragraph 2.

35 Grant, *Propaganda and the Role of the State*, pp. 85–87.

36 This is not to say that Kingsley Wood did not politically benefit from this show of magnanimity. Wood's efforts to rouse the GPO were praised across the House and in 1935 he joined the national government's Propaganda Committee. See *Hansard*, 6 June 1934, vol. 290, col. 1019 and cols 963–964, 993–935, 1014.

37 Wood wrote, 'Any references you felt able to make in public speeches, especially during October, to the desirability of extending the telephone service of the country as an essential part of our national equipment, would be very happily timed and much appreciated. We want to put this country higher among the telephone using nations of the world. It stands at present third in the total number of its telephone instruments in use, but ninth only in the percentage of telephones to its population.' BT Archive, POST33/4856, 'Publicity: Telephone Week 1934', K. Wood, 'Draft Letter', 30 July 1934.

38 Postal Archive, POST 33/5699, 'Public Relations: Committee Notes from the Review of Tallents (1935) and Crutchley (1936)', S. Tallents, 'Report of Committee of Enquiry into Post Office Publicity, 1935'.

39 Qtd in M. J. Daunton, *Royal Mail: The Post Office Since 1840* (London & Dover, NH, 1985), p. 298. Until his removal by Woods, the aloof Murray – whose father had occupied the same position – was feared throughout Whitehall. Stanley Baldwin had warned the incoming PMG Clement Attlee in 1931 that 'you'll find your real difficulty will be Murray'. R. Jenkins, *Mr Attlee: An Interim Biography* (London, 1948), p. 135.

40 The Lever Committee appointed by PMG Mitchell Thomson in 1927 under the Chairmanship of Dunlop Rubber's Sir Samuel Hardman Lever consulted modern corporate figures such as the Underground's Lord Ashfield and ICI's Sir Harry McGowan to develop new suggestions to reinvigorate the telegraph trade. The Simon Committee similarly addressed the problems of the telegraph trade but, by bemoaning the expense and lack of flexibility of GPO staff and the obligation to provide a national

service, alienated GPO staff. See Clinton, *Post Office Workers*, p. 284.

41 Postal Archive, POST 33/3576, 'Public Relations Department: Formation, Part 1', S. L. Y, 'Memorandum', 9 February 1933.

42 Postal Archive, POST 33/3576, 'Public Relations Department: Formation, Part 1', Whitley Council, 'Minutes', 2 July 1926.

43 Postal Archive, POST 33/4308, 'Publicity: Post Office Services, Posters, Signs', February 1925, Various minutes.

44 Postal Archive, POST33/4308, 'Publicity: Post Office Services, Posters, Signs', 'PMG of Canada to GPO', 28 August 1924.

45 Ogilvy-Webb's official history of the government communication services places Tallents's appointment at the GPO in the pioneering context of the Post Office's mid-nineteenth-century promotional campaigns to sell government annuities, life assurance and the virtues of the Post Office saving bank. See M. Ogilvy-Webb, *The Government Explains: A Study of the Information Services* (London, 1965).

46 A. C. Stewart, 'Post Office Publicity and Green Papers', *Public Administration*, Vol. XIV, No. 3, July 1936, p. 70.

47 Kingsley Wood wrote to Union staff regretting the 'considerable amount of hardship' that existed among the GPO's lowest-paid staff, but determined to keep wages down 'out of due regard for national finances'. Qtd in Clinton, *Post Office Workers*, p. 480.

48 Ostensibly introduced to guarantee the loyalty of the Civil Service in the wake of the General Strike, the Act was popularly resented as a political gesture. Only postal workers' participation in Workers Education Association programmes survived this draconian edict.

49 To give two examples, John Newlove (editor of the *Civil Service Socialist*) and George Middleton (editor of *Post* and later a Labour MP) both studied under Cole. The Union gradually abandoned its commitment to more participative managerial structures after the Second World War. See M. Moran, *The Union of Post Office Workers. A Study in Political Sociology* (London & Basingstoke, 1974).

50 The Whitley committee complained, 'The Staff Side were not satisfied that what the department was doing was sufficient to advertise its services or to defend itself against the various attacks made on it in the Press and elsewhere.' Postal Archive, POST 33/3576, 'Public Relations Department: Formation, Part 1', Whitley Council, 'Proposal to Set up a Separate "Publicity" Branch of the Post Office', 2 July 1926.

51 Postal Archive, POST 33/4308, 'Publicity: Post Office Services, Posters, Signs', February 1925, Various minutes.

52 Tallents, *Post Office Publicity*, p. 12.

53 Postal Archive, POST33/5699, 'Public Relations: Committee Notes from the Reviews of the Tallents (1935) and Crutchley (1936) meetings', S. Tallents, 'Report of Committee of Enquiry into Post Office Publicity, 1935'.

54 Postal Archive, *The Post Office Magazine*, 'Our Working Day', May 1934, p. 215.

55 Postal Archive, *The Post Office Magazine*, 'Telephone Exchanges on Historic Sites: Switchboards where Dandies Once Danced', October 1934, pp. 453–454

56 Tallents did not edit the magazine, but he frequently penned its editorials and contributed articles. GPO technophilia is even more evident in the Post Office 'Green Paper' publications later commissioned by Tallents. Early titles included, 'Ship–shore Wireless', 'Submarine Cable Engineering', 'Pneumatic Tubes and Telegram Conveyors', 'Room Noise and Reverberation' and 'Porcelain Insulators'.

57 See Postal Archive, *The Post Office Magazine*, 'Speeding up Telegraph Delivery', May 1934, pp. 211–214.

58 Postal Archive, *Post Office Magazine*, January 1934.

59 Tallents conceptualised all this in typically personal terms: 'Your work is a passport into every home in the country. I'm not thinking only of the postman and the boy messenger, the counter clerk and the telephone operator, who meet or speak to the public in person. The same thing is true of the sorter speeding letters to every city and every farm in the Kingdom, of the telegraphist to whom are confided the urgent messages of the rich and poor (and internationally) I'm not thinking only of your telegraph and telephone services, your Empire and foreign mails, and your swiftly growing Air Mails. I'm not forgetting that the broadcasting of the King's voice to the Empire at Christmas depends on the efficiency of Post Office engineers. But I'm remembering particularly some papers I happened to see when I was shown round your Money Order Dept – carrying the wages of a Lascar crew back to their families in the Far East.' S. Tallents, *Post Office Magazine*, March 1935, 'Windows on the World', p. 77.

60 The GPO's foray into the world of paid advertising after the departure of Evelyn Murray extended only to the nationals, much to the frustration of regional papers. Postal Archive,

POST 33/3577, 'Public Relations Department: Formation, Part 2 (end)', 'Briant to Daish', 11 June 1935.

61 Postal Archive, POST33/3576, 'Public Relations Department: Formation, Part 1', 'Tallents to Welch', 1 May 1934.

62 Unlike a commercial publisher, however, Tallents did not run the magazine at a profit. He informed the Treasury, 'There is a reasonable possibility that it [*The Post Office Magazine*] will make sufficient profit to carry its overheads, but in order to stabilise its position it ought to be developed slightly more, so that there will be a reasonable prospect of being able to increase its advertising revenue still further.' Typically, Tallents's ever-expanding ambitions did not ever allow this profit to be realised. Postal Archive, POST 33/3576, 'Public Relations Department: Formation, Part 1', 'Tallents to Welch', 1 May 1934.

63 For example, 'The Up Special' feature published in the February 1935 issue focuses heavily on the difficulties of the travelling sorters as well as the beauty of the Beattock climb. According to Forsyth Hardy this practice was not unusual, with Edgar Anstey's article 'SOS' in the April 1935 magazine eventually leading to Harry Watt's much-praised *North Sea* (1938). *The Post Office Magazine* was also used by Tallents's unit to scope suitable material for radio broadcasts. See POST 108/91, 'History of The GPO Film Unit 1933–1940'.

64 LMS interest was possibly stimulated by the success of the Great Western Railway (GWR) centenary celebrations in 1935. GWR's celebrations included commissioning Edward Heath Robinson to produce *Railway Ribaldry*, a book of satirical cartoons, and the film *The Romance of a Railway* by the *One Family* director Walter Creighton. See R. Burdett Wilson, *Go Go Great Western: A History of GWR Publicity* (Newton Abbot, 1987) and S. Anthony, *Night Mail* (London, 2007).

65 Tallents was an early enthusiast for Auden's poetry. Interview with Miranda Pemberton-Piggot, 11 February 2007.

66 It could be argued that the documentaries of the GPO Film Unit, with their emphasis on the comradeship of small groups working without hierarchy in the interests of 'getting the job done', unconsciously reflected the UPW's political ethos. This character of the Film Unit is expanded on in D. Vaughan, *Portrait of an Invisible Man: The Working Life of Stewart McAllister, Film Editor* (London, 1983).

67 He told the *Night Mail* team, 'Can we imagine a society without letters? Of course we can't. But does anyone appreciate the

postman? Of course not. We take him for granted. We take
him for granted like the milkman, the engine driver, coal miner,
the lot of them. We take them all for granted, yet we are all
dependent on them, just as we are all interdependent one to
another. It has nothing to do with class or education. The simple
fact is that we are all in each other's debt. We must acknowledge
it and pay it with respect and gratitude one to another. This
is what we must get over. This is what this documentary is all
about.' Qtd in P. Jackson, *A Retake Please!*, p. 24.

68 All newspaper quoteations are drawn from clippings in the
Postal Archive file, POST 121/430, 'Grierson, John; Chief Film
Officer, GPO Film Unit: Appointment Papers'.

69 Postal Archive, POST 33/5699, 'Public Relations: Committee
Notes from the Reviews of the Tallents (1935) and Crutchley
(1936) Meetings', S. Tallents, 'Report of Committee of Enquiry
into Post Office Publicity, 1935'.

70 Basil Wright and John Grierson – both members of the '1917
Club' – appear to have written the English credits of *Turk–Sib*.
See B. Wright, *The Long View*, p. 117.

71 Tallents, *Post Office Publicity*, p. 6.

72 This is an understanding of the Post Office which can apparently
be tracked back to the Victorian era. See K.-L. Thomas, 'A
National Correspondence: Postal Reform and Fictions of
Communication in Nineteenth Century British Culture', D.Phil.
dissertation, University of Oxford, 2002.

73 See N. Fishwick, *English Football and Society, 1910–1950*
(Manchester, 1989).

74 Postal Archive, *The Post Office Magazine*, 'FA Cup Final', June
1935, pp. 202–203.

75 M. J. Wiener, *English Culture and the Decline of the Industrial
Spirit, 1850–1980*, 2nd edition (Cambridge, 2004). John
MacKenzie makes a similar argument from the different end
of the political spectrum. See J. MacKenzie, *Propaganda
and Empire: The Manipulation of British Public Opinion,
1880–1960* (Manchester, 1985), p. 84.

76 In this context it is apt that the British artists most frequently
drawn on by the public relations pioneers were invariably those,
like the Nash brothers, Graham Sutherland and Eric Ravilious,
engaged in Janus-faced communion with a mystically defined
Albion, as well as the modernist impulses of continental Europe.
See P. Nash, 'Going Modern and Being British', *The Weekend
Review*, 12 March 1933, pp. 322–323.

77 This is clearly a reference to Robert Blatchford's *Merrie England*, a classic evocation of medieval 'socialism'. Postal Archive, *The Post Office Magazine*, 'Grand Parade', March 1934, pp. 114–115.

78 Tallents further expounded on the intended symbolism of Barnet Freedman's designs ('triumph and reward, stability, peace') in a broadcast to the nation. *BBC Radio*, S. Tallents, 'Jubilee Stamps', 23 April 1935.

79 E. Percy, *Some Memories* (London, 1958), p. 160.

80 For more on the production of the King's Jubilee stamps, see Postal Archive, POST 33/4887, 'Postage Stamps: Special Issues, Jubilee 1935, Coronation 1937, Publicity Arrangements'.

81 Postal Archive, POST 33/3576, 'Public Relations Department: Formation, Part 1', 'Robinson to Sambrook', 13 April 1934. Wood apparently shared Tallents's loose attitude to staffing, apparently using the GPO public relations department to find work for the children of ex-lovers. See Jackson, *A Retake Please!*, p. 10.

82 Tryon was a long-established critic of free trade and stout proponent of imperial preference. His cool attitude to Tallents, and general suspicion of promotional work, might have been influenced by Tallents's EMB background. See G. C. Tryon, *A Short History of Imperial Preference* (London, 1931).

83 Postal Archive, POST 33/3577, 'Public Relations Department: Formation, Part 2 (end)', 'Tryon to Tallents', 13 July 1935.

84 Postal Archive, POST 33/5699, 'Public Relations: Committee Notes from the Reviews of the Tallents (1935) and Crutchley (1936) Meetings', S. Tallents, 'Report of Committee of Enquiry into Post Office Publicity, 1935'.

85 Tallents's work continues to be held in high regard in the Post Office: the new British Philatelic Bureau in Edinburgh was named after him in 2000.

86 Postal Archive, POST 33/5699, 'Public Relations: Committee Notes from the Reviews of the Tallents (1935) and Crutchley (1936) Meetings', S. Tallents, 'Report of Committee of Enquiry into Post Office Publicity, 1935'.

87 The redesigning of Giles Scott's kiosk proved an exceptionally fraught process and Scott was infuriated by Tallents's attempts to meddle. See BT Archive, POST 33/5155 'Telephone Kiosk: Descriptions for Nos 1–5 for Use on Temporary Shows, Jubilee Design (No. 6) Sir Giles Scott'. Also G. Stamp, *Telephone Boxes* (London, 1989) and J. Timson, *Requiem for a Red Box* (London, 1989).

88 Postal Archive, POST 33/5253, 'Post Office Service Publications: Poster Work, Formation of Advisory Group'.

89 Tallents, *Post Office Publicity*, p. 8.

90 Mechanics rejected this particular proposal on the grounds that 'locking bars and other projections would interfere with the mounting of posters'. Postal Archive, POST 33/5253, 'Post Office Service Publications: Poster Work, Formation of Advisory Group', 'Minutes', 2 May 1934.

91 This was a considerable set-back to Tallents, whose commissioning of Valentine telegrams was not universally welcomed. GPO management cautioned that they would be sabotaged by 'practical jokers who would think of sending bad news on a decorated form'. See Postal Archive, POST 33/4879, 'Greetings Telegrams: Introduction, Designs, Special Issues', 'Minutes', 17 May 1935.

92 The *Post Office Magazine* hopefully reported that, 'He helped his father prepare his naval memoirs.' There were, however, some similarities between the two men. Crutchley had served the Chief Secretary in Ireland during the early 1920s, before moving to Australia to become the British government's representative, helping to defuse the 'Bodyline' cricket scandal. In 1938, Sir John Anderson, his mentor in Ireland, would appoint him as Public Relations officer to the Ministry of Home Security, where he was responsible for liaising with the second Ministry of Information. Equally, Crutchley shared his predecessor's frustrated literary ambitions. As a young Post Office Surveyor he had modelled himself on Anthony Trollope. See B. Crutchley, *Ernest Tristram Crutchley: A Memoir* (Cambridge, 1941).

93 See Postal Archive, POST 33/5253, 'Post Office Service Publications: Poster Work, Formation of Advisory Group', E. T. Crutchley, 'Memorandum on Poster Advisory Group', 15 October 1937.

94 Postal Archive, POST 33/5699, 'Public Relations: Committee Notes from the Reviews of the Tallents (1935) and Crutchley (1936) Meetings', S. Tallents, 'Report of Committee of Enquiry into Post Office Publicity, 1935'.

95 Postal Archive, POST 33/5699, 'Public Relations: Committee Notes from the Reviews of the Tallents (1935) and Crutchley (1936) Meetings', S. Tallents, 'Report of Committee of Enquiry into Post Office Publicity, 1935'.

96 Postal Archive, *The Post Office Magazine*, 'The Girl with the Golden Voice', August 1935, p. 262.

97 See BT Archive, POST 33/5537, 'Telephone Speaking Clock Service: Purchase of Mr Wender's Apparatus, Miscellaneous Papers, Enquiries and Suggestions'.

98 Qtd in Clinton, *Post Office Workers*, p. 294.

99 50,000 Valentine's telegrams were sent, two and a half times the average number of telegrams sent in a week. See Postal Archive, POST33/5448 'Valentine's Day greetings telegrams: introduction and supply of special forms'.

5

The limits of public relations:
The BBC and the Ministry of Information

John Grierson would later describe Tallents's pioneering publicity work during the interwar period as one of 'the more curious feats of Civil Service bravery'.[1] Tallents was a generous and far-sighted patron of artists, administrators and thinkers, and the success of his reformist conception of public relations rested upon the freedom of an enlightened individual to negotiate between competing internal and external priorities. In Tallents's definition, public relations was an imaginative process of arbitration that interpreted competing demands into forms that its practitioners deemed as best serving the majority interest. Introducing public relations at the BBC and the Ministry of Information, however, pitted Tallents's subtle sensibility against more powerful ideological, institutional and political competition. After Tallents's death, his contribution was recognised as having made the BBC 'more accessible and more widely understood by the public and more readily responsive to public opinion'.[2] At the time, Tallents's determinedly liberal notion of public relations helped curtail his career.

The development of public relations at the BBC

Between 1929 and 1933 the number of radio licences in Britain doubled and by 1935 almost all of Britain (98%) had access to the BBC. A once tightly knit organisation that had been forged by John Reith's driving personality was growing into a more complex national institution.[3] As the BBC grew, the nature of its relationship with a mass audience began to be debated. Tallents's appointment as Controller of Public Relations in 1935 recognised that the BBC could no longer neglect public opinion. Reith remained contemptuous of what he saw as the triviality of the mass commercial media, but he realised that the BBC's privileged position had to be publicly defended.

Tallents's modestly graded predecessor, Gladstone Murray, had been responsible for managing the BBC's publications and running its press office. In contrast, Tallents was given control of managing the BBC's public persona. *The Mirror* described him as the BBC's Assistant Director General. *The Yorkshire Post* characterised Tallents as a '"sympathetic listener" who will help John Reith shed his reputation for autocratic aloofness'.[4] Indeed, when Tallents was recruited, Reith's poor relationship with the press dominated media coverage of the BBC. Forthright and pious, Reith was easy to parody, while the BBC's Sunday programme policy alienated 'ordinary' listeners – a weakness that the commercial media were able to capitalise on in the run-up to charter renewal in 1935. Tallents was appointed to help protect the BBC, to deflect and depersonalise the criticism aimed at it.

In practice, Tallents showed little interest in fulfilling the role that Reith had assigned him. While it had been stressed at interview that managing the press would be an integral part of his new 'public relations' role, Tallents took a relaxed attitude to press criticism.[5] 'Distortion is the stuff out of which the huge circulations of popular papers are made', he counselled, 'those who suffer from the distortion of BBC programmes and affairs should read what is said about them in the perspective of what is said about everything else in the same papers'.[6] Although Tallents was keen to correct simple factual inaccuracies, he understood that the popular press demanded 'sensational material and exclusive stories; and in the gathering of them none dares let another get a lead'.[7] His public response to the resultant sensationalism was accordingly weary but amused. Tallents told *World Press News*:

> I sometimes feel as if I were Public Relations Officer in the Department of the Clerk of the Weather. Rain or shine, frost or heat-wave, we generally seem to manage to excite somebody. When we don't do things then things are invented for us to have done. They are generally things that in the view of the inventor, we ought to have left undone.[8]

Tallents's placid outlook was often taken for complacency by unimpressed colleagues. Tallents's fundamental lack of interest in the agenda of the popular press saw him endlessly repeat lines such as 'by and large, the BBC gives us as good a ten shillings-worth as it would be possible to buy in this world', and delegate his Press Office responsibilities to Patrick Ryan.[9] Ryan was a robust ex-newspaper man who had managed the press for Tallents at the EMB and wrote (in Tallents's name) the Board's annual reports.[10] The difference between the priorities of Tallents and his Assistant Controller of Public Relations is revealed by a quick glance through their respective script outputs during the immediate postwar period. Ryan wrote 'Japanese Independence', 'Chinese Aggression', 'The Future of the Korean War' and 'The Future of Sudan'. Tallents completed 'The Mole', 'Kentish Autumn', 'Accidents and First Aid' and 'In My Library'.[11]

Unsurprisingly, since he had been recruited to appease the press, Tallents's attitude towards Fleet Street irritated senior BBC management. Senior staff complained of the hypocrisy of the press attacks on the corporation, and the crescendo of criticism in the run-up to charter renewal further panicked BBC management. 'Is it safe to ignore the popular press?' wrote the Controller of Administration; 'much dripping wears away the stone, and I am absolutely certain that we are losing a great deal of our once impregnable goodwill'.[12] By instructing BBC bosses to philosophically accept hostile and inaccurate coverage as 'a good jest', Tallents appeared to be both naive and ineffective. His colleagues worried that the BBC's display of restraint in the face of premeditated aggression encouraged further assaults.[13] Most damagingly, *The Daily Mail*'s sustained campaign against the Corporation's alleged 'Red Bias' ('The wireless masts of the BBC lean as noticeably as the tower of Pisa – and always to the left') appeared to have fundamentally altered people's perceptions of the BBC.[14] Reith complained to his diary:

> Feeling annoyed with Tallents' apparent futility; our press relations are quite rotten. Most newspapers write more or less congratulating the government on its decisions. They are ignorant and have been hoodwinked.[15]

To make matters worse, the press sniggered that Tallents's capacity to intervene at press conferences appeared to be limited to ensuring 'that cups of soothing tannin and biscuits are served out at the crucial moment, so handling the proceedings with tact and decorum'.[16] Adding insult to senior management injury, while remaining aloof from the campaigns of the popular press, Tallents took pains to encourage 'the responsible body of radio criticism' that he had identified in newspapers such as *The Manchester Guardian*, *The Times* and *The Yorkshire Post*, and from which he believed that the BBC had much to learn. Tallents's chutzpah – in convenient conjunction with his extracurricular writings for many of the papers he admired – enraged Reith. After their first meeting Reith had recorded his concern that Tallents might prove to be 'a sycophant, disinclined to press his own views if they are likely to prove unpopular'.[17] Tallents's later conduct at the BBC cemented Reith's belief that his PR chief was obsessed by his own social standing.

Stephen Tallents at the BBC

The minor tragedy of Tallents's problematic spell at the BBC was that he joined the Corporation as an enthusiast. He idealised the BBC, its programmes, its creative staff and its semi-official status. It is possible that Tallents's enthusiasm blinded him to the public stresses that such a unique organisation must withstand, as well as the peculiar nature of the BBC's internal politics. Certainly, by aiming to encourage 'good' criticism rather than manage press headlines, Tallents took an idealistic as well as an idiosyncratic approach to his public relations brief. His intellectual thesis, however, was sound enough. As Tallents had it, the BBC's physical, technological and organisational remoteness encouraged uninformed attacks and enabled the BBC to resist legitimate public demands. Building a closer relationship with the audience was therefore vital because 'in the long run public ill will and lack of understanding leads to an unintelligent application of inappropriate remedies by inexpert outside forces'.[18] Although Tallents tempered the tone of his criticism, his view of the BBC's failings was invariably pointed. He wrote:

> Some important sections of BBC staff differ in quality from those of other big undertakings, in that they contain no solid core of homely men and women of all ages such as is found in the lower divisions of a government department. A newcomer to Broadcasting House gets in these quarters the impression of a highly educated and cultured community that has tended to prolong into its working life not only the desirable qualities of intellectual curiosity and an interest in ideas, but also sometimes the airs and theories and jargon of an undergraduate society ... Such mannerisms and tendencies

as these get the BBC staff the reputation of superior persons.
Time and training alone can remove them.[19]

In historical context, Tallents's observations on the upright social
protocols of the BBC are far from unusual. A. J. P. Taylor noted
that Reith 'used what he called "the brute force of monopoly"
to stamp Christian morality on the British people. He stamped
it also on his employees'.[20] Joseph Macleod claimed the hierarchical working atmosphere made Broadcasting House 'something
of a Royal Palace and Embassy'.[21] Robert Silvey remembered,
'Reith was dictatorial and Admiral Carpendale, his deputy, had
never realised that he had left the quarter decks'.[22] However, in
the context of his appointment, Tallents's behaviour was particularly provocative. Far from acting as a press shield, Tallents
frequently joined the chorus advocating reform. 'The more lively
and well-informed criticism the BBC has to face, the better', he
wrote in *The Spectator*, 'only so can it hope to achieve a virtue
that, like Olivia's beauty, will be in grain and will endure wind
and weather'.[23]

Since the publication of *The Projection of England*, Tallents
had argued that modern Britain must shake off 'the reputation of
superior persons'.[24] At the BBC the practical effect of Tallents's
plea was to upset managerial protocol. He corresponded with
John Maynard Keynes on the inferiority of 'thin, wretched
cultured accents' against strong regional accents.[25] He told *John
Bull* that he was committed to reform because 'I remember very
well, as a temporary soldier training for the Front in 1914, the
terror with which one walked down Piccadilly for fear one should
overlook or fail to salute a passing "brass hat"'.[26] He furthermore
encouraged the workforce to take greater initiative and accept
more responsibility for improving relations with the public. For
instance, he suggested that engineers might regularly meet with
radio manufacturers on an informal basis.[27] Tallents believed that
the BBC's participation in informal social networks would correct
the 'fairly general impression that the BBC is a highbrow body,
aloof from the interests of the man on the street and lacking the
common touch'.[28] To the old Reithian guard Tallents's comments
were something akin to inciting anarchy. Organisational growth,
technical developments and employee pressure might have made
these changes inevitable, but Tallents made altering the working
atmosphere at the BBC a point of public relations principle.

When Tallents arrived at the BBC the Press Office was seen as the natural home of the unwell and the unruly. 'Mr Hawtayne is a trier [but] his physical defects make him quite useless', as one appraisal of press office staff began; 'his is a hard case as he was badly wounded in the head during the war with adverse mental effect'. [29] Gladstone Murray's regime had also been accused of 'favouritism', with a subsequent report cryptically ruling that his methods were 'not in keeping with the prestige of a big institution such as the BBC'.[30] During his reign Tallents did much to raise he status of the BBC's Press Office. He began by implementing the practice of open monthly press conferences, the nine Press Office staff of 'limited professional qualifications' were bolstered and, as well as responding to more than 350 enquiries and hosting over a hundred visitors, he pushed Press Office output to 7,500 words per week. Most importantly, he encouraged the BBC to provide new forums for public interaction. Repeating experiments first developed at the EMB and GPO, Tallents wanted the BBC to participate in exhibitions and trade shows, fund documentary films and produce a collection of Green Papers. Tallents believed the coverage provided by the BBC's magazines also needed to be 'popularised and made more topical'.[31] He further sought to encourage the BBC to publicise itself co-operatively with amateur radio organisations, to provide lecturers for voluntary organi- sations and answer public correspondence 'in a simpler style, free of jargon' and with 'greater individual discretion'. Lastly, he outlined plans to increase the number (and widen the character) of people allowed to visit Broadcasting House.

Although his critics were liable to portray Tallents as an intellectual lightweight, he doggedly pursued a non-prescriptive vision. Early in his tenure, Tallents had told colleagues that he understood that 'the BBC depends chiefly for good public relations upon the quality of its programmes. The main instrument of BBC public relations will always be its broadcast programmes.'[32] However, by developing an understanding of the BBC that differ- entiated between 'minority' and 'majority' interests, he also challenged the Corporation's existing ethos and proselytised structural reform.[33] The most radical example of this was Tallents's introduction of Listener Research, which aimed to redistribute greater power to the general public. While Reith had appointed the BBC a 'civilising' mission, Tallents conceived it as providing a forum through which distinct strands of national life could discover commonalities of purpose.

The introduction of Listener Research

By the mid-1930s the BBC received more than 150,000 letters a year, but the volume of letters did not equate to a variety of correspondence. Tallents judged the correspondence dominated by issues of morality and bad language, to be articulating only middle-class anxieties. The BBC had become a national institution, but it received feedback only from a minority of listeners who 'wrote so often they might have been called BBC pen friends had their letters been consistently friendly'.[34] Establishing Listener Research at the BBC gave Tallents further opportunity to pursue a national priority which he had identified in *The Projection of England*, the need to build up a 'full picture of this very rich and ample life of our country'.[35]

Unlike Listener Research in America, which segmented audience by socio-economic status for the benefit of advertisers, Tallents's programme of Listener Research developed out of an idealistic discourse of public entitlement. Tallents believed Listener Research would enable the BBC to gauge public opinion just as 'an expert will judge, say, a large butter consignment by taking a sample at random from a few boxes or barrels'.[36] The head of Listener Research, Robert Silvey, was a Fabian whose self-professed mission was to ensure that the BBC served 'an obligation to the whole of its public which could not be met simply by seeking to satisfy the majority'.[37] The perceived failure of written correspondence to do this legitimised Tallents's establishment of Listener Research.[38] Tallents briefed the *The New Statesman and Nation* that he believed in 'the possibility of making democracy function through the work of the sympathetic interpreter of chaotic group opinion'.[39]

Until the appointment of new BBC governors, such as the Toynbee Hall warden J. J. Mallon, Tallents's pursuit of Listener Research was marginalised.[40] Among the few enthusiasts for Tallents's project was Val Gielgud, the BBC's Head of Drama.[41] Gielgud believed that good theatre was impossible without a good audience and thus looked to Listener Research as a mechanism by which the cheers, applause, laughs, groans and tuts that guided actors on stage could be recreated.[42] For instance, as part of the Public Relations department's 'Variety Barometer', two thousand volunteers were asked to keep a log of their listening. The idea was to cast some light on the habits and routines of listeners by building up a picture of how people chose, listened and responded to BBC programmes. Tallents broadcast an appeal for volunteers:

We welcome frank and honest criticism. We want to give
you programmes that you'll enjoy, and we want to put on
those programmes at times that are convenient to you ... The
planning and producing of good, attractive programmes, to
run for fourteen hours out of every twenty four, is a difficult
and complicated job. It takes two to make a success of it – the
BBC and those who broadcast on the one hand; listeners on
the other. That's why I have been talking to you tonight not
simply as listeners but as partners.[43]

The rhetoric of partnership and co-operation had long been a
hallmark of Tallents's addresses but his tone was something
of an anathema to a Reithian BBC set up in opposition to the
'dictatorship of the percentages'. The experimental establishment
of Listener Research was approved only because of a Byzantine
bureaucratic manoeuvre by which Tallents's proposal reached the
Chairman of the BBC's Advisory Council, the Archbishop of York
William Temple, but bypassed Reith.[44]

Away from Broadcasting House, Tallents's ideas gained greater
traction. The early establishment of television 'sampling' prompted
a subscriber to write hoping that 'television would not become
inhuman like the BBC'.[45] Indeed, Tallents's plans for the BBC's
television service, which began operation in 1936, were expansive.
He even went as far as planning a London versus New York
television take-up competition, with the city that sold fewest
televisions at Christmas having to address a grovelling broadcast
to the other.[46] The eager informality with which every television
subscriber was invited to Alexandra Palace for tea and cigars in
1937 was indicative of the more informal lines along which the
BBC would develop in the wake of Reith's departure. With much
organisational and linguistic awkwardness, prewar television can
be judged the most successful home of early Listener Research.

Although Tallents's imaginative democratic ambitions for
Listener Research were being translated into a considerably
more prosaic reality, the press were vociferous in their criticism.
'Listener Research is a useless idea founded on a fallacy', wrote
The Morning Post, 'for the average listener does not know what
he wants. His one desire is to be entertained.'[47] To a degree, this
criticism reflected widespread ignorance of market research. Few
companies had commissioned such research – the Gas, Light and
Coke Company was among the British pioneers – and still fewer
organisations were qualified to undertake it.[48] The American

advertising firm J. Walter Thompson, along with Crawford's and the London Press Exchange, were among the handful of isolated practitioners.[49] Tallents's efforts to better identify the 'super glow worms' of public opinion by working with voluntary organisations were also mocked. *The Birmingham Post* ridiculed the idea that organisations such as the Women's Freedom League, the Women's Gas Council, the Electrical Association for Women and the National Adult School Union were able to provide insight into the mentality of 'everyday women'.[50] Tallents believed he was putting the BBC in touch with a wider strand of opinion; the popular press argued that he was merely substituting one strand of middle-class opinion for another.

Concern about the future of the licence fee ensured that Reith retained an open-minded interest in social research.[51] Indeed, as Minister of Information, he would treat 'Home Intelligence' with unfashionable seriousness.[52] He did, however, oppose directly applying research into popular taste on to the BBC's output. Nevertheless, in Reith's mind Listener Research entailed fundamentally compromising the BBC's mission to inform, educate and entertain. Reith's personal antipathy towards Tallents was inextricably linked to his sense that Tallents's philosophy of 'public relations' entailed resigning cultural leadership. In 1937, Reith promised to resign if Tallents was appointed Deputy Director General ahead of Cecil Graves. In June 1940, Reith blamed the unpopularity of his successor, Frederick Ogilvie, on Tallents's malign influence. In December 1940, he encouraged senior staff to draft a note threatening a mass walk-out if Tallents was appointed Director General.

The limits of public relations at the BBC

Appointed to provide a press shield, Tallents was perceived to have instead 'opened up' the BBC to new strands of criticism. It was a tactic that made him appear naive to experienced BBC hands. Moreover, the dominant corporate culture was one of control and compulsion. Tallents's attempt to shift some emphasis on to individual initiative and voluntarism made his initiatives appear safe to ignore. Cost-effectiveness aside, on the face of it, there was little to object to. 'The only point of attending exhibitions', wrote one official, 'is to prevent people remarking on our absence'. Elsewhere, it was felt that elements of Tallents's planned lecture series and educational material had 'a facetious, parish magazine touch'.[53] Senior management were inclined to regard Tallents, and his public relations project, as an excuse for all manner of ineffective but time-consuming meddling. Tallents's standing was further damaged by his managerial failings. In particular, Tallents's failure to manage sensitively R. S. Lambert, the eccentric editor of *The Listener*, saw the BBC roundly mocked in newspapers, led to questions being raised in Parliament and compromised the organisation as it went through charter renewal.[54]

Before his appointment to the BBC, highbrow publications had praised Tallents's ability to combine 'the gifts and experience of an able Civil Servant with the imagination and sympathy capable of directing temperamental and individualistic workers'.[55] In actuality, the corporation's prickly and educated staff tended to regard Tallents's initiatives with suspicion. The Lambert debacle showed Tallents in his worst light. He had encouraged Lambert to use his position on the British Film Institute board to take a harder line against commercial film companies, but then refused to support him publicly after this tactic had precipitated controversy. While neglecting to dampen the growing political friction, Tallents had instead increasingly begun to interfere with Lambert's editorial work. Lambert accused his Public Relations chief of pushing unwanted self-penned articles on *The Listener* and of 'constant interference, often over petty trifles, such as style of grammar and punctuation'.[56]

In the short term, Tallents's reign was judged to have been one where 'the Programme Division felt, rightly or wrongly, that it was becoming more and more the servant of Public Relations'.[57] Reithians saw press praise for Tallents's personality ('he is a cultured and progressive man') and his track record in 'the art of tactful propaganda' as testament to Tallents's lack of concrete beliefs.[58] By contrast, the 'professionalism' which Tallents introduced – which saw sloppy broadcasters rebuked for not acknowledging their sources of information and its likely bias – was seen to stem from a pedantic unimaginativeness.[59] Tallents's critics were liable to see him as narrowing the BBC's vision rather than opening the organisation up; consequently Tallents's post was abolished during the war. Although it was subsequently recognised that 'much useful work that was being done under the control of one man has lapsed', future public relations chiefs would never have such creative and intellectual freedom at the BBC. Tallents's eventual successor, Kenneth Adam, was appointed at a much lower grade and given a much narrower 'publicity' brief.[60] Listener

Research would eventually become its own department although it was initially accorded minor importance – Robert Silvey was given equivalence to the Head of Catering.

Stephen Tallents and the shadow Ministry of Information

The Committee of Imperial Defence had been prompted to establish a shadow Ministry by the unfavourable press comment attracted by the Abyssinian crisis. The Ministry of Information was sited at the Home Office and initially focused on agreeing how coverage of any future conflict should be censored.[61] No department would cede its right to censure to a new ministry; thus, after his appointment in October 1936 Tallents would spend a disproportionate amount of time trying to broker an agreement between the Admiralty, the Air Ministry, the War Office and the Home Office's War Press Bureau. Tallents made little headway; indeed he was unable even to attend these discussions until his shadow Ministry was allowed to join the Inter-departmental Committee on Censorship on 11 February 1937. Even more absurdly, he found himself – the Director General Designate of the Ministry of Information – advising his junior staff that they 'could not rely on official sources of information'.[62] A civilian Civil Servant adrift in an overwhelmingly military organisation, Tallents was forced to revise his plans continually on the basis of incomplete and second-hand information as his embryonic Ministry was pitted against rival initiatives such as the Civil Emergency Organisation. 'The Home Office have not proved a very amiable or interested parent' as the shadow Ministry of Information's secretary later observed; 'indeed, if there was a national society for the prevention of cruelty to war babies, I expect that they would have instituted a prosecution against The Home Office'.[63] Tallents's failure to persuade the military and security establishment that there would be a place for 'positive' wartime propaganda resulted in the Ministry of Information's initial wartime reputation as the 'Ministry of No Comment'.

Tallents's loyalty to the BBC added a further layer of intrigue to the departmental turf war. He had been appointed to the shadow Ministry on the recommendation of Reith.[64] In a 1935 paper entitled 'The Position of the BBC in War', Reith had proposed a scheme whereby the BBC would fall directly under government control during wartime. The Board of Governors would be temporarily disbanded and in their absence the Director General

would personally answer to the Minister of Information rather
than the Postmaster General. Reith's pre-emptive report served
two purposes. Firstly, its apparent loyalty to government was
calculated to find favour in the run-up to charter renewal. Secondly,
it represented an attempt to secure the most beneficial compromise
with central government possible. Reith gambled that his personal
relations with Baldwin and his powers of persuasion, as well as
his general political skill, would keep governmental interference at
arm's length. By placing Tallents in the Ministry Reith sought both
to neuter political criticism and to attack analogous government
broadcasting groups such as the Committee on General Policy
of Broadcasting in Time of War. 'I do not quite know what his
[Reith's] motive is', as one official complained, 'except perhaps an
inherent dislike for the Broadcasting Committee, of which he was
not a member'.[65]

Indeed, until Reith's departure in 1938, Tallents's attempts to
articulate the shape of a wartime government communication
network were partially subordinated to the strategic objectives
of the BBC. At the most basic level this meant ensuring that the
BBC would be able to continue broadcasting during wartime.[66]
More significantly, Tallents and Reith worked hard to build a
cross-governmental consensus to expand the BBC's news service.
The perceived impact of speeches by Stanley Baldwin, Ramsay
MacDonald and Lloyd George in the general elections of 1931 and
1935 – along with the boom in radio ownership which followed the
mass production of 'people's sets' and the advent of hire purchase
– allowed Tallents to frame a long-pursued sectarian objective in
the national interest. Wartime restrictions offered a pretext for the
corporation to encroach upon the territory of newspapers.[67]

Of course, Tallents's pursuit of BBC objectives damaged the
integrity of his recommendations. An ex-*Times* journalist at the
India Office, H. McGregor, proved an especially troublesome
critic. According to McGregor, radio broadcasts could be easily
disrupted and it was the global reach of the news agencies that
should have commanded Tallents's attention. 'As media of distribution they (Reuters, the Central News, Exchange Telegraph
Co. and the British United Press) are the greatest of all', argued
McGregor, 'and should receive particular treatment'.[68] Not
only was Tallents's focus on broadcast news wrongheaded in
McGregor's view but he had allotted the news agencies only a
modest spot in a sub-section of his report's 'Press (Verbal or
Written)' category. Possibly the BBC's break with Reuters in

1932 had led Tallents to overestimate the BBC's news-gathering abilities, but his neglect of the news agencies – the importance of which the Foreign Office had recognised with funding as early as 1915 – demonstrated a surprising naivety.[69] This embarrassment was compounded by McGregor's observations about the insulated character of Tallents's scheme. Tallents had created sections for disseminating home, foreign and empire news, when a more outward-looking plan might have provided facilities for home, foreign and empire correspondents. McGregor dismissed Tallents's recommendations as bureaucratic irrelevancies:

> The present scheme would seem to take up propaganda as it existed on November 11, 1918, when as a systemised feature of war it was still novel and, instead of experts fully staffing the ministry, the manning is to be done by the Civil Service ... 'the purpose of the news division will be to ensure the rapid dissemination of "quick news" as opposed to prepared propaganda.' And the provision of this quick news is, according to Appendix E, to be led by a counsellor of the Foreign Office, and conducted by two principals, two assistant principals and half a dozen military assistants. Nowhere is there essential provision for a single member of the journalistic profession who have been trained in news all their professional lives.[70]

McGregor's criticisms of the unimaginative blueprint were well founded.[71] Tallents had drawn heavily on books and clippings passed to him by the Foreign Office librarian H. O. Lee, and admitted that his own report borrowed much from Sir Edward Cook's 1920 book, *The Press in War Time*.[72] The atypical conservatism is demonstrative of the lack of freedom under which Tallents worked. For example, McGregor suggested that Tallents should approach Geoffrey Dawson of *The Times*, Howell Gwynne of *The Morning Post*, Sir Roderick Jones of Reuters and Wickham Steed for advice. In fact, Tallents had repeatedly petitioned his political masters to allow him to consult with both Dawson and Jones, as well as a much wider pool of film-makers, writers and cartoonists.[73] Although he was eventually granted permission to discuss the specific shortcomings of newspaper censorship in the First World War with Geoffrey Dawson, Tallents's more ambitious schemes were blocked on the grounds that the fads and fashions of the contemporary media industry were too fickle to be trusted.[74]

The historian Temple Wilcox has argued that Tallents's inability to organise an effective shadow Ministry of Information implied a praiseworthy moral stance by the British establishment. Wilcox has argued that the proposals contained within Stephen Tallents's blueprint for the second Ministry of Information verged on the totalitarian. He portrays Tallents's removal in the wake of the Munich crisis as something of an ideological triumph, arguing that the decentralised form which the Ministry subsequently took may have impaired its effectiveness, but it protected the public.[75] He argues:

> The fundamental issue was whether the British government should build up a propaganda machine with the purpose of competing with totalitarian states or whether this activity should be organised in a way more appropriate to a 'democratic' or 'open' society.[76]

It is true that both the Civil Service and political establishment were wary of the implied 'totalitarianism' of centralising communications. As soon as the existence of the shadow Ministry had been acknowledged, the press hysterically envisaged it as an all-powerful authority. *World Press News* inaccurately reported, 'what is now known is that the entire suppression of the Free Press is envisaged'.[77] This lasting fear of legitimate political authority being usurped by media power would later see Clement Attlee ensure that the Ministry's postwar reincarnation, the Central Office of Information, was a non-ministerial service department. Nevertheless, the British establishment also had less idealistic reasons for opposing the creation of a powerful and independent-minded Ministry of Information.

The shadow Ministry had initially been created to devise a more effective scheme of censorship. The security and armed forces had simply wanted to improve the mechanisms for controlling the flow of information to the public and remained unconvinced by the idea of 'positive' media work. 'There is sometimes, in non-military quarters', argued Lord Stanhope, 'a tendency to think a war can be won without fighting – by the effect, for example of propaganda and economic pressure'.[78] Having dismissed the need for 'positive' media work, the centralisation proposed by Tallents could be rejected for managerial reasons because it implied either an inefficient lengthening of the managerial chain or a loosening of departmental control. The fundamental function of the Committee of Imperial Defence was not resisting totalitarian methods but preserving the status quo of revealing as little information to the public as possible. 'Clearly, this Ministry of Information has no conception of its work as a modern war weapon', noted John Hargrave on the outbreak of war, 'Its whole job is to stop information and gag almost every form of effective propaganda'.[79]

The policy of appeasement further exacerbated the dominant governmental tendency to silence and secrecy. While Tallents wanted to openly define and outline the role of foreign propaganda, senior Civil Servants took the view that 'this kind of subject is one which should not be spoken about much and, if possible, should not be written about at all'.[80] The emphasis on secrecy belied a conscious desire to limit, if not block, Tallents's progress. Richard Cockett has argued that by ruthlessly manipulating lobby journalists through his press agent Sir Robert Topping, and employing ex-MI5 agent Joseph Ball to build a media intelligence unit, Neville Chamberlain was able to marginalise media coverage of opposition to appeasement.[81] Tallents's removal in the wake of the Munich crisis is directly related to this trend.

There is a Rosencrantz and Guildenstern aspect to Tallents's removal from the shadow Ministry as he appears to have been at times almost comically oblivious to the severity of the political crisis.[82] Tallents's interest in constructing a garden of historic plants, for example, led him to contemporaneously make friendly enquiries into the botanical preferences of the great European dictators.[83] However, while Tallents was not in the vanguard of anti-appeasement activists, his arguments for a positive propaganda and public relations campaign closely mirrored those of the Foreign Office News Department, a department in the sway of radically anti-appeasement Civil Servants such as Sir Robert Vansittart and Rex Leeper.[84] Vansittart had been sidelined with the grand but empty role of Chief Diplomatic Adviser to the Foreign Office in 1937, while Leeper was moved from his post in the wake of the Munich crisis.[85] Regardless of whether Tallents had a strong view on appeasement or not, his proactive approach to organising the Ministry was deemed a threat.[86] By attempting to contact opposition radio stations such as Deutsche Freiheitssender and authorising an experiment that saw fifty balloons explode a shower of pacifist literature over Germany, Tallents's maverick measures had the potential to cause serious diplomatic embarrassment.[87] After his removal it was agreed that the shadow Ministry should in future 'concern itself with preparing the outline of the machine, the actual steps to be taken should be left to be dealt with when the actual time comes'.[88] 'The press', noted one shadow Ministry official, 'were going to be asked not to be publicly rude to Herr Hitler or Signor Mussolini'.[89]

In context, governmental opposition to Tallents's wide-ranging plans for the Ministry of Information did not centre on the degree to which they consciously or unconsciously represented a drift towards authoritarian propaganda. It appears more accurate to say that no sincere military or political imperative to ensure the war-readiness of the Ministry of Information existed.[90] The calm reaction of Civil Servants to the resignation of Tallents's shadow Minister, John Colville, was revealing.[91] The eve-of-war appointment of Lord Perth ('one of those appointments in the bad British tradition that, when there is a tricky job to be started, the best person for it is a tired old man [who] can be relied on to play safe') confirmed the Ministry's lack of standing.[92] For the first part of the War an enfeebled Ministry of Information was a convenient Aunt Sally for the political and military establishment.[93] Tallents's 'failure' would be followed in quick succession by the 'failures' of Sir Ernest Fass, Sir Samuel Hoare, Lord Perth, Findlater Stewart, Kenneth Lee, Frank Pick, Walter Monckton and Cyril Radcliffe. There was, as Robert Bruce Lockhart later described it, 'more political warfare at home than against the enemy'.[94]

Tallents had benignly, if at times eccentrically, been concerned with ensuring the shadow Ministry's likely competence. 'The mere herding together of a number of scattered schemes will never produce effective Ministry of Information', he argued, 'any British government, from the eve of peace or war, will in future need an efficient and unified [publicity] machine'.[95] Tallents further explained to Warren Fisher that the British public – accustomed to being told the truth – had an unassailable psychological advantage over a German population that was routinely deceived. Tallents's plans had merely set out to rectify the nation's temporary 'mechanical handicap'. In wartime the truth of Tallents's arguments was realised. Officials recognised that the lack of co-ordination between the new Ministry of Information and the government's existing press and publicity functions rendered it ineffective.[96] It was not until Churchill appointed his political fixer, Brendan Bracken, Minister of Information in 1941 (the fourth minister to be posted to the 'unquiet graveyard') that the department – as a corporate entity – began to operate effectively.[97]

Tallents's development of the BBC Overseas Service

Before Tallents's appointment in May 1940, the BBC Overseas Service had been the poor relation of the Empire Service, recruiting its first specialist journalist, A. E. Barker, only in February 1938.[98] War with Germany prompted a belated increase in output, with the Service given the enormous task of serving the Americas, the Near East and Europe. In the autumn of 1940, Tallents and Frederick Ogilvie outlined plans for the 'triple expansion' of the Overseas Service. 'Triple expansion' included the recruiting of an additional 2,750 staff to facilitate an increase in broadcast output from 48.5 hours per week to 152.5 hours. The BBC aimed to produce a variety of programmes that, for example, could 'not only satisfy those in the sophisticated cafes of Egypt, but would be appreciated by people in the remote places of the Persian Gulf'.[99] After the War the wartime network created by Tallents would become part of what is now known as BBC World Service.

As Controller of Public Relations, Tallents had played an important role in the development of the BBC's services in Latin America. His approach combined the innovations of the civilian Listener Research programme with an emphasis on diplomacy and intelligence that were a legacy of his secondment to the shadow Ministry of Information.[100] By developing a BBC library on Latin America and establishing contacts with organisations such as the Ibero-American Institute and the Sociedade Paulista de Cultura Anglo-Brasilia Relations, Tallents had created an important cultural infrastructure. Such sensitivity was at the time highly unusual at the BBC.[101] Under Tallents's direction the Overseas Service sought to build closer relationships with an international audience and moved away from 'the cold delivery of translated material'.[102] Tallents was determined to ensure that a more thoughtful approach to foreign broadcasts was adopted. It was noted:

> Such questions as the length of a news bulletin, the arrangement of items, the speed of delivery, and the kind of voice have become of the gravest importance. Furthermore, in occupied countries where listening is both difficult and dangerous, it is important that the limited number of listeners should remember as much as possible in order to increase the circulation by word of mouth; in other words, the memory value of the programme must be studied.[103]

The appointment of Mark Abrams as Overseas Publicity Organiser (aka Head of Propaganda Research) was indicative of this new emphasis on intelligence gathering and applied market research.[104] Foreign correspondence was used to gather information and generate new programme ideas.[105] Of particular importance was BBC Monitoring, which, after recruiting scholars such as William Empson, began production of a 100,000-word 'Daily Digest of World Broadcasts' alongside shorter summaries and more tightly focused reports such as 'America and the War'. The information provided by Monitoring also enabled the Overseas Service to identify, and then recruit, key foreign broadcasters. As Tallents reflected, 'one of the surest ways of securing the goodwill of a country is to reflect its personalities and its doings in the UK's press or broadcast programmes'.[106] By allowing air time to prominent foreign correspondents such as Ed Morrow and Michel St Denis, and providing an institutional umbrella for the staff of radio stations that had fled from occupied Europe, the BBC was understood to empower a plurality of voices.[107] Asa Briggs describes the Tallents-directed service as one of the few areas where the British propaganda machine comprehensively defeated Goebbels's organisation.[108]

Furthermore, in programmes such as 'Listening Post', 'The Ear of Britain' and 'The World Hears London', the work of BBC Monitoring was itself championed throughout the world. The particular appeal of the Britain projected by Tallents's Overseas Service was that it demonstrably listened to minority languages – such as Maltese and Kurdish – rather than persecuting them. The BBC Overseas Service aggregated the widest possible range of independent activity by the use of 'background' initiatives, such as the commissioning of thousands of Overseas Service handkerchiefs embroidered with the BBC's wavelengths.[109] Ultimately, the BBC Overseas Service refined an international version of the national address that Tallents had created at the GPO. Listeners to 'Letters from Abroad' were told:

> A trapper in a lonely spot in Alaska regularly listens to the best concerts from London. We hear of milking sheds in New Zealand where wireless sets have been installed so that farmers may get their BBC news. While a writer from India, almost the only critic of Big Ben, complains that its chimes wake the baby.[110]

While Tallents believed that this inclusive method had ensured

Britain's 'leadership of the oppressed peoples', the BBC managers, Civil Servants and politicians became increasingly wary. The Overseas Service fondness for J. B. Priestley – the series 'Letters from Abroad' was originally constructed out of the mass of responses provoked by his talks – hinted that a Britain that boasted about its 'listening' credentials might have to begin thinking and acting differently.[111] Overseas staff garnered a reputation for taking maverick initiative and stood accused of committing 'His Majesty's Government to political actions which certainly have been disapproved if the FO had been consulted beforehand'.[112] In July 1940, the German Service's Sefton Delmer turned down Hitler's 'final' appeal for peace without any recourse to government, prompting questions to be raised in the House.[113] The security services eventually curtailed the 'V' campaign on the grounds that it was running ahead of the Allied government's readiness to co-ordinate a resistance movement.[114] More seriously, there were continual allegations that unfriendly governments had placed agents in the Overseas Service. 'Several hundred aliens, including Germans, are employed at Broadcasting House in the foreign language service', reported *The Daily Telegraph*; 'a purge of these employees is felt to be desirable'.[115]

The transfer of Ivone Kirkpatrick from the Foreign Office brought a halt to Tallents's haphazard management. Kirkpatrick judged that the BBC's Overseas staff too readily followed their own 'individual ideas of policy' and outlined the need for a substantial reorganisation.[116] Tallents's trusted lieutenant, A. P. Ryan, agreed. He complained:

> What is required is a unified control of output ... at present there is unfortunately no co-ordination between news, news talks and programmes. In some cases news editors and programmers are working in completely water-tight compartments.[117]

The absence of editorial controls in Tallents's Overseas Service was coupled with more rudimentary failings. In the first two years of the War staff numbers had massively expanded, and, while the BBC had gained the ability to broadcast in thirty-one different languages, new services were introduced piecemeal, at short notice and without recourse to strategic control. Transmitters, studio facilities and office space lagged even further behind. Worse, despite the increased financial outlay, the actual volume of foreign-language broadcasting appeared to be in danger of falling.[118]

The appointment of Brendan Bracken as Minister of Information in July 1941 bought Tallents's reign to a close. By creating the Political Warfare Executive, Bracken attempted to unify the British propaganda effort. As Tallents did not impress Bracken as someone who could ensure the political accountability of a re-focused European Service, he was replaced by Kirkpatrick in September 1941.[119] Tallents rejected the opportunity to determine the BBC's long-term plans for Empire broadcasting as 'face-saving or otherwise unreal employment'.[120]

However, Tallents's commitment to national projection led him to spend the next eighteen months writing *Man and Boy*. Ostensibly the first chapter of his autobiography, the book's focus on Britain's relationship with the margins of Europe had clear political intent. By recounting his own role in securing an armistice between Estonia and Germany, consolidating Latvia's independence and calming a land dispute between Estonia and Latvia, Tallents portrayed Britain as the disinterested but just international policeman.[121] As one contemporary had it, the book filled a gap between 'the German reminiscences of von der Goltz and Noske and the French reminiscences of du Parquet and Niessel' and reasserted the importance of Britain's humanitarian intervention.[122] Moreover, the book exemplified the dictum of Tallents's Overseas Service that 'propaganda is not just a question of cleverness, astuteness and technique. It is a question of authentic feeling.'[123]

Notes

1 Grierson's remarks deserve fuller quotation: 'Tallents marked out the habitation and the place for our new teaching of citizenship and gave it a chance to expand. In relating it to the art so variously called "cultural relations", "public relations" and "propaganda", he joined it with one of the driving forces of the time and guaranteed it patronage ... It was a strange alliance for Whitehall. The intangibles of art – whether of propaganda or of film – were hardly "to be packed into the narrow act" of a Treasury file; and Tallents' contribution at the time deserves to go down among the more curious feats of Civil Service bravery.' Grierson archive, G3:14:5, 'Story of the Documentary Film' article in *Fortnightly Review*, August 1938.

2 BBC Archive, Tallents L2/211/1, 'E. I. C. Jacob to Lady Tallents', 23 September 1958.

3 See D. LeMahieu, 'John Reith: Entrepreneur of Collectivism', in S. Pedersen and P. Mandler (eds) *After the Victorians: Private Conscience and Public Duty in Modern Britain* (London & New York, 1994), pp. 189–206.

4 BBC Archive, P13/1, 'Changes at the BBC', *The Yorkshire Post*, 10 July 1935.

5 At interview Tallents admitted that he would 'Be quite happy about the general publicity part, and he did not seem unduly alarmed on the score of the wider promotion of general good will. As regards the press relations, this would be, generally speaking, a new field to him, and he seemed to rely on the assumption that he could count upon one or more highly experienced subordinates to do the greater part of his work under his general direction. On this point I disillusioned him.' BBC Archive, Tallents L2/211/1, 'Notes on First Interview', 12 June 1935.

6 BBC Archive, R44/442, 'BBC Public Relations: Memorandum by Controller', September 1936.

7 BBC Archive, R44/442, 'BBC Public Relations: Memorandum by Controller', September 1936.

8 BBC Archive, P573, 'Sir Stephen Tallents Answers His Critics', *World Press News*, 30 July 1936.

9 BBC Archive, P13/1, 'BBC Sins – the Answer', *John Bull*, 14 December 1935.

10 Though Ryan was married to C. P. Scott's granddaughter he quickly left *The Manchester Guardian* – 'finding its politics at some points too far to the left for his taste' – for *The Daily Telegraph* before joining the EMB. On joining the BBC as Tallents's deputy he demanded wage parity with the private sector and a chauffeur. See BBC Archive, L2/178/1, Alfred Patrick Ryan.

11 So great was Tallents's dependence on Ryan that, when Tallents was seconded to assist Beveridge with Fuel Rationing in 1942, he again attempted to bring his former protégé along with him. This was a ridiculous ploy that much annoyed Ryan (who described Tallents as 'an old and unemployed Chief') who believed himself to be on the brink of the Director Generalship. See BBC Archive, L2/178/1 'Alfred Patrick Ryan'.

12 BBC Archive, R44/442, 'Comments by Controllers on Controller (PR) Memorandum on Public Relations', 16 October 1936.

13 R. Eckersley, *The BBC and All That* (London, 1946), p. 119.

14 BBC Archive, P15, 'Bias and the BBC', *The Daily Mail*, 13 June

1937. However, in his autobiography, Macleod (who was a Communist) complains that Tallents extensively rewrote scripts on Soviet Russia and ensured that all statements made by the USSR had the prefix 'in its opinion' attached. See J. Macleod, *A Job at the BBC: Some Personal Reminiscences* (Glasgow, 1946), p. 12.

15 Qtd in C. Stuart (ed.), *The Reith Diaries* (London, 1975), p. 172.

16 BBC Archive, P573, 'High Spots', *The Mirror*, 25 February 1936.

17 Tallents's pursuit of membership of the Athenaeum through a badgering correspondence with Reith adds a certain amount of substance to this judgement. Reith wrote after their first meeting, 'I was not tremendously impressed at the result of this first contact. From the start he gave me the feeling, instinctively, that it would be unwise to talk of our more intimate affairs with that complete freedom [... indistinct ...] a sycophant ... disinclined to press his own views if they are likely to prove unpopular.' This document has been damaged by fire. BBC Archive, Tallents L2/211/1, 'Notes on First Interview', 12 June 1935.

18 BBC Archive, R44/442, 'BBC Public Relations: Memorandum by Controller', September 1936.

19 BBC Archive, R44/442, 'BBC Public Relations: Memorandum by Controller', September 1936.

20 A. J. P. Taylor, *English History 1914–1945* (London, 1965), p. 204.

21 J. Macleod, *A Job at the BBC*, p. 12.

22 R. Silvey, *Who's Listening: The Story of BBC Audience Research* (London, 1975), p. 19.

23 S. Tallents, 'What's Right with the BBC', *The Spectator*, 24 March 1939, p. 478.

24 Tallents, *The Projection of England*, p. 37.

25 Keynes wrote, 'I feel strongly that the cultured voice of the Universities is very unsuccessful, particularly when the announcers put on a tone which is reverend as well as cultured.' King's College, Cambridge, Keynes Papers, BR/3/116, 'Keynes to Tallents', 12 July 1937.

26 BBC Archive, P13/1, 'BBC Sins – the Answer', *John Bull*, 14 December 1935.

27 BBC Archive, R44/442, 'BBC Public Relations: Memorandum by Controller', September 1936.

28 BBC Archive, R44/442, 'BBC Public Relations: Memorandum by Controller', September 1936.

29 The report continued, 'Miss Lyons is a good worker but has a

very unfortunate manner. I think she is being paid too much.'
BBC Archive, R13/319/1, 'Confidential Report on Staff and
Organisation', 10 November 1926.

30 In full, 'Murray's method of handling the Press was open
to criticism, and was certainly, as investigation subsequently
proved, not in keeping with the prestige of a big institution such
as the BBC.' BBC Archive, R13/319/2, 'BBC Public Relations',
Graves to DG, 27 December 1940.

31 BBC Archive, R44/442, 'BBC Public Relations: Memorandum
by Controller', September 1936.

32 BBC Archive, R44/442, 'BBC Public Relations: Memorandum
by Controller', September 1936.

33 Even DIA members, Tallents's supposed allies, were moved
to complain about the radical nature of his work at the BBC.
London Transport Archive, Frank Pick papers, F 11/84, 'Jefferys
to Boult', 30 April 1940.

34 Silvey, *Who's Listening*, p. 28.

35 BBC Archive, P573, 'Great Problems Ahead', *The Yorkshire
Telegraph & Star*, 18 March 1936.

36 BBC Broadcast, Stephen Tallents, 'What Every Listener Knows',
BBC Radio, 2 January 1938.

37 Silvey, *Who's Listening*, p. 19.

38 Indeed, it has been argued that, although market research in
America may have been corporation-led, it was the education
lobby in Britain that petitioned the BBC to expand the scope of
its listener surveys. See A. Briggs, *The History of Broadcasting
in the United Kingdom Volume II: The Golden Age of Wireless*
(Oxford & New York, 1995), pp. 238–251.

39 'A London Diary', *The New Statesman and Nation*, 13 July
1935, p. 55.

40 Joseph Macleod asserted that Mallon's appointment was the
work of Attlee. See Macleod, *A Job at the BBC*, p. 12.

41 See V. Gielgud, *Years of the Locust* (London & Brussels, 1947).

42 See V. Gielgud, *British Radio Drama, 1922–1956* (London,
1957).

43 BBC Broadcast, Stephen Tallents, 'What Every Listener Knows',
BBC Radio, 2 January 1938.

44 Silvey amusingly recalled the BBC's bureaucratic practices:
'I learnt the subtle difference between sending a memo to X
"through" Y, which meant that Y had the right to add his
comments ... and addressing a memo to X "with a copy to Y",
which gave Y no opportunity to comment before X got it but did

keep him in the picture, or addressing it 1.X 2.Y, which meant
that Y only received it after X had done so and perhaps had added
a minute of his own. I learnt about some personal eccentricities:
that P was fierce in writing but mild to meet so that it was always
better to go to see him rather than write him a memo, or that as
Q tended to somnolence after lunch he was best approached in
the morning if he was required to apply his mind to the subject
but in the afternoon if you didn't want him to look at the problem
too closely.' Silvey, *Who's Listening*, p. 23.

45 See BBC Archive, T1/6/1, 'Audience Research Memos 1A,
   1936–1939'.
46 BBC Archive, T1/6/1, S. Tallents, 'Television Campaign', 23
   January 1939.
47 BBC Archive, P15, 'Sounding the Listener', *The Morning Post*,
   13 January 1937.
48 Ironically, after the Second World War, 'Market Research' was
   celebrated in a special BBC series dedicated to great British
   accomplishments of the modern age. It saw the profession
   beginning with the Liverpool ship merchant and philanthropist
   Charles Booth, before being further developed by Seebohm
   Rowntree and then Professor Arthur Bowley at the London
   School of Economics. See BBC Archive, 'Talks: Abrams Mark
   Dr, File 1, 1946–1955', and M. Abrams, 'Market Research
   (British Achievements)', *BBC Radio*, 8 October 1948.
49 Sir William Crawford sent Tallents several listener surveys.
   See, for example, BBC Archive, R34/1 Tallents to Crawford,
   24 February 1939. Tallents recruited both Mark Abrams and
   Robert Silvey from the London Press Exchange. Abrams and
   Silvey both worked on *The Home Market: A Book of Facts
   about People* promoted by Frank Pick (London, 1939).
50 BBC Archive, P15, 'The Big Idea for the BBC', *The Birmingham
   Post*, 10 April 1937.
51 How to best estimate the future impact of a decreasing
   population on BBC revenue was a Reith-approved investigation
   that prompted correspondence between Tallents and Beveridge.
   See, for instance, LSE Archive, Beveridge Papers, 'Tallents to
   Beveridge', 4 January 1937.
52 Reith asked the BBC's television producer and consumer rights
   pioneer Mary Adams to direct the MoI's own Home Intelligence
   Department. For more on the use of market research to launch
   the Latin America service see BBC Archive, R34/1, 'Reith to
   Tallents', 25 March 1938.

53 BBC Archive, R44/442, 'BBC Public Relations: Summary of Comments by the VC, Mrs Hamilton and Control Board (Excl. DG) on Memorandum by Controller PR', September 1936.

54 To give a brief resume of the scandal, as well as editing *The Listener*, Lambert was also a governor of the fledgling British Film Institute (BFI). At the time, the BFI was funded through a tax on cinema tickets, an arrangement which Tallents and Lambert both regarded as compromising. In their opinion, the BFI merely provided a fig leaf of respectability for commercial companies whose main activities were directed towards marginalising educational cinema. Encouraged by Tallents, Lambert began to speak out on the issue, his strong public criticisms of commercial film companies stirring up considerable controversy, as it was interpreted – without foundation – that the BBC was seeking to move into film production. Lambert's subsequent co-authoring of *The Haunting of Cashen's Gap* with the ghost hunter Harry Price ('a true life tale' that detailed the pursuit of a talking mongoose named Gef) provided convenient impetus for one BFI governor (Sir Cecil Levita) to seek Lambert's removal. Levita unofficially approached the BBC Chairman, R. C. Norman, to supply information on Lambert's mental state (Lambert was continually moving house, as he believed that he was being pursued by the Evil Eye) and fitness to continue working for the BFI. When news of Levita's enquiry filtered down to Lambert, he panicked. Worried that his position at the BBC was under threat, Lambert instructed his solicitor to sue Levita for defamation. At this point the BBC attempted to intervene, eventually obtaining a retraction from Levita's lawyers. However, it proved too little too late and, despite the apology, Tallents was unable to prevent Lambert from pursuing the case. Lambert later claimed (and an enquiry upheld) that Tallents had obliquely threatened to curtail his career if he continued his personal legal action at the expense of the good name of the BBC. After Lambert was awarded £7,500 in damages for libel, the Labour Party, which had long harboured the suspicion that the degree of control that Reith's BBC exerted on its workforce was unacceptable, eagerly seized upon his complaint. Although Attlee did not manage to persuade Baldwin that the BBC should be opened up to the unions, the end result of this long-running legal saga saw the creation of a new staff organisation and led to BBC vacancies being advertised externally. See BBC Archive, R22/135/11a.

55 BBC Archive, P13/1, 'Changes at the BBC', *The Observer*, 14 July 1935.

56 Characteristically, Tallents contributed articles on afforestation in the Lake District, the National Dahlia Society show and the art of scything. BBC Archive, R22/135/1a, 'Lambert to Reith', 12 November 1935.

57 BBC Archive, R13/319/2, 'BBC Public Relations', 'Graves to DG', 27 December 1940.

58 'We owe it to him', continued the correspondent, 'that Empire Marketing is associated in our minds, not with Beaverbookian boost, but with a real advance in the design of the art of the poster'. 'A London Diary', *The New Statesman and Nation*, 13 July 1935, p. 55.

59 For instance, Ryan was critical of reporting norms. He berated staff on their naive use of sources 'a happy-go-lucky spirit still seems to prevail here after ten or fifteen years of broadcasting ... If a propagandist body can seriously be regarded by any department of the BBC as fitting authority to justify what is said at the microphone, then it is indeed time that the worldly wisdom of the most junior sub-editor on a country weekly was infused into our staff'. BBC Archive, R34/1, A. P. Ryan, 'Advertising in Programmes', 7 April 1937, and also S. Tallents, 'Newspaper Acknowledgements', 7 February 1939.

60 However, like Tallents, Kenneth Adam eventually moved into an editorial role at the BBC. Adam was made Controller of Television in 1957. 'Mr Kenneth Adam', *The Times*, 19 October 1978, p. 18.

61 For example, the Admiralty censors wanted seniority over the other armed forces. See NA, CAB 104/87, Committee of Imperial Defence Sub-Committee on the Ministry of Information, 'Campbell Stuart to C. N. Ryan', 24 November 1938.

62 For example: 'I gathered the other day that there was a proposal, in case of isolation but not, I think, inevitably in case of war, to divide the country into a heptarchy, with regiments for certain services, on the lines of the civil emergency "civil commissioner". Any such plans would be material to our publicity, and would presumably look to us for the necessary provision.' NA, CAB 104/86, 'Tallents to Ryan', 20 June 1938.

63 NA, CAB 104/88, 'E. E. B. to H. J. Wilson', 25 November 1938.

64 One explanation of this is that it offered Reith a way of marginalising – and if war should come – dispensing with Tallents. His official reason was that he already had 'greater or lesser ideas for

myself for the next war if it comes'. See M. Balfour, *Propaganda in War 1939–1945* (London, 1979), p. 56.

65 NA, CAB 104/84, Committee of Imperial Defence Sub-Committee on the Ministry of Information, 'Hankey to Warburton', 1 November 1935.

66 For example, the Air Ministry had to be reassured that the BBC's new shortwave radio transmitters could not be used as guidance systems by enemy bombers.

67 Reporting to the new DG, Tallents explained, 'He [Lord Burnham, an important newspaper owner and lobbyist] told me that the press were very anxious about this as they felt there would be serious competition with the newspapers to their detriment ... I said that the BBC would stand firmly by its opinion as to the desirability of such a practice in wartime and indicated that it was for the government to consider the situation dispassionately in the light of the evidence which we could bring forward and which I imagined would weigh heavily with them.' BBC Archive, R34/941, 'Tallents to Ogilvie', 18 July 1938.

68 NA, CAB 104/84, H. McGregor, 'Report on the Ministry of Information', 26 February 1937.

69 See S. J. Potter, *News and the British World: The Emergence of an Imperial Press System, 1876–1922* (Oxford, 2003).

70 NA, CAB 104/84, McGregor, 'Report'.

71 Tallents's MoI preparations can be seen to echo the initatives of First World War pamphleteers like Campbell Stuart, H. G. Wells and John Buchan. On reading Tallents's memo, Campbell Stuart noted the 'curious co-incidence that just over 20 years ago a (similar) paper of mine on "Propaganda in War Time" should have gone before the cabinet – the first paper of mine to do so'. NA, CAB 104/87, Committee of Imperial Defence Sub-Committee on the Ministry of Information, 'Campbell to Ryan', 24 November 1938.

72 See NA, CAB 104/87, Committee of Imperial Defence Sub-Committee on the Ministry of Information.

73 On being appointed shadow Designate, Tallents had appointed Jack Brebner from the Post Office as his deputy. He also attempted to recruit former collaborators such as Jack Beddington and Gervas Huxley. NA, INF 1/13, 'Tallents to Woodburn', 25 April 1938.

74 Tallents was informed, 'Apart from those who hold from time to time outstanding offices, such as that of Chairman of the

Newspaper Proprietors Association, the public reputation of those who are occupied in the world of "information" change rapidly. Who, for example, in 1938 would be rash enough to forecast the future outstanding figures in the film industry? Any attempt to single out in advance of a crisis individuals, as distinct from office-holders, as suitable members of the advisory council would be liable to land the ministry on its occurrence with a very unconvincing body of advisers.' NA, CAB 104/86, Committee of Imperial Defence Sub-Committee on the Ministry of Information, 'Plans for the Establishment of a Ministry of Information', 6 April 1938.

75 However, Tallents was never officially sacked; rather, 'owing to his BBC duties, it has been found necessary for Sir Stephen Tallents to relinquish the post of DG (Designate)'. NA, CAB 104/88, Committee of Imperial Defence Sub-Committee on the Ministry of Information, 'Tallents to Fisher', 21 December 1938.

76 T. Wilcox, 'Projection or Publicity? Rival Concepts in the Pre-war Planning of the British Ministry of Information', *Journal of Contemporary History*, Vol. 18, 1983, p. 98.

77 BBC Archive, P16, 'First Details of Britain's Ministry of Information Revealed', *World Press News*, 8 October 1938.

78 He continued, 'It is no use threatening your enemy with the disasters he will suffer when he loses the war if, for the time being, he is clearly winning it.' NA, CAB 104/87, 'Stanhope to Ryan', 24 November 1938.

79 He further exclaimed, 'Here is a department staffed with nearly one thousand people, calling itself a Ministry of Information, yet the daily output of information issued for publication in British newspapers was so meagre it would hardly fill one typed foolscap sheet.' J. Hargrave, *Propaganda the Mightiest Weapon of All Words Win Wars* (London, 1940), pp. 7–8.

80 NA, CAB104/87, 'H. J. W to Sir Warren Fisher', 20 October 1938.

81 The press, asserts Cockett, 'had become not so much the watchdogs of democracy as the harlots of democracy – at every level forfeiting their independence for power and fortune (and frequently a peerage)'. R. Cockett, *Twilight of Truth: Chamberlain, Appeasement and the Manipulation of the Press* (London, 1989), p. 187.

82 There can, for instance, be few shadow Ministries whose DG Designates could have simultaneously been orchestrating public

protests to reduce the environmental damage done by fighter planes. S. Tallents, 'Bombing Near Holy Island: the Beauty of Northumbria', *The Times*, 8 February 1936, p. 8.

83 Through the pages of *Country Life* and *The Times* Tallents chronicled his efforts to construct a 'historic' garden that preserved the saplings of famous plants in history such as the apple tree which Newton sat beneath. He recalled, 'Between the wars I thought it might be prudent to lay down some stock associated with the European dictators. I began to make enquiries about Hitler's favourite flower. But a visitor to Berchtesgaden reported that he wasn't a likely contributor. She had pointed one day to vase of sweet peas on the table and asked what the German name for them was. Hitler had replied peevishly – "how should I know?" – discouraged by this evidence of botanical ignorance among the dictators, I decided to waste no stamps on a letter I had thought of composing and sending to Mussolini.' S. Tallents, 'A Garden of Historic Plants', *BBC Radio*, 10 July 1948. See also S. Tallents, 'Plants with a History', 12 April 1939, *The Times*, p. 11. The dates of Tallents's interest suggest that Hitler's decision to personally present all Gold medal winners of the Berlin Olympics with an oak sapling might have been an influence. See P. Radford and D. Smith, 'Hitler's Olympic Oak Gift to Briton Axed', *The Observer*, 19 August 2007, p. 21.

84 See Taylor, *The Projection of Britain*, pp. 216–259.

85 There are many similarities between Tallents's and Leeper's thinking. Leeper's conviction that 'publicity is the best form of propaganda', and predilection for non-political soft-edged cultural activity is almost indistinguishable from Tallents's conception of 'background publicity'. For instance, in *The Projection of England*, Tallents had argued that there was a need for a national agency of cultural diplomacy while Leeper had synchronistically created the British Council. Perhaps significantly, both Tallents and Leeper had served in the Baltics at the close of the First World War.

86 Indeed, Leeper and Tallents had often clashed. Tallents wanted to merge the Foreign Office News Department into the MoI, Leeper wanted it to remain independent. I see this disagreement stemming both from departmental pride and from the anti-appeasers' fear of having their public voice quashed.

87 These leaflets released after the detonation of a clockwork fuse apparently utilised 'up-to-date enemy type faces' without

disguising 'the fact that they were issued by the British government'. NA, CAB 104/87, Committee of Imperial Defence Sub-Committee on the Ministry of Information, 'S. Tallents – Notes on the Preparation of Plans for the Establishment of the Ministry of Information/Information in Enemy Countries', 7 November 1938.

88 These remarks were made after 'the position of Sir Stephen Tallents was discussed and tentative arrangements made as regards the future'. NA, CAB 104/88, 'Meeting in Sir Warren Fisher's Office', 2 December 1938.

89 NA, CAB 104/88, E. E. B., 'Audience with Rogerson', 29 November 1938.

90 Unable to convince 'insiders' of his loyalty, or persuade them of the values of his innovations, John Grierson would face the same frustrations as his mentor. See J. Fox, 'John Grierson, His "Documentary Boys" and the British Ministry of Information, 1939–1942', *Historical Journal of Film, Radio and Television*, Vol. 25, No. 3, 2005, pp. 345–369.

91 They resolved to find a replacement once it was discovered 'what ministers are ear-marked for something else: then we can suggest a name or names to the PM'. NA, CAB 104/87, 'HJW to Bridges', 3 August 1938.

92 Qtd in Balfour, *Propaganda in War*, p. 56.

93 The supposed decadence of the Ministry was famously parodied in Evelyn Waugh's *Put Out More Flags* (London, 1943).

94 R. H. Bruce Lockhart, *Comes the Reckoning* (London, 1947), p. 96.

95 NA, CAB 104/88, 'Tallents to Fisher', 21 December 1938.

96 'I have this morning obtained from The Treasury a complete statement of the staff in government departments now employed wholly or mainly in publicity (which really means anything from news to propaganda, plus advertisement). The annual cost of this work now reaches the astounding figure of £650,000 a year. Is it not fairly certain in the case of all departments, old and new, most vitally concerned with war problems, that they will in fact insist on retaining when the time comes either the whole or at least the nucleus of their existing public relations organisation? ... Where then does the Ministry of Information, sine qua news and publicity come in? The answer would seem to be that the Ministry of Information will simply not come in at all.' NA, CAB 104/88, J. Beresford, 'New Memorandum on Ministry of Information', 13 May 1939.

97 See A. Boyle, *Poor, Dear Brendan* (London, 1974), pp. 265–310.

98 He was the son of the Liberal professor Ernest Barker, and a confidant (from his period in Warsaw at *The Times*) of Rex Leeper.

99 BBC Archive, P575, 'Broadcasting', *The Birmingham Post*, 26 April 1938.

100 The diplomatic sweep of Tallents's thinking saw A. S. Calvert transferred from the Foreign Office to assist the BBC. NA, CAB 104/87, Committee of Imperial Defence Sub-Committee on the Ministry of Information, 'S. Tallents, Publicity Work in Central and South America'.

101 *The Daily Mirror*, for instance, accused the BBC of believing that 'the world is populated by two plainly divided classes of people – Englishmen and others.' BBC Archive, P382, 'Bill Grieg says ...', *The Daily Mirror*, 7 December 1940.

102 BBC Archive, R13/187/2, Assistant Controller, 'Use of Foreign Staff', 15 November 1940.

103 BBC Archive, R13/183, 'Overseas Publicity Section & Propaganda Research Section', 'Propaganda Research Section', 20 September 1940.

104 See BBC Archive, R13/183, 'Overseas Publicity Section & Propaganda Research Section'.

105 This idea of creating an international 'mail bag' programme was suggested to Tallents by A. P. Ryan. 'It is a fascinating picture – Bulgarians quoting Isaiah in block capitals, and Greeks writing from New South Wales. It seems to me that there would be real interest in you coming to the microphone and saying that you had just been rummaging about in our overseas post bag and would fish up some random catches to show how world-wide and various a reception we get.' See BBC Archive, 910 Tal File 1, 'Ryan to Tallents', 31 July 1940.

106 NA, CAB 104/87, Committee of Imperial Defence Sub-Committee on the Ministry of Information, 'S. Tallents – Publicity Work in Central and South America'.

107 Tallents later claimed that Michel St Denis's theatrical troop 'La Compagnie de Quinze', a company whose actors were trained not only to act but to 'sing, draw, design and make costumes and accessories, even improvise scenarios, write or compose music' provided a model for the EMB/GPO Film Units. S. Tallents, 'The Birth of the British Documentary (Part II)', p. 29.

108 Briggs, *War*, p. 173.

109 See BBC Archive, R13/183, 'Overseas Publicity Section & Propaganda Research Section', 'European Publicity', 20 November 1941.

110 BBC Broadcast, Stephen Tallents, 'Letters from Abroad', *BBC Radio*, 11 August 1940.

111 Priestley's 'home' broadcasts had, of course, proved equally contentious. See J. B. Priestley, *Postscripts* (London, 1940), and S. Nicholas, *The Echo of War: Home Front Propaganda and the Wartime BBC, 1939–1945* (Manchester & New York, 1996).

112 BBC Archive, R13/187/4, 'Work of the Liaison Department', 13 May 1941.

113 Sefton Delmer later achieved national notoriety as a 'black' propagandist. See S. Delmer, *Trail Sinister* (London, 1961) and *Black Boomerang* (London, 1962).

114 See C. Cruickshank, *The Fourth Arm: Psychological Warfare 1938–45* (London, 1977), p. 124 Originally the brainchild of the BBC's Belgian Programme Organiser, Victor de Laveleye, use of the 'V' as a non-violent protest against Nazi occupation soon spread throughout mainland Europe and across the Atlantic. What began as an incitement for people to chalk Vs in public places was ingeniously extended into a campaign of civil disobedience as BBC radio programmes instructed listeners how to create 'V' sounds in Morse code. See C. Rolo, *Radio Goes to War* (London, 1943), p. 139.

115 BBC Archive, P382, 'BBC to Have New Chief', *The Daily Telegraph*, 6 December 1940.

116 See I. Kirkpatrick, *The Inner Circle: The Memoirs of Ivone Kirkpatrick* (London, 1959), pp. 149–155.

117 BBC Archive, R13/187/3, 'A. P. Ryan – Proposed Organisation of Overseas Propaganda Department', 25 February 1941.

118 Vernon Bartlett told the House of Commons that 'at present less time is devoted to broadcasting in foreign languages than was the case the year ago, yet you have all those European countries which have come under Nazi domination and which can only be reached by the spoken word'. BBC Archive, P32, 'British Propaganda', *Manchester Guardian*, 22 February 1941.

119 'The minister [Bracken] continued that, in addition to special oversight of the cost of the service, the government was entitled to satisfy itself that the persons in charge of the service enjoyed its confidence and approval ... the minister said that he was satisfied for several reasons that there should be a change in the present controller [Tallents] of the Overseas Division.' BBC

Archive, R13/187/3, 'Powell – Memo on BBC Overseas Service', 17 September 1941.

120 BBC Archive, 'Powell – Memo on BBC Overseas Service', 17 September 1941.

121 See S. Tallents, 'Baltic Adventure', *BBC Radio*, 27 March 1949.

122 J. Hampden Jackson, 'Review', *International Affairs Review Supplement*, Vol. 19, No. 13, September 1943, pp. 694–695.

123 BBC Archive, E2/453, 'Foreign Gen: Overseas General: Prop Research, Sept 1940–March 1942', 'A Plan and Basis for Propaganda', 4 May 1931.

Rebuilding the nation:
The Festival of Britain and
the formation of
the Institute of Public Relations

'There are two ways of starting a new enterprise', Tallents argued. 'You can either work out careful plans on paper then order them to be carried out; or you can pick the best men that you can find for your purpose and put them to grips with a still disorderly material.'[1] As Tallents's stilted work at the Ministry of Town and Country Planning was to attest, the postwar world did not well reward those who had their feet placed in the latter camp. The vogue for larger organisational units, the return of political sectarianism and the first stirrings of the Cold War all militated against the individualistic brand of public relations pioneered by Tallents. Instead, aspects of Tallents's thinking were codified into a profession by the newly created Institute of Public Relations. Somewhat bizarrely, Tallents's personal idiosyncrasies would become the template of a fast maturing industry.

Not for the first time, Tallents was rescued from the wilderness by Beveridge. The popular and political interest in 'reconstruction' excited by the publication of the Beveridge report into social insurance prompted the Prime Minister Winston Churchill to launch a 'four-year plan' to ensure that the country was prepared for the challenges of the postwar world.[2] An important part of Churchill's conciliatory gesture was the establishment of a new Ministry of Town and Country Planning (MTCP) in January 1943. The extensive bombing of cities such as Coventry, Glasgow, London, Portsmouth, Plymouth and Southampton had given symbolic weight to the rebuilding of Britain and pushed the town planning profession from the political margins in to the spotlight.

Under Reith, the Ministry of Works had commissioned the Scott Committee to consider the problems of rural development, founded the Uthwatt Committee to suggest how a system of compensation and betterment might operate, and tasked Patrick Abercrombie with developing a London plan. Though Reith was a non-party appointee, the administrative and organisational changes he championed were understood politically. Although in principle the concept of establishing a central planning agency and the nationalisation of development rights enjoyed cross-party support, the mechanisms necessary for implementing them were coming to be understood as left-wing. William Morrison's appointment as the first Minister of Town and Country Planning was thus an exceptionally tricky one. On the one hand, the Conservative MP was appointed to allay fears that the state intended to limit the rights of landowners. On the other hand, Morrison had to convince both Labour and Liberals that the MTCP possessed the power and political will to effectively tackle the problems of planning. Following the lead of politicians at the GPO and the Ministry of Information, Morrison responded to contradictory demands for rapid change by appointing a public relations officer. In 1943 Sir Stephen Tallents was appointed as Morrison's Principal Assistant Secretary (Tallents's wage demands exceeded Civil Service scales for publicity work) and took charge of the MTCP's public relations department.[3]

Although the MTCP did succeed in passing the Town and Country Planning (Interim Development) Act in 1943 it made little political headway.[4] Morrison was a circumspect figure and tended to talk abstractly about the need for collective effort. Morrison's opening address to the Town and County Planning Association (penned by Tallents) was typical:

> It would be out of place to paint a picture of the England and Wales as we want to see. Probably, none of us would agree precisely in our mental pictures of the country which to-day so many millions of eager hearts are expecting. Yet, in broad outline, we all have the same picture of a community worth preserving, creating a worthy present and laying the foundation of a noble future fit for our children's needs.[5]

At the Empire Marketing Board, Tallents had often used vague language of progress, modernity and science to neutralise more political interpretations of the Board's imperial mission. He employed a similar tactic at the MTCP, toning down the rhetoric of reconstruction and advising: 'it is important not to build such castles in the air as were raised after the last war and brought

contempt upon the phrase "homes for heroes"'.[6] The 'realism' and
rhetorical caution of the MTCP quickly resulted in an aura of
faint disappointment attaching itself to the department. *The Times*
wearily noted on the MTCP's inception in 1943, 'it is difficult to
say what the value of the new Ministry is likely to be [and] it must
be repeated that good intentions will achieve nothing, and may
even do more harm than good'.[7]

Paradoxically, in practice the MTCP's relative political
conservatism gave Tallents a stronger platform from which to
encourage contributions from architects, town planners and
engineers than a more directive organisation might have allowed.
As Minister for Works and Planning, Reith had revelled in the
existence of differences of professional opinion because the lack
of consensus enabled him to frame his department's agenda.[8] His
officials mused:

> There is one particular gap in the preparatory work ... We are
> doing the barest public relations. It is my view that preparatory
> public relations on planning should go beyond the normal
> task of explaining the department to the public, and aim at
> educating public opinion to the right form of reconstruction. I
> believe that our public relations should be part of our planning
> organisation.[9]

By contrast, Tallents's public relations work did not look to
propound a particular vision. Tallents was able to speak the
technocratic language of the town planning movement, and unlike
Reith was prepared to examine more discreet ways of building
consensus. During his three years at the MTCP Tallents would
develop (often very personal) channels to engage with town
planners, building professionals and environmental activists. He
became 'a frequent visitor' to the Royal Institute of British
Architects (RIBA) and was made an Honorary Associate in
1946.[10] Furthermore, Tallents's friendship with William Beveridge
(Tallents's well-received 1943 autobiography *Man and Boy* used
their early Civil Service partnership at the Ministry of Food as
its promotional spearhead) gave him the reformist credentials
necessary to forestall, if not impress, potential critics.[11]

While ideological cracks were beginning to show in the high
political consensus, the MTCP peddled the line that science and
statistics would bring about an unproblematic realignment of the
divergent concerns of architects, planners and builders.[12] In this
context, the two main aims of the public relations and publicity

work pursued by Tallents were understandable. One strand of work concentrated on helping the industry define and then prepare for the challenges ahead, while the second strand of work sought to enlist the active support of the wider population in anticipation of the postwar reforms to come. As Tallents put it:

A half century, at least, of intense planning and construction lies ahead of us. Designers and builders and materials are all for a while going to be short. We cannot afford to waste either men's time or materials on unnecessary experiments or mistakes. To look at the future from another point-of-view, those responsible for long term programmes of physical reconstruction will be wise to invite the criticism, and secure the active consent, of the public; and that involves both the creation of a popular understanding of the ends at which the proposals are aimed and the maintenance of popular confidence during the early and unspectacular stages of their work.[13]

Since his tenure at the EMB, Tallents's philosophy of public relations had been underpinned by education and cultural exchange. However, the MTCP took the encouragement of pedagogical activity to the outer limits of credibility. Tallents petitioned universities to teach spatial planning 'as an independent subject and not as an adjunct to some other field' and warned planners that, in addition to surveying, engineering and law, they should be prepared to master the disciplines of political science, geography and economics.[14] The MTCP further sponsored textbooks, outlined the possible shape of future industry organisations and suggested codes of best practice.

Despite the reassurance of Morrison ('this is not academic research, it is administrative reconnaissance, undertaken as a necessary preliminary to action')[15] radicals such as Edward Carter became increasingly suspicious of the department's ever-growing enthusiasm for sponsoring research activity.[16] The MTCP's endless interest in collating ever more knowledge was judged as a diversion from, rather than a step towards, realising the era's proudest ambitions. With hindsight, the period's emphasis on 'competency' can appear rather cynical.[17] Although there is a ring of truth to such retrospective criticism, it was a judgement few could easily admit at the time.[18] In 1943 town planning was still a comparatively new profession. During the interwar building boom its theoreticians had not been influential, while the construction industry was generally uninterested in the relationship between town planning and wider social and economic problems.[19] In the space of a little over twenty years a profession which had previously concentrated the majority of its efforts on improving the sanitary conditions of working-class estates was agitating for an unprecedented increase in power and responsibility.

Recognising that town planning was a profession still in its infancy, the MTCP worked to build forums through which planners and the construction industry could share information. Often working in tandem with (although, admittedly, sometimes against)[20] the Ministry of Health and the Ministry of Works, the MTCP identified areas where further research was required and published summaries of technical knowledge, current industry practices and likely future trends.[21] Although planners were encouraged to fundamentally rethink previously cherished assumptions, this spirit of critical self-reflection ('the current method of designing houses for rehousing projects appears to be based largely upon intuition') was balanced by an almost unshakeable confidence in the applied sciences. It is tempting to see the fetishisation of figures, facts and the language of rationality as a psychological totem being waved at cold hard reality. As a prominent planner admitted in 1947, the profession's skill set was hardly deep-rooted:

> I started by being appointed Chairman of the Town Planning Committee of the City Council of Sheffield, a not inconsiderable appointment. I probably possessed no equipment for the great task except the love of natural scenery, developed by rambling excursions in the Peak District of Derbyshire, and a fair acquaintance with the works of William Morris and Ruskin.[22]

Furthermore, the horrendous economic, human and material cost of fighting the Second World War ensured that the planners would gain extra responsibility at the precise moment when the profession was perhaps least equipped to fulfil it. Wartime restrictions prevented the free exchange of the economic, physical and sociological information that planners required. These restrictions were so severe that it was not until September 1945 that the MTCP was able to produce – with the Ordnance Survey – detailed maps illustrating the human, economic and political geography of Britain.[23] Indeed, even these resources were problematic as, for example, Depression-era budget cuts had prevented the Ordnance

Survey from carrying out much systematic survey work.[24] Most importantly, the fighting of the Second World War invalidated some of the existing population data by displacing thousands of British citizens.

Ultimately, progress would be delayed not by the MTCP's enthusiasm for encouraging further training and collaboration but by the political stalemate over the Uthwatt report. Just as Uthwatt's attempt to secure a political consensus that delineated the rights and responsibilities of landowners faltered between competing ideologies, Tallents's public relations work would be similarly stymied. In the bureaucratic confines of war, external collaboration was increasingly frowned upon, and the MTCP's menial status further reduced the creative outlets available. The limited ambition of Tallents's work at the MTCP also reveals some of the more fundamental problems that the early practitioners of public relations were beginning to face. At the EMB, GPO and, to some degree, the BBC, it had been possible to take an entrepreneurial approach to public relations. Reflecting both the modern character of the organisations that sponsored it and the novelty of the work, early public relations practitioners developed an independent sensibility that could stimulate both external and internal changes.

Ironically, while the public relations profession grew speedily on the back of such idiosyncratic successes, the rapid growth in PRO numbers prompted commercial organisations to begin to systemise the role by sub-dividing their functions. In consequence, public relations officers were less able to take an objective or pan-organisational viewpoint and experimentation was curtailed by categorisation and central oversight. Here it is instructive that Tallents's work on the presentation of Patrick Abercrombie's Greater London Plan proved his most successful initiative at the MTCP. Abercrombie's idealistic Plan stood outside departmental boundaries and crossed simple commercial, political and organisational lines. It was exactly the kind of imaginatively reformist scheme that Tallents had so often coaxed into a national media monument.

Patrick Abercrombie's Greater London Plan of 1944 recommended that London should be encircled by a green belt of countryside that would preserve space for agriculture and recreation, as well as prevent the metropolis encroaching further upon the countryside.[25] The plan also proposed moving industry, and some 600,000 people, out of the over-populated centres of

London and into a number of satellite 'new towns'. To sceptics much of Abercrombie's supposedly rational plan was simply fanciful. *Building* magazine complained that instead of sculpting his plan round the valleys of the Thames, Lea, Brent, Colne, Darent, Wandle and Mole, Abercrombie had laid down his plan with a compass. 'There is too much space given to purely descriptive writing of imaginary things', its correspondent continued, 'the whole plan indicates an over emphasis of the circle. The author seems to be obsessed with rings.'[26] Pragmatic Conservatives were also unsettled by Abercrombie's idealism (his report declared that 'we can build the new England which has been the inspiration and must be the reward of the citizen soldier who "knows what he fights for and loves what he knows"') and his stress on larger, regional planning agencies.[27] Equally, radical architects considered elements of Abercrombie's thinking (as well as vast swathes of the Scott Report)[28] to be little more than a warmed-over version of what they saw as Ebenezer Howard's anachronistic Garden City utopia.[29]

Whether the criticisms were ideological, political or pragmatic, the considerable influence wielded over Abercrombie by easily caricatured bodies for social improvement such as the YMCA, the Council for the Preservation of Rural England, the Ramblers' Association, the Young Ornithologists and Toynbee Hall, were seen to undermine the Plan.[30] Abercrombie's intellectual debt to the unorthodox sociological thinking of Patrick Geddes was also problematic.[31] Abercrombie explained that his plans were underpinned by a 'biological triad' that blended the demands of environment, function and organism into a harmonious 'philosophy of progress, sharply opposed to dialectical materialism, which seeks to proceed by means of a series of head-on collisions'.[32] The art critic Herbert Read acclaimed Abercrombie's plan as:

> A revolution which humanises industry at the same time as it disperses industry; which will give the worker responsibility for the work he does and a deep satisfaction in the place of his work so that when his work is done, he does not seek to escape from that place, but stays there in joy and pride. The modern proletariat has no roots: it is 'mobile labour' drifting like cattle over the land, seeking nourishment where it may be found.[33]

Thus the loudest enthusiasts for the Greater London Plan were apt to approve of the dispersal of both industry and people to newly created satellite towns for reasons that were all but alien to both the building industry and the government administrator. It was Tallents's task to ascertain, and then demonstrate, both the rationality and achievability of Abercrombie's ambitions.

Tallents's presentational work on the Greater London Plan operated on two main fronts. The first recognisable aim – and the easiest to achieve – was to stress the Plan's material aims. It was insisted that the Greater London Plan had been deliberately configured to address the '1) Congestion of traffic 2) Depressed housing; 3) Intermingling of housing and industry; and 4) Lack and mal-administration of open space'.[34] To bolster these key messages the MTCP began to share publicly the statistical bedrock of Abercrombie's plans.[35] Tallents's breezy reflection that the MTCP must help 'the interested citizen who wishes to understand the changes going on around him' became entrenched. This innovation also had the welcome side-effect of concentrating critical attention on practical points of detail rather than knottier ideological questions. More interesting than the rhetorical shift of emphasis were Tallents's attempts to 'bring the plan alive'. This entailed reconciling the seemingly contradictory goals of demonstrating the Plan's achievability while simultaneously appealing to the general public's imagination. For all their social ambitions, wartime planners had done little to dispel the secrecy that surrounded their grandiose visions. Instead planners acted, as Edward Carter later recalled, like 'a nervous woman concealing her pregnancy'.[36] By contrast, Tallents had commissioned various visual aids, including illustrative photographs and sketches, to widen the popular appeal of the Greater London Plan.[37] On Tallents's prompting the MTCP also commissioned Halas and Batchelor to produce *New Town*, an explanatory cartoon film.[38] One anecdotal testament to the effectiveness of Tallents's promotion was the response of British prisoners of war held in Stalag III. 'The lecture [on the London Plan] lasted for two hours and aroused so much interest that it was necessary to repeat it on three successive evenings in order to admit the people to whom this is a subject of great national importance', a POW wrote; 'may I ask you to send me another copy together with any other plans which may have been completed for the reconstruction of other parts of Britain?'[39]

Promoting the Greater London Plan also led Tallents to develop what would become an important personal and professional enthusiasm for architectural models. After a meeting with Robin Darwin of the Directorate of Camouflage, Tallents began commissioning high-quality models from a range of interesting artists. Having introduced Listener Research at the BBC, Tallents evangelised the use of public models at the MTCP. He explained:

> Many an architect must have been reduced to despair by the inability of a client to understand his simplest proposals on the drawing board ... This wide spread deficiency no doubt explains why many modern American schools of architecture contain, as I read, fully equipped modelling branches. [Indeed] The most casual visitor to an exhibition cannot fail to notice how the crudest model is a magnet for the public. It calls them away from even the most finished maps or diagrams, even the most engaging perspectives. And if any part of it moves – even a single wheel of it only – visitors will stand and watch it attentively for longer than I am patient enough to count.[40]

Persuading planners and architects to make fuller use of amendable models that evolved with the suggestions of public and professional critics became a point of public relations pride for Tallents. 'Provided that they are stoutly made', he wrote, 'they should enable us to bequeath, to those that come after us, the most vivid historical record that there could be of the ideas which a generation entrusted with a unique opportunity for the reconstruction of our country, bought to the discharge of its task'.[41] By encouraging the production of such lavish models and sketches Tallents had, in the best traditions of 'two-way communication', built a simple mechanism that could alert planners to previously hidden defects in their own designs. For example, building a model of one of Abercrombie's suggested satellite developments at Ongar in Essex revealed its likely monotony.[42] 'The citizens of the town were our clients', a planner told the BBC, 'and it would have been as foolish for us to try and plan without consulting them as it would be for a doctor to prescribe a cure for a patient he didn't see.'[43]

Of course, it is not surprising that proponents of new towns believed that they had secured public support. In truth, the planning industry's consultations remained almost entirely one-sided and it seems unlikely that the public's contributions to the 'new town' debate organised by Tallents were ever meaningfully taken into consideration.[44] It is only when Tallents's attempts to communicate with a wider audience are compared with the BBC's previous efforts that the MTCP's relative openness becomes apparent. The MTCP's appeal admitted, 'We are only the experts and we are expert enough to know how often the experts go wrong'.[45] The rural everywoman selected by the BBC's 1940 series, in contrast, was told to discuss how it was 'difficult to get female domestic servants to stay in a country place' and the programme's findings were ruthlessly (if 'progressively') predetermined.[46] The MTCP's initiatives set a promising precedent, perhaps, even if their actual immediate effect was limited.

Interestingly, the soft-sell realism of the MTCP's 'New Jerusalemite' project stands in striking contrast to how the rebuilding of Britain was projected abroad. When opening RIBA's exhibition of the Middlesbrough Plan in 1945, Tallents congratulated the planners for eschewing 'a chocolate box portrait' and instead building up 'a truthful picture of the dark spots as well as the bright ones'.[47] The talks prepared by the MTCP for the BBC Overseas Service, on the other hand, were more strident. It had long been Tallents's conviction that the rebuilding of the nation would 'be reflected throughout the world as the British response to an urgent challenge'.[48] Utilising his contacts at the BBC, Tallents was able to organise frequent talks on subjects such as 'The Rebuilding of British Cities', 'The Art of Town Planning' and 'Town Planning in Britain' for Arabic, Latin American, Pacific and Turkish audiences. The note struck by the broadcasts of Tallents's associate Clem Leslie was typical:

> Even amid the resounding successes in Normandy, the British have more than a thought to spare for new proposals ... The way has been opened for the planning of England, Scotland and Wales to an extent never before contemplated in practical politics. London and Manchester, Cardiff and Glasgow, Counties and County Boroughs up and down the land, will be able to arrange the development of their areas in the interest of the communities with whose wellbeing they are concerned.[49]

This direct approach reflected the fact that 'reconstruction' in Axis-occupied nations had an enormous emotional purchase. Patrick Abercrombie's foreword to a book on Lidice, the Czechoslovakian town all but annihilated by the Nazis, provided a particularly pertinent example.[50] Unfortunately for the MTCP, 'planning' gained considerably less grip on the British public's imagination. As the war stretched on, popular attention increasingly focused on homes rather than communities. There was a growing feeling in the BBC, for example, that nascent consumerist fantasies of 'dream kitchens full of knobs you press, upon which every possible appliance descends from the ceiling or shoots up from the floor' should take journalistic precedence over the logistical struggle to actually build them.[51]

The phoney war in planning that had indulged Tallents's methods ended in 1945. After Labour's landslide victory, potential defects in the system could be less readily admitted as pressing shortages demanded a rapid response. Labour's manifesto pledge to create a new Ministry of Housing and Planning was quietly abandoned, and when *Building* magazine profiled Labour's ministerial team in September 1945 it concentrated its attention on Nye Bevan at Health ('a typical Welshman, fluent, fiery, gesticulating') and George Tomlinson at the Ministry of Works.[52] Lewis Silkin, the new Minister for Town and Country Planning, was afforded just two paragraphs, only a few lines more than Fred Marshall, his Permanent Secretary.[53] Presumably for reasons of administrative efficiency, power over planning had shifted back to the Ministry of Health. As Tallents's friend G. M. Trevelyan, bemoaned:

> How ominous are the facts – how ominous the weak position of the Ministry of Town and Country Planning, its lack of recognised status in such recent legislation as the Water Bill, the Forestry Bill, and the Distribution of Industry Bill ... The protection of good agricultural land rests on no sure foundation; the beauty of the sea coast, with which the English people have some concern, is just about as defenceless. One could prolong the mournful catalogue. Soon – in a few months maybe – the full tide of 'development' will begin its levelling and destructive sweep over the green and pleasant parts of England that survive.[54]

The postwar political and administrative changes were accompanied by a hardening of rhetoric. Bevan announced a 'finish the houses' drive. Silkin called it a 'penal offence' that architects were submitting proposals to local authorities that were not in harmony with the best town planning principles.[55] Meanwhile, the construction industry called for the problem of reconstruction to be treated as 'a campaign under a supreme Commander-in-Chief'.[56] The change in rhetoric was accompanied by a change in the style and scope of public relations methods employed. Even if Tallents had not been of retirement age, it seems unlikely that he would have remained at the MTCP.

The personal connections between Stephen Tallents, the Ministry of Town and Country Planning and the Institute of Public Relations

When Edward Heath addressed the Silver Jubilee conference of the Institute of Public Relations (IPR) in 1973 he attributed the Institute's 'sense of public service and public responsibility' to its roots in local government.[57] Just as Geoff Lewis owed his term as President that year to the Greater London Council, Tallents was offered the inaugural Presidency by officials from the National Association of Local Government Officers (NALGO) in 1947. This was not a ceremonial appointment. Tallents's personal profile would be crucial to determining the character of an organisation of local government officials that had split down the middle before it had even formed.

The IPR's formation was part of a NALGO initiative to exert greater influence on Labour's anticipated programme of local government reform. In 1937, only thirty-seven public relations officers served Britain's 1,530 local authorities. As a result local councillors believed that the press was 'liable to give the public a burlesqued portrayal of local government work. The highlights of scandal and disorder are featured, but there is not enough regular and informed comment.'[58] Local government, it was felt, needed a platform to approach both central government and the general populace. The IPR was envisaged as a diplomatic forum that would enable practitioners from central and local government to meet. In America 'public relations' was dominated by corporate interest, but its British counterpart was to retain the curious quirks of its local government origins for some time. Tim Traverse-Healy remembered, 'all the early IPR meetings were, "on point of order, Mr Chairman, excuse me you can't vote on that till you've done this", it was very much like running a sort of council meeting in the Wigan Town Council'.[59] More specifically, Labour's promise to introduce a comprehensive planning system was perhaps the biggest communication challenge that local authorities had ever faced. This partly explains why Tallents's Vice President, R. S. Forman, had arrived at the IPR from the town planning profession. Coventry Corporation, the Harlow Development Corporation, the Hemel Hempstead Development Corporation and the Stevenage Development Corporation were also prominent early supporters of the IPR. One of the IPR's goals was to spread best presentational practice, and the exhibition of redevelopment and reconstruction plans was judged

to be the lone triumph of local government publicity to date.
It was argued:

> Exhibitions of housing and town planning schemes have
> proved valuable, not only in arousing the public's interest but
> in obtaining for the council useful criticism and suggestions
> from local citizens. A box for suggestions is an important
> feature of this kind of exhibition and it has frequently been
> supplemented by meetings for the discussion of the plans being
> displayed.[60]

However, while local government officials provided the majority
of the IPR's members, their responses to Labour's proposed
reforms varied. The passing in 1947 of the Town and Country
Planning Bill, which transferred planning powers from 1,444
borough councils to 145 major regional authorities, was particularly divisive. In addition to ideological opposition, the Bill
also awakened a determination on the behalf of the smaller
London Borough Councils to protect their political patch.[61] If the
Development Corporations were one large constituent group of
the IPR, they were more than matched by a coalition of smaller
London Borough Councils such as Holborn, Hornsey and St
Pancras.[62] In short, the IPR was split between government bodies
who welcomed the administrative changes necessary to implement
'planning' and those bodies whose interests were most threatened
by it.

In such a fraught political environment it is not too much to
say that the immediate future of the IPR rested on Tallents's
personal integrity.[63] Part of Tallents's broad appeal was generational. He belonged to a passing liberal tradition that favoured
an emollient approach over a factional one and which spoke in
soothing tones rather than aggressive ones.[64] Tallents was part
of a generation ready to admit that 'some of the worst offenders
in promoting misuse of good land in the immediate past have
been the planners themselves'.[65] More to the point, Tallents had
enacted the tricky reconciliation he encouraged all IPR members
to make. The general line offered by the MTCP press office had
been that 'a house can't be considered by itself – it's got to be
considered in relation to the community'.[66] Tallents had personally
propagated the necessity of change at the MTCP by penning a
speech lecturing the CPRE on the need for some rural areas to
be set aside for urban expansion.[67] However, he had also been an
important contributor to Lionel Curtis's campaign against ribbon

development and donated his house, St John's Jerusalem, to the National Trust in 1943.[68] *Country Life* recorded:

> It is highly fitting that St John's should now be a National Trust property, in view of the Hospitalliers dedication to public service, and the house's close association with the history of Kent. Moreover, Sutton-at-Hone may not always remain a country village, and St John's meads must be kept green. As such they will also be a memorial to an officer of the MTCP, who, with his skill in the pleasant ways of trees, especially of the walnuts and willows that he cultivates, has revived at St John's the interests of Abraham Hill.[69]

Indeed, not only was Tallents seen to exemplify a modestly progressive tradition, he was also exceptionally skilled at presenting himself as such. The fact that Tallents was related to – and took inspiration from – the socially progressive architect and builder Thomas Cubitt, for example, was frequently quoted in the press.[70] Tallents's well-documented achievements also contributed substantially to his standing as an enlightened member of the establishment. On retirement from the MTCP he had encouraged the Leverhulme Trust to investigate how English villages should be developed. He volunteered his home village of Sutton-at-Hone in Kent as a test bed for a range of public participation-in-planning programmes.[71] Such actions ensured that, when Tallents spoke of the need for a vehicle to bring the citizen, Westminster and local government into 'a full understanding of the needs, wishes and difficulties of the other two partners, for the good of the community as a whole', he spoke from a position of impeccable authority.[72]

Tallents's personal reputation was initially able to hold together a range of apparently competing political, professional and industrial interests. Indeed, the IPR's involvement in the staging of large exhibitions like the British Army Exhibition in 1945, and Britain Can Make It in 1946, demonstrated the profession's efforts to extend the conciliatory practices of coalition government into the postwar era.

The Festival of Britain and the triumph of 'the Tallents tradition'

Although *The Projection of England* was widely discussed when it was published, Tallents's ideas were initially better disseminated than understood. At the first and most common level of contemporary analysis, Tallents's argument was discussed purely as a call

to advertising arms. 'England, he says, must Tell the World, Shout
the Odds', as *The Evening News* review put it, 'only, being a Civil
Servant, he calls it, in the more reserved manner of Whitehall,
"the art of national projection"'.[73] Honourable exceptions to the
rule included lengthy reviews in *The Manchester Guardian*, *The
Observer* and *The Listener*. Ivor Brown's review in *The Guardian*
is worth thinking through:

> Now I do not know to what extent Sir Stephen Tallents accepts
> Mr Wells' hatred of nationalism or to what extent he supports
> the continued section of the world by empires, armies, flags,
> tariffs, and so on. But the possibility of a cosmopolitan
> cohesion is still so remote that even the best internationalist
> may conscientiously apply himself to improving nationalism,
> and that, in fact, is what 'national projection' is intended to
> do.[74]

The lineage of the 'improved nationalism' identified by Brown is
significant. You don't have to strain too hard to see an embryonic
form of the warts-and-all patriotism of Orwell at the time of *The
Lion and the Unicorn* present in the pages of *The Projection of
England*. Orwell characterised Britain as a family with the wrong
members in charge, Tallents bemoaned how utterly 'our memory
of England yesterday beclouds our projection of the England
of to-day'. Orwell famously grappled with a nation of concrete
roads, magnetos and the naked democracy of swimming pools,
Tallents began his pamphlet with a list of typical British icons,
before moving on to extol the virtues of 'less familiar excellencies'
such as animal genetics and nutritional science, 'which no-one has
heard of but which might project the best of what is happening in
Britain today'.[75] Over the course of the war, what had looked like
a manifesto for advertisers in 1932 had transmuted into a more
imaginative discourse of citizenship. The change in establishment
attitudes prefigured by *The Projection of England* was to be
realised by the Festival of Britain. The Festival may have been
prompted by the Royal Society of Arts, and commissioned by
Labour minister Herbert Morrison, but organisationally and
ideologically it was recognisable as the product of progressive
bureaucracy.[76] As Hugh Casson put it:

> The Establishment suspected it was all a smoke screen for
> advancing Socialism. The Left decided it was middle class;
> the academics that it was populist; Evelyn Waugh that it was

pathetic; Sir Thomas Beecham said it was imbecilic; Noel Coward that it was worth more than a mild giggle.[77]

A self-consciously non-partisan popular demonstration of Britain's artistic and scientific potential, as well as a celebration of the national character, there is an argument that the Festival was the *sui generis* culmination of twenty years work by Tallents's public relations movement.

Following the template established in *The Projection of England*, the Festival sought to educate popular taste and encourage technical enthusiasms. Radars and efficient factory layouts were exhibited alongside modern British artists and indigenous arcana such as the Tempest Prognosticator.[78] The Festival's bold confidence in British design followed Tallents's argument that national prosperity depended on Britain's ability to reimagine itself as a pioneer of new industry.[79] The Festival also addressed the key problem of British exhibitions in the interwar years by allowing experts the freedom to curate it. All the objects displayed at the Festival were selected on aesthetic or technological merit rather than because a manufacturer was prepared to pay to have them exhibited, as had been the norm during the interwar period. Indeed, the Festival site on the South Bank (where advertisements were banned) represented an attempt to realise the hinterland between officialdom and the hurly-burly of the commercial world idealised in *The Projection of England*.

Tallents exerted a considerable influence on the presentation of the Festival from the margins. After leaving the MTCP, Tallents had founded Cockade, a consortium of designers, artists, craftsmen and craftswomen dedicated to raising the aesthetic standards of model-making. As well as employing the Cassons – the architect Hugh Casson was arguably the controlling imagination behind the Festival – it found work for other ex-MTCP designers such as Richard Guyatt. According to the V&A retrospective conducted on the Festival's twenty-fifth anniversary, Cockade's presence was all-pervasive.[80] With doubtless pleasing personal resonance, Tallents's firm was responsible for centrepieces such as the replica Crystal Palace of 1851 (Tallents frequently boasted of his familial link to Joseph Paxton) and the model of the BBC's proposed Television Centre at White City. Indeed, Tallents's written contribution to the Festival programme was a celebration of British television design that lingered lovingly on the walnut finishes of contemporary sets.[81]

To illuminate the national character, the Festival also drew heavily on the cultural topography outlined in *The Projection of England*. Cockade produced replicas of Magna Carta, Habeas Corpus and the King James Bible, as well as models of Shakespeare in performance for the Lion and Unicorn pavilion. Using Tallents's familiar aggregative method, this pavilion compounded diverse aspects of the British character into a whole that was cohesive only in its diversity. As well as celebrating native authors, the Lion and the Unicorn pavilion reminded visitors, 'the British do not simply leave the development of their language to the professionals of literature. The Cockney has added a local vocabulary to the national one; and every British county has contributed a proverb, or a telling phrase.'[82] The Festival writ large the associational and collaborative approach pioneered by Tallents's experimental programme of public relations.

Of course, the South Bank exhibitions that attracted over eight million visitors were merely the centrepiece of a larger range of regional displays – such as the ship *Campania* touring Britain's ports – and community activism.[83] This proliferation of spin-off village firework displays, improvements to rural bus stops and road safety weeks were similarly descended from the pioneering national jamboree of publicity activity that Tallents had unleashed at the GPO.

What had been good for the IPR's founder President was good for the profession. The presence on the Festival Committee of Paul Wright, public relations officer to the Coal Board, was indicative of the profession's increasing stature. According to the IPR's journal, 1951 was the year when public relations as an industry began to make a significant economic impact.[84] From the 'Keep Britain Tidy' campaign to Abram Games's stark logo, the Festival stimulated a phenomenal range of public relations activity.[85]

The Festival of Britain even allowed Tallents a material legacy. The decision to preserve part of Wells Coates's cinema as a permanent National Film Theatre fulfilled a British Film Institute need identified by the Radcliffe Committee served by Tallents in 1948. However, the prominence of Tallents, and the strand of public relations which he had sponsored, proved to be short-lived. Michael Frayn famously argued that 'The Festival was the last, and virtually the posthumous, work of Herbivore Britain'.[86] For Frayn, the Festival marked the demise of a *Guardian*-reading, BBC-listening, Crown Film Unit watching and petition-signing liberal elite. Although this was an exaggeration, the weakening of the modest reformism of the benevolent administrator class pinpointed by Frayn would be demonstrated by the future development of public relations in Britain.

'The Tallents tradition' and the high politics of the post-war era

During the eight years which it took to organise the Festival of Britain the nature of the British media landscape altered considerably. As the spirit of wartime coalition evaporated, public rhetoric became increasingly aggressive and sectarian. Key to this development was Labour creation of the Central Office of Information (COI) in April 1946.

Ironically, it was the 'Festival Minister', Herbert Morrison, who sponsored the government's decision to retain elements of the wartime Ministry of Information. Morrison reasoned that 'it is in the national interest that the citizen and tax payer should be adequately informed by the government on its administration and policy. The people "have a right to know."'[87] Here Morrison was in step with the broader inclinations of the Labour Party, who believed that the successful implementation of their nationalisation programme needed to be accompanied by a correspondingly large degree of official explanation and information. Indeed, in September 1945, Clement Attlee had taken the significant step of appointing Francis Williams, a former editor of The Daily Herald, as press adviser to Number 10.[88] During its six years in office the postwar Labour administration funded more than 100,000 lectures, 500 films, 170 exhibitions and 30 national advertising campaigns and published innumerable pamphlets and books.[89] As one historian has it: 'no former government of the UK had allocated so great a proportion of its resources to the tasks of informing and cajoling its citizens'.[90] Labour's enthusiasm for government communication aroused the ire of Conservatives and, more significantly, encouraged both commercial interests and local government to begin formally organising their own channels of communication in response. The establishment of the 'non-partisan' COI prompted a very political response.

A further driver of politicisation was Labour's decision to appoint a Royal Commission into the Press. Formed out of a general awareness of interwar malpractice, the Commission attempted to discover how far commercial interests and the opinion of newspaper barons influenced the content and presentation of Britain's printed news media.[91] However, postwar austerity and the beginnings of the Cold War – governments in Hungary and Czechoslovakia had begun to restrict the freedom of journalism and journalists – saw the Commission conclude that a greater threat to democracy was posed by the government's new information service than by the existing commercial media.[92]

The Royal Commission were particularly concerned by the rapid expansion of governmental public relations. Hence, Sir Stephen Tallents, the first government PRO and then inaugural President of the IPR, was asked to defend the profession's impact on public life. Giving evidence in April 1948, Tallents confided that he shared the Commission's anxiety that government public relations officers could occasionally be distracted to 'exalt a person rather than the work of a department'. He also admitted that government press officers are 'concerned, of course, to put over the point of view of your department; that is what you are there for'.[93] However, unlike the more strident criticism journalists made to the Commission ('the kind of subtle innuendo and distortion which appears regularly does incalculable damage when circulated amongst members of the public with little knowledge of the facts') Tallents sought to put the work of the public relations officer in a fuller context.[94] He convinced the Commission that, 'far from restricting the flow of information, the information divisions make more information available to a wider circle'.[95] He stressed that press office work was but a narrow aspect of a grander public relations function to improve all lines of communication between an institution and the public. He argued that the PRO should affect 'the style of letters that go out from a department and the types of building in which the public are received'.[96] According to Tallents, the proper role of the PRO was to serve the public's wider information needs and not become obsessed with tawdry day-to-day tussles with journalists. He told the Commission:

> The increasing complexity of the processes of government, scientific research and the need to get the co-operation of the public on the one hand; on the other, the interests of the public, as you get a larger electorate and a better educated public, necessitate the Public Relations Officer system. Again, new media, films and broadcasting in particular, have become available in the last thirty years, so that [communicating with the public] becomes a much more specialised job than it was in the days when a government mainly relied on speeches.[97]

Tallents's broader explanation of both the necessity and the desirability of public relations was accepted. Public relations was understood as an urbane profession able to educate Civil Servants, journalists and the general public. The Commission even drew the revealing, if not wholly convincing, comparison between the public relations practitioner and the university college tutor. One far-reaching result of the Commission was to entrench the primary importance of 'ethics' as, although the accusations made by the commercial media to the Commission were specifically aimed at the government information services, there was a sense that the public relations profession as a whole was under scrutiny.

The Projection of England had been prompted by the interwar dictators' sophisticated use of the mass media. It modestly emphasised the necessity of providing an antidote to negative stereotypes about Britain by projecting the nation's 'real' nature abroad. After the war, Tallents often quoted UNESCO's charter: 'since wars begin in the minds of men, it is in the minds of men that the defences of peace must be constructed'.[98] However, Tallents's idealist paradigm struggled to survive growing international tension. The birth of the Cold War saw public relations professionals define themselves as 'a group of crusaders whose job is to carry the torch of understanding into areas where discord and dissension may be eliminated by information and explanation'.[99] Practitioners were encouraged to think of themselves as apostles of freedom. Rather pompously, the IPR began to position itself as an institution that could spread western civilisation's 'flame of truth'. The organisation even adopted the image of a burning torch and the Latin motto 'Pro fide'. The Chief PRO of London Transport, for example, took this argument to a rather shrill extreme:

> Evil propaganda must be met and beaten by Truth. She will always win ... Give her wings! Let the air be hers and the press and the film and the posters ... Let it not be a question so much of countering communist propaganda but of getting in first ... Faith exemplified in our adherence to Christian principles and thought is essential to the preservation of Western life as we know it.[100]

Indeed, the Labour government's nationalisation programme allowed the public relations industry to materially demonstrate its independence from the state that had nurtured it. 'The Aims of Industry' campaign underwritten by important IPR constituents, such as Ford and the Austin Motor Company, was an example of a concerted public relations campaign that attacked Labour's policies. While the IPR *Journal* described 'The Aims of Industry' as a 'non-profit-making campaign with no connexion with any political party', its organisation of, for example, a mass-media campaign to prevent the nationalisation of the sugar industry ('Tate not State') was an undeniably political intervention.[101] IPR members spoke euphemistically of the need to counter 'national bureaucracy', even referring to public relations as 'the dock leaf growing beside the bureaucratic nettle in the perpetual war for the soul of man'.[102] Moreover, the IPR appeared to scrutinise disproportionately the public announcements of the nationalised industries.[103]

Shifts in the political pronouncements of IPR members accompanied a boom in the growth of public relations consultancy. Tallents and the early practitioners of public relations had been employees of large organisations pursuing long-term visions. The postwar world was more fragmented, more project-driven and more goal-orientated. The 'two-way' public relations practised by Tallents in the era of national government could be compared to a negotiated exchange of ideas; the 'two-way' practices of postwar practitioners merely indicated the profession's willingness to sit on either side of the political fence. In addition to the burgeoning portfolio of corporate work, IPR members continued to act as consultants for a Labour government committed to reviving export trade. Public relations practice in Britain was in the process of becoming a limited type of public advocacy.

'The Tallents tradition' and the internal politics of the Institute of Public Relations

Tallents had been appointed President of the IPR in 1948 partly in an effort to resist the tide of Americanisation. The term 'public relations' apparently originated when the American publicist Edward Bernays appropriated the title 'Counsel of Public Relations' from 'Council of Legal Relations' in the early 1920s.[104] The term probably crossed the Atlantic courtesy of the British railway administrator John Elliott who had met Ivy Lee while on secondment to *The New York Times*.[105] Later in life, John Grierson claimed that he had appropriated the term from 'that old thug Sam Insull', whose blanket advertising campaigns he had experienced first-hand while studying at the University of Chicago in the early mid-1920s.[106] It was not until 1949 that J. H. Brebner published Britain's first 'public relations' text book.[107]

The formation of the IPR may have accepted that British labels for 'public relations' such as 'projection' had been superseded, but it also continued to define itself against American practices. IPR members had different political views but they all agreed that the American excesses of the early stages of the Cold War (the 'adolescent character' of Americans was blamed for their susceptibility to ranting and free-market propaganda) was something that the they particularly wished to avoid.[108]

Tallents had appointed many of the nascent profession's senior figures to jobs in 'projection', 'publicity' and 'salesmanship' and therefore stood at the head of a family tree of public relations in Britain that included luminaries such as John Grierson, Patrick Ryan, Gervas Huxley and Jock Brebner. Tallents's appointment at the IPR thus represented a defence of native traditions that were rapidly being challenged by the flood of new entrants who had joined the profession post–1945. While in 1931 there were just 44 people employed in government publicity work, by 1946 there were 2,400.[109] Private sector growth was equally rapid and further eroded the authority of 'the Tallents tradition'.

In one sense the IPR was established to provide a vehicle through which the interwar practitioners of public relations could regain control of the profession. Tallents's IPR organised conferences, published journals and established a comprehensive library as it sought to educate new entrants. 'The Arts and the Public' lectures at the Royal Academy of Arts sponsored by the IPR – which saw Dame Ninette de Valois talk ballet and Anthony Asquith hold forth on film – were typical of a wider push to ensure that PROs possessed the correct cultural capital. One consequence of the Royal Commission had been that practitioners felt compelled to continually play up their 'honourable character' – public relations began to posit itself as a gentlemanly pursuit as much as a hard-nosed profession. It became common for the IPR *Journal* to extol such virtues as 'great understanding, great forbearance and a great spirit of attunement with one's fellow beings'.[110] Or as a future President of the IPR put it, 'Public Relations is the comparatively recent expression by business of the old precept "do unto others as you would have them do to you"'.[111] In the long term, this failing led to Tallents's impressive track record as an innovative patron of the arts and sciences being institutionalised by the IPR into a kind of public-school behavioural code. Thus, while the films, posters, books and models created by the first generation of public relations practitioners in Britain retain a striking eloquence, the dynamic and idealistic understanding of the profession that animated them quickly perished.

Interestingly, Tallents's IPR was not afraid to chastise the new intake of public relations practitioners. A *Brains Trust*-style panel discussion on the future of public relations hosted by Richard Dimbleby revealed the IPR's deep-rooted anxieties about recent recruits. As one sarcastically dismissive commentator had it:

> We've had a splendacious and most luxurious crop of public relations in this country during the last ten years ... like poppies in the corn. Plausible, charming types mainly, who are too good for Fleet St, too clever for advertising agencies – briefless barristers and MPs without seats – sophisticated gentlemen who know how things can be worked – who know how to organise a lively press conference – and how to get paragraphs about their bosses into the papers ... They are a sort of juvenile rash – the measles of a young profession.[112]

IPR debates about new entrants to the profession reflect the more general anxieties of an older generation struggling to come to terms with the postwar world. The specific consequence of this feeling, however, was that the IPR leadership became increasingly anxious, introspective and withdrawn. Public relations had become an essential element of the postwar world but the IPR forfeited the opportunity to define the profession's proper form and function. As one IPR member complained, the commercial world used public relations 'as a euphemism to cover advertising activities – in much the same way as a lavatory cleaner may call himself a cloakroom attendant'.[113]

Awarded a second term as IPR President in 1952, Tallents regretted that 'there is no body of experience put down in writing in books that are worth much'. Tallents was not even able to praise the IPR's book on public relations: 'I miss in Mr Brebner's approach to the subject', he wrote, 'any insistence on what I regard as an essential characteristic of the best modern publicity – that it should not merely impart information to the mind but should also stir the imagination'. [114] Tallents's liberal instincts and faith in the transformative powers of science and emerging technologies made him constitutionally averse to prescribing the proper limits of the profession, but without achieving professional status the new breed of private sector public relations officers found it difficult to persuade management that they possessed a unique skillet. 'I can well imagine how aggrieved a colleague might be as seeing in a

newspaper one morning that a schoolmaster had been appointed
to an important public relations post', complained one member,
'as I tremble to think what would happen if a public relations
officer was appointed to a headmastership'.[115] Tallents's refusal
to sanction any definition of public relations (on the grounds that
the IPR must 'not get too formal and not get too deeply embedded
in paper')[116] was contested by new members convinced that 'it is
imperative that both the status of the craft and its service to the
community should carry the corporate recognition of a professional body'.[117] This generational impasse prevented the IPR from
agreeing any definition of what public relations actually was. As
an angry correspondent put it in 1951:

> Must we consider ourselves incapable of getting down on
> paper an acceptable form of words to describe what we are,
> what we do and how we do it? We are supposed to be experts
> in conveying ideas and persuading the public. Must we confess
> that we, the experts, find the writing of a few descriptive
> lines of plain English beyond our powers ... I suggest we cut
> the cackle, get our heads out of the clouds and get our feet
> planted on the ground. I suggest we become realists and not
> visionaries.[118]

Although this appeal for 'realism' did belatedly prompt the
production of practical 'toolkits' such as 'Brightening up the
Company Report', 'How to Exhibit', 'How to Commission Films'
and 'How to Produce House Magazines', such pamphlets did not
convince sceptical managers that public relations constituted a
profession.

In the end, it was not until 1963 that figures such as Sam Black
were finally able to establish a Code of Professional Conduct
and not until 2005 that the IPR managed to obtain chartered
status.[119] This failure to define public relations would perhaps
explain why fewer than 10% of the 60,000 public relations
officers in Britain had joined the IPR by the end of the twentieth
century. Little wonder that Tallents's description of Alan Hess, a
future IPR President, as 'a wonderful chap so much more than
a PRO' and his insistence on quoting Sir William Crawford's
motto that 'no-one knows anything about publicity', so provoked
the younger postwar generation.[120] Tallents was a Civil Servant
whose interest in social and imperial administration had led him
to develop new public relations techniques at a time of revolutionary scientific, technological and administrative change. The

generation that followed him were focused on codifying those techniques into a profession that suited the needs of a growing economy.

Notes

1 Tallents papers, File 26, 'The Start'.
2 The sincerity or otherwise of Churchill's 'plan' was a subject much commented on. *The Economist* wrote in 1945, 'the new Parliament will inherit a legacy of unfinished plans, a mountain of White Papers to be translated into Acts of Parliament ... Mr Churchill's words to the Conservative conference might be paraphrased: "Never was there a time when so much was planned and projected with so little hope of being turned into action."' Qtd in K. Jeffrey (ed.) *War and Reform: British Politics during the Second World War* (Manchester, 1994), p. 113.
3 Tallents earned more than £1,200. NA, HLG 124/5, Ministry of Town and Country Planning: Setting-up, Organisation and Complement, 'Minutes of meeting', 8 December 1942.
4 This Bill was passed to prevent 'undesirable' wartime development rather than to prompt future action.
5 'Annual General Meeting', *Journal of the Town Planning Institute*, Vol. XXIX, No. 9, May–June 1943, p. 174.
6 'Annual General Meeting', *Journal of the Town Planning Institute*, Vol. XXIX, No. 9, May–June 1943, p. 176.
7 'Progress in Planning', *The Times*, 13 January 1943.
8 'I had heard what responsible individuals had to say about the past, present and future of this particular world – representatives of professional bodies, engineering, architecture, and town planning; representatives of associations of employers and employees. There was much contradictory advice. That made it all the easier to decide on what was required.' J. C. W. Reith, *Into the Wind* (London, 1949), p. 410.
9 NA, HLG 124/5, Ministry of Town and Country Planning: Setting-up, Organisation and Complement, 'Beaver to Reith', 4 April 1941. Despite his poor opinion of Tallents, Reith had apparently been converted to a very Tallents-esque conception of public relations. He later recorded in *Into the Wind*, '[A Public Relations Officer] is, in fact, an essential member of an executive management board. He works outside and inwards; the only one who looks at, and judges, the organisation and its performance from a detached point of view. He is, of course, responsible

for the projection of his organisation to the outside world; to Parliament, Press and public. But, from what he sees and hears and anticipates outside, he is equally responsible for projection inwards; he has a part to play in the shaping of policy, not just in it explanation and defence; perhaps a determining part.' Qtd in 'So a Public Relations Officer Was Appointed', *Journal of the Institute of Public Relations*, Vol. 2, No. 3, March 1950, p. 3.

10 RIBA Library, 'Stephen Tallents Personal File'.

11 Beveridge would provocatively open the 'When We Build Again' exhibition on 1 December 1943 with the words, 'We must be in a position to control the location of industry and so the population before we start building ... That is the subject of the Barlow Commission report and the Uthwatt Committee report ... The problems dealt with by the Barlow Commission and Uthwatt Committee are much harder and more controversial than those in my report on social insurance: squalor is a tougher giant than want. A government which hedges on Beveridge is only too likely to be ditched on Barlow and Uthwatt.' '"When We Build Again" Exhibition', *Journal of the Town Planning Institute*, Vol. XXX, No. 3, Jan.–Feb. 1944, p. 73.

12 'A brief tour of suburbia must convince even the most sceptical that any dwelling no matter how badly built or how fantastically designed could have been sold in the inter-war period for a deposit of £25 ... It is to the social sciences that the architect, the builder and the planner must look for some parts of the answers to the questions of "what to build" and "where to build", the basic problems of house design and town planning.' D. Chapman, 'The Social Survey Technique of Obtaining Housing Information', *Journal of the Royal Institute of British Architects*, Vol. 51, No. 7, June 1944, p. 191.

13 S. Tallents, 'In Praise of Models', *Building: A Journal for Architects, Builders and Specialists*, September 1945, Vol. XX, No. 9, p. 229.

14 'Better Training for the Planner', *Journal of the Town Planning Institute*, Vol. XXXI, No. 3, Jan.–Feb. 1945, p. 60.

15 'Building Plots in Rural Areas', *Journal of the Town Planning Institute*, Vol. XXXI, No. 7, May–June 1945, p. 137.

16 Edward Carter co-wrote Penguin's popular explanation of Abercrombie's County of London Plan. Carter, a Communist and architectural radical, worked during the 1930s as librarian at RIBA where he was influential not only in introducing many continental ideas and architects to Britain, but securing refugee

status for the likes of Walter Gropius. He also implemented with John Summerson, Kenneth Clark and John Betjeman the wartime plans for a National Buildings Record. After the War Carter went with Julian Huxley (who recruited him) and John Grierson to UNESCO. See RIBA Library, 'Edward "Bobby" Carter Personal File'.

17 Writing in 1962, Carter bemoaned how 'the enthusiasm of those early days was quickly tamed by the great Whitehall negation – "we have no money" – by the realisation that we lacked administrative powers to do speedily those things which everyone wanted done, and by the worthy flood of intellectual reservations that perhaps these schemes were immature and faulty. The post war plans were written in an exultant mood – courageous, optimistic, and adventurous. Now we have come down to the technically impeccable presentation of the plans of the administrative county in which anxiety and sense of urgency are concealed (if they are present at all) beneath the words and phrases of polite encouragement and self-esteem.' E. Carter, *The Future of London* (London, 1962), p. 16.

18 These included Carter, who had already approached Tallents for promotional advice and, as Anthony Cox remembered, wanted 'to create a demand for knowledge, in which he thought in some respects the profession dreadfully lacking'. Or in Carter's own words, 'in practice architects have shown themselves far less responsive to the impact of science than, for instance, the medical and surgical professions ... we all know the excuse that failures in modern buildings are inevitable because modern techniques are still experimental, but if we are honest we would admit that not a single failure is due to anything other than someone or other's crass ignorance'. See RIBA Library, 'Edward "Bobby" Carter Personal File'.

19 See W. Ashworth, *The Genesis of Modern British Town Planning: A Study in Economic and Social History of the Nineteenth and Twentieth Centuries* (London, 1968).

20 One point of frustration for MTCP officials was that they might be forced to move into Dolphin Square in Pimlico, 'a psychologically inferior address to the Office of Works'. See NA, HLG 124/5, 'Ministry of Town and Country Planning: Setting-up, Organisation and Complement'.

21 For example, the Ministry of Health and Works issued its Housing Manual of 1944 (which includes much planning material) without consulting Tallents, who was humiliated by

the snub. See NA, HLG 110/11, 'Ministry of Health Housing Manual: Comments by Ministry of Town and Country Planning'.

22 'An Address by Mr Fred Marshall', *Journal of the Town Planning Institute*, Vol. XXXIII, No. 10, July–August 1947, p. 134.

23 'Guides to Policy', *The Times*, 12 September 1945, p. 5.

24 Brigadier K. M. Papworth of the OS lectured planners, 'you will not get the maps and plans you now require either to-day or to-morrow. The situation is bad because virtually no systematic survey work has been carried out since 1914. The false economy of the reduction of staffs and output in the 1920s is only too apparent. The sins of the fathers go far beyond the third and fourth edition.' 'The Post War Programme of The Ordnance Survey', *Journal of the Town Planning Institute*, Vol. XXXIII, No. 4, March–April 1947, p. 64.

25 Though, of course, the Greater London Plan was an extension of his and J. H. Forshaw's earlier County of London Plan.

26 S. D. Adshead, 'Greater London Plan', *Building: A Journal for Architects, Builders and Specialists*, Vol. XX, No. 1, January 1945, pp. 16–17.

27 Qtd in Carter, *The Future of London*, p. 189.

28 The Scott Report's emphasis on preserving the character of the countryside could appear to stem from a long-held fear that dispersing the urban working class would lead to disaster. For instance, Sir Herbert Baker had long complained of London's sprawl into Kent: 'these people have no experience of owning property and have come from districts where they simply paid a weekly rent. They do not realise the further liabilities, such as rates and road charges, railway fares, and the necessities of setting aside money for maintenance and repairs. After they have been in their homes a short time they get into debt and are obliged to take a second family on the first floor in order to pay their way. This is a very frequent occurrence and the danger to the local authority is that the district may become a new slum.' Victoria and Albert Museum, RIBA Archive, Sir Herbert Baker Papers, BAH/68/2, 'Notes on development,' 10th January 1936.

29 The renewed intensity of debate around the issue of national planning prompted a searching re-examination of Howard's thinking. Howard's disciples were frustrated by the many slights the Garden City pioneer suffered and they responded by defending him as, 'An idealist in the sense in which an engineer conceiving and wanting to try out a better sort of bridge is an idealist ... Howard and his associates made one propagandist

mistake in siting Letchworth and Welwyn – building them in
England within an hour's journey of London. One should have
been built on some remote island like Mauritius, and the other in
the Soviet Republic of Uzbezchakistan. Planners and journalists
would then have visited them and written them up, and we
should have had lots of illuminating books on them. Also we
should be excited about them as wonderful achievements, and
be wanting to know why we can't have towns of the new type in
Dear Old Stick-in-the-Mud England.' F. J. Osborn, 'The Garden
City Movement: a Re-evaluation', *Journal of the Town Planning
Institute*, Vol. XXXI, No. 6, April–May 1945, pp. 198–199.

30 The priority given to (frequently courted) contributions from
these organisations is evident in Abercrombie's working papers
and, of course, Abercrombie had been personally active in
establishing the CPRE. See NA, HLG 85/34, 'Ministry of
Town and Country Planning and Predecessors: Greater London
Plan, Working Papers of Professor Abercrombie: Miscellaneous
Correspondence'.

31 For more on Geddes see A. Defries, *The Interpreter Geddes:
The Man and His Gospel* (London, 1927), P. Boardman, *The
Worlds of Patrick Geddes* (London, 1978), and H. Miller,
'Patrick Geddes' in G. Cherry (ed.), *Pioneers in British Planning*
(London, 1981), pp. 46–71.

32 P. Abercrombie, 'The Townsman's Use of the Country', *Country
Life*, 24 October 1941, p. 770.

33 'Dr Herbert Read: The Decentralisation of Art', *Journal of the
Town Planning Institute*, Vol. XXXI, No. 2, Nov.–Dec. 1944,
p. 23.

34 'The County of London Plan: First Steps Towards Realisation',
Journal of the Town Planning Institute, Vol. XXXI, No. 9,
July–August 1945, p. 180.

35 On Reith's orders planning officers had begun to compile an
atlas of the nation's physical features – how its land was used,
where its industries were based, the migrational trends of its
population and the extent of its communications infrastructure
– and Tallents ensured this information was shared with an
unprecedented generosity of spirit.

36 Carter, *The Future of London*, p. 35.

37 See NA, HLG 85/16, 'Ministry of Town and Country Planning
and Predecessors: Greater London Plan, Working Papers of
Professor Abercrombie: Correspondence on Proposed Model to
Illustrate the County of London Plan'.

38 *New Town* can be viewed on the BFI YouTube channel. See http://www.youtube.com/user/ BFIfilms#p/u/64/60phEYd4A-Q. The MTCP also collaborated with MoI newsreels and appears likely to have aided documentary-makers, such as Paul Rotha, to produce films such as 1944's *Children of the City.*

39 See 'Prisoners of War and the County of London Plan', *Journal of the Royal Institute of British Architects*, Vol. 51, No. 7, June 1944, p. 190.

40 S. Tallents, 'In Praise of Models', *Building: A Journal for Architects, Builders and Specialists*, Vol. XX, No. 9, September 1945, p. 228.

41 Tallents, 'In Praise of Models', p. 230.

42 NA, HLG85/16, 'Ministry of Town and Country Planning and predecessors: Greater London Plan, Working Papers of Professor Abercrombie: Correspondence on Proposed Model to Illustrate the County of London Plan', 'Darwin to Tallents', 18 April 1944.

43 Your Questions Answered, 'Town Planning in Middlesbrough', *BBC Radio*, 14 December 1945.

44 The most striking example of this was a survey of BBC listeners (and *Listener* readers) that Tallents organised to investigate the size, type and location of the public's ideal 'new town'. The MTCP's appeal was meek: 'while a new town could avoid defects that some of these towns (towns of around 100,000 people such as Reading, Walsall and South Shields) have, it might also lack their sense of tradition and community spirit'. However, the results were overwhelming: new towns (1109 votes) were greatly preferred to the countryside (315 votes) and traditional cities (200 votes). For more on the public response see NA, HLG 84/17, 'New Towns Committee: Town and Country Planning Broadcast by Mrs Monica Felton: Replies from Public to Questions Posed'.

45 *The Listener*, 24 January 1946, Vol. XXXV, No. 889, p. 102.

46 For example, 'We want two witnesses, one from a new housing estate (Thomas suggests Sheffield) and one from a block of flats (Thomas suggests Leeds). Thomas has sketched out the sort of testimony he is hoping to get from them and I attach a copy of his notes.' BBC Archive, R51/598, 'Talks – Town and Country Planning', 'Luker to Boyd', 15 December 1938.

47 S. Tallents, 'The Middlesbrough Plan at RIBA', *Journal of the Royal Institute of British Architects*, Vol. 53, No. 1, November 1945, p. 16.

48 'Annual General Meeting', *Journal of the Town Planning Institute*, Vol. XXIX, No. 9, May–June 1943, p. 177.

49 S. C. Leslie, 'Town and Country Planning', *BBC Radio Pacific Service*, 14 December 1945.

50 C. Merhout, B. Stross, E. Sternberk, W. Lawther, foreword by P. Abercrombie, *Lidice* (London, 1945).

51 As the quotation perhaps implies, the senior male managers at the BBC were rather sceptical of the (mostly American) innovations promised by new technology. BBC Archive, R51/242/3, 'Ed (RT) to Benzie', 3 April 1944.

52 'There should be a Ministry of Housing and Planning combing the housing powers of the Ministry of Health with the planning powers of the Ministry of Town and Country Planning.' Labour Party, *Let Us Face the Future* (London, 1945), p. 8.

53 Marshall is approvingly described as 'a great believer in maintaining high standards of beauty both in the things of nature and those that man has made'. 'The New Ministers', *Building: A Journal for Architects, Builders and Specialists*, Vol. XX, No. 9, September 1945, p. 243.

54 Although Trevelyan's assessment is overstated, it is true that Silkin barely features in town planning literature (other than as an object of cross memoranda) and does not appear to have addressed RIBA until May 1946. However, while in intellectual and industrial circles Silkin was considered unimpressive ('a rather heavy, thoughtful and legal type of mind'), many citizens of areas marked out for 'new town' development quickly came to understand him as a high-handed bully. G. M. Trevelyan, 'Planning the Countryside', *The Times*, 7 July 1945, p. 5.

55 'Building Now', *Journal of the Royal Institute of British Architects*, Vol. 53, No. 7, May 1946, p. 268.

56 'One Ministry', *Building: A Journal for Architects, Builders and Specialists*, Vol. XX, No. 12, December 1945, p. 289.

57 '25th Anniversary of the IPR', *Public Relations*, April 1973, p. 55.

58 Political and Economic Planning, *Public Relations and the Town Hall*, No. 265, 2 May 1947, p. 8.

59 Qtd in L'Etang, *Public Relations in Britain*, p. 66.

60 Political and Economic Planning, *Public Relations and the Town Hall*, No. 265, 2 May 1947, p. 11.

61 These figures are taken from J. B. Cullingworth, *Town and Country Planning in Britain* (London, 1988).

62 The interwar period had seen local authorities continually resist

attempts by regional or central government to take control of their land planning function. For example, twenty-three of the local authorities potentially affected by Abercrombie's Greater London plan had refused to assist his research. See NA, HLG 85/34, 'Ministry of Town and Country Planning and Predecessors: Greater London Plan, Working Papers of Professor Abercrombie: Miscellaneous Correspondence'.

63 Tallents's background was also represented by the participation of press officers and institutional support from the Colonial Office, the General Post Office and the Ministry of Town and Country Planning.

64 Tallents had latterly been associated with more 'gradualist' planners such as George Pepler ('the object of the planner is to provide a fair field for life – not to dictate how life shall be lived') who had also left the Civil Service at the end of the Second World War. Pepler was perhaps the key figure in instigating the creation of the Town and Country Planning Institute as well as a loyal (and senior) advocate of the National Playing Fields Association and the Campaign for the Protection of Rural England. G. Cherry, 'George Pepler', in G. Cherry (ed.) *Pioneers in British Planning* (London, 1981), pp. 131–149.

65 L. Dudley Stamp, 'Land Utilisation', *Country Life*, 26 September 1941, p. 575.

66 The MTCP's (quoted) contribution to the BBC Radio programme 'The Citizen's Home' is entirely typical. See BBC Archive, R51/242/3, 'The Citizen's Home', 19 July 1943.

67 W. Morrison, 'Council for the Protection of Rural England AGM', *Journal of the Town Planning Institute*, Vol. XXX, No. 3, Jan.–Feb. 1944, p. 70.

68 See Victoria and Albert Museum, RIBA Archive, Sir Herbert Baker Papers, BAH/68/1 and 68/2.

69 However, Tallents's lavishly praised gesture was also financially motivated. C. Hussey, 'St John's Jerusalem, Sutton at Hone, Kent – The Home of Sir Stephen Tallents', *Country Life*, 31 March 1944, p. 555.

70 He also featured prominently in *Man and Boy*. See, for example, 'The Cubitts', *The Times*, 30 March 1938, p. 15.

71 See S. Tallents, 'Planning of Villages', *The Times*, 10 August 1946, p. 5, and later work on the skilful enlargement of villages in 'Perils and Prospects in Town and Country: a Second Conference at the Royal Society of Arts', *The Journal of the Royal Society of Arts*, February 1958, pp. 149–195.

72 Qtd in A. Spoor, *White-collar Union: Sixty Years of NALGO* (London, 1967), p. 438.

73 Tallents papers, File 19, Press cuttings, *Evening News*, 14 April 1932.

74 Tallents papers, File 19, Press cuttings, I. Brown, 'Telling the World', *The Manchester Guardian*, 16 April 1932.

75 Tallents, *The Projection of England*, p. 16.

76 See F. M. Leventhal, '"A Tonic to the Nation": The Festival of Britain, 1951', *Albion: A Quarterly Journal Concerned with British Studies*, Vol. 27, No. 3, Autumn 1995, pp. 445–453.

77 Qtd in J. Manser, *Hugh Casson: A Biography* (London, 2000), pp. 125–126.

78 In addition to artistic and technical achievements the Festival celebrated British idiosyncrasy. The Tempest Prognosticator was a replica (made by Tallents's company Cockade) of an elaborate nineteenth-century device which utilises the hysteria of fresh water leeches prior to a storm to warn of imminent bad weather.

79 Tallents, *The Projection of England*, p. 19.

80 See T. W. Hendrick, 'The Achievements of Cockade', in M. Banham and B. Hillier (ed.) *A Tonic to the Nation: The Festival of Britain, 1951* (London, 1976), pp. 163–165. Hugh and Margaret Casson were significant twentieth-century designers. Hugh achieved popular recognition, and a knighthood, for his pivotal role in the 1951 Festival of Britain.

81 S. Tallents, 'Design for Leisure', in Council of Industrial Design (ed.) *Design in the Festival* (London, 1951), pp. 46–47.

82 Qtd in B. E. Conekin, *The Autobiography of a Nation: The 1951 Festival of Britain* (Manchester & New York, 2000), pp. 96–97.

83 Just one year later the *Campania* demonstrated a different kind of scientific prowess to the world by testing a British atomic bomb in the Pacific. P. Hennessy, *Never Again: Britain 1945–51* (London, 1992), p. 431.

84 A. Hess, 'The Conference Speech', *Journal of the Institute of Public Relations*, Vol. 3, No. 2, December 1950, pp. 5–7.

85 This was launched on the basis that 'During the festival of Britain there will be many visitors from overseas countries, some of which have a better record for tidiness than our own'. 'Nationwide campaign for Festival Year', *Journal of the Institute of Public Relations*, Vol. 3, No 4, June, 1951, pp. 13–14.

86 M. Frayn, 'Festival', in M. Sissons and P. French (eds) *The Age of Austerity 1945–1951* (London, 1963), p. 308.

87 NA, CAB78/37, 'Memorandum by Lord President', 14 September 1945.

88 Williams had just completed *Press, Parliament and People*, a consideration of how government might best inform the public of its policies without impinging on the freedoms of the press.

89 The Labour government's publicity initiatives included the creation of the Empire Publicity Committee, an organisation whose approach obviously derived from the EMB.

90 W. Crofts, *Coercion or Persuasion? Propaganda in Britain after 1945* (London, 1989), p. 250.

91 However, the Conservatives tended to see the Commission as motivated by the offended personal sensitivities of Herbert Morrison, whose handling of the Food Crisis saw him personally vilified in the press. Morrison submitted personally collated files of clippings that 'misrepresented' him to the Royal Commission as evidence. See B. Donoughue and G. W. Jones, *Herbert Morrison: Portrait of a Politician* (London, 2001), p. 359.

92 The motion to establish the Commission that was put before the House read: 'having regard to the increasing public concern at the growth of monopolistic tendencies in the control of the press, and with the object of furthering the free expression of opinion through the press and the greatest practical accuracy in the presentation of news, the House considers that a Royal Commission should be appointed to inquire into the control, management and ownership of the press'. NA, HO251/394, 'Royal Commission on the Press (1947–1949): Evidence and Papers: Full Report', p. 3.

93 Qtd in 'Royal Commission on the Press', *The Journal of the Institute of Public Relations*, Vol. 1, No. 2, December 1948, p. 10.

94 NA, HO251/155, 'Royal Commission on the Press (1947–1949): Government Information Services', 'McKechnie to Nunn', 15 September 1948.

95 NA, HO251/394, 'Royal Commission on the Press (1947–1949): Evidence and Papers: Final Report', p. 147.

96 Qtd in 'Royal Commission on the Press', *The Journal of the Institute of Public Relations*, Vol. 1, No. 2, December 1948, p. 13.

97 Qtd in 'Royal Commission on the Press', p. 12.

98 For example, S. Tallents, 'What I Believe', *BBC Radio*, 2 September 1956.

99 Qtd in L'Etang, *Public Relations in Britain*, p. 69.

100 G. Dodson-Wells, 'Bulwark of Freedom', *The Journal of the Institute of Public Relations*, Vol. 4, No. 1, September 1951, p. 8.

101 'Items of News', *The Journal of the Institute of Public Relations*, Vol. 1, No. 2, December 1948, p. 12.

102 R. Wimbush, 'The Presidential Address', *The Journal of the Institute of Public Relations*, Vol. 5, No. 2, January 1953, p. 11.

103 See, for example, 'British Railways: a Criticism', *The Journal of the Institute of Public Relations*, Vol. 1, No. 4, June 1949, p. 2.

104 For more on Bernays transformation see S. Ewen, *PR! A Social History of Spin* (New York, 1996), pp. 159–173.

105 Elliott began his life as a journalist – his father was editor of *The Daily Express* – but after being sacked from *The Evening Standard* he found work as head of publicity at Southern Railways in 1925. This was a post engineered for him by the politicking of the Underground's Lord Ashfield (who was a friend of his father) and whose 'duties' were directly copied from those of the Underground's Frank Pick. Elliott chose the title 'Public Relations Consultant' because he thought it made him sound important, and his boss, Sir Herbert Walker, agreed, because 'No one will understand what it means and none of my railway officers will be upset'. See J. Elliott and M. Esau, *On and Off the Rails* (London, 1982).

106 University of Stirling, Grierson archive, G6/37, notes for article 1954. Insull's Christmas promotion of 1925 subjected the city to $7.5 million worth of newspaper copy, 25,000 advertisements in church bulletins and theatre programmes and 1.6 million flyers. Insull, an English émigré, was then President of the Commonwealth Edison Company, whose aggressive sales efforts had made Chicago the most energy-intensive city in the world. See Harold L. Platt, *The Electric City: Energy and the Growth of the Chicago Area, 1880–1930* (Chicago & London, 1991).

107 Jock Brebner learnt his trade as Tallents's junior at the General Post Office. S. Tallents, 'Review', *Public Administration*, Vol. 27, No. 3, Autumn 1949, p. 218.

108 'Dimbleby Asks Some Questions', *The Journal of the Institute of Public Relations*, Vol. 1, No. 1, September 1948, p. 11.

109 Figures quoted in M. Grant, *Propaganda and the Role of the State in Inter-war Britain* (Oxford, 1994), p. 45.

110 'The Conference Speeches: Alan Hess', *The Journal of the Institute of Public Relations*, Vol. 3, No. 2, December 1950, p. 6.

111 R. A. Paget-Cooke, 'Good Business', *The Journal of the Institute of Public Relations*, Vol. 3, No. 3, March 1951, p. 9.

112 Qtd in 'Dimbleby Asks Some Questions', p. 11.

113 'Public Relations in Industry', *The Journal of the Institute of Public Relations*, Vol. 1, No. 1, September 1948, p. 4.

114 S. Tallents, 'Review', *Public Administration*, Vol. XXVII, No. 3, Autumn 1949, p. 217.

115 S. Duncan, 'A Provincial Member Is Disturbed', *Public Relations: The Quarterly Journal of the Institute of Public Relations*, Vol. 5, No. 2, January 1953, p. 17.

116 'Speeches at the Luncheon', *The Journal of the Institute of Public Relations*, Vol. 1, No. 2, December 1948, p. 5.

117 R. Wimbush, 'The Birth of an Institute', *The Journal of the Institute of Public Relations*, Vol. 1, No. 1, September 1948, p. 2.

118 A. A. Garnett, 'That Definition', *The Journal of the Institute of Public Relations*, Vol. 3, No. 3, March 1951, p. 16.

119 The achievement of Charter has seen the number of IPR members rapidly increase, making it the largest organisation of its kind in Europe. The annual award of the Tallents medal keeps its Founder President's name alive, although it is impossible to credit that he would have been impressed by the narrow scope of the award. The Tallents medal was first awarded in 1984 for 'the most informative and efficient press pack for an audio visual press event, such as a programme, press show, an AV launch, film festival or conference'. *Public Relations: The Quarterly Journal of the Institute of Public Relations*, Vol. 3, No. 2, Winter 1984, p. 32.

120 As well as working as PRO for Austin Motor Company, Alan Hess worked as the BBC's motoring correspondent and competed as a racing driver. Indeed, in many respects his PRO job merely looks to have been an excuse to bring all these interests together. The popularity of a promotional pamphlet, *Gullible's Travels*, encouraged Austin to send Hess on PR stunts like competing in Indiana and asking him to drive an Austin from the equator to the Arctic Circle. Hess recorded his adventures in best-selling books such as *The Indianapolis Records* (London, 1949), *Wheels around the World* (London, 1951) and *Crazy Journey* (London, 1953).

7

Conclusion

This book was first prompted by the publication of the Phillis report into government communications in 2004. It's fair to say that popular affection for public relations practitioners had never been widespread but, it was argued, their malign influence had sunk British public life further into the gutter than ever before. 'Most PR activity does not involve outright falsehood,' Nick Davies argued persuasively, it distorts 'a gentler, albeit almost equally destructive, art.'[1] Common wisdom had it that modern state propaganda began with Winston Churchill's foundation of *The British Gazette* newspaper and had been going downhill ever since. But it soon became clear, to my surprise, that Churchill's initiative was far from typical.

The deeper I ventured into archives the clearer it became that public relations was the initiative of Civil Servants. As I read on, an unexpected portrait of a strand of the British Civil Service emerged: technocratically inclined officials (often profoundly marked by the experience of the Great War) determined to apply new scientific knowledge to the nation's social and economic problems. Through a series of friendships and semi-official networks, these public sector pioneers could also claim to be influencing (if not leading) the development of private sector public relations, as they brokered imaginative collaborations in an effort to circumvent the austerity of the post-slump years. Any default assumptions about the origins and politics of the British public relations profession were swiftly turned upon their head.

As an administrator, initiator and tactician, Sir Stephen Tallents played a crucial role in the development of public relations in Britain. 'The skills of many [inter-war] progressives', as Dan

LeMahieu put it, 'especially the bureaucrats, lay in the not inconsiderable tasks of organisation and implementation'.[2] LeMahieu's observation perfectly encapsulates Tallents's contribution to the development of public relations in Britain. He was not the 'Great Man' of British PR, but an intellectual entrepreneur around whom the majority of the period's most interesting experiments orbited.

Tallents was an Asquithian Liberal and his path through the great political, economic and social transformation of the twentieth-century landscape carried a broader resonance. A Liberal graduate of Toynbee, as the economic and social activities of the state expanded in the wake of the slump he would be appointed by both Conservative and Labour ministers to finesse creative compromises. Tracking the development of 'public relations' offers a way of examining the transformation of Liberalism, and the role played by Liberal intellectuals in that transformation. Like Keynes and Beveridge, Tallents can be seen to have played a part in saving capitalist parliamentary democracy from itself. Against the hysteria and negativity of the commercial British media during much of the interwar period, the attempt by Tallents and his fellow pioneers both to project accurate, positive images of modern Britain and to distribute factual information can look thanklessly heroic. In that specific historical context, an obvious but glib explanation for the poor image of public relations practitioners is that popular understanding of their work has overwhelmingly been framed by journalists.

My book closes by attempting to explain why Tallents's methods were less applicable in the postwar world ushered in by Clement Attlee's Labour administration. The creation of the more economically and socially active state that Tallents and his peers had propagated ironically pulled the organisational rug from beneath the feet of the freer-spirited bureaucratic class of which they were a part. Nevertheless, the formation of the IPR rather bizarrely saw something of Tallents's personality – his idiosyncratic rhetoric, his idealism, the breadth of his imaginative vision – transmuted into a template for a fast-expanding profession. At the Silver Jubilee conference of the Institute of Public Relations in 1973, to take an illustrative example, Prime Minister Edward Heath was joined by Professor H. J. Eysenck (who spoke on the social implications of the permissive society), the broadcaster Mary Stott ('What power do women have now?') and the theatrical impresario Sam Wanamaker. Meanwhile, the IPR President, Geoff Lewis, lectured delegates of the necessity of a 'collective, deliberate, planned and sustained effort to maintain mutual understanding between *all* peoples of the world *wherever* they may be and *whoever* they are'.[3] The peculiarly cultured heritage of the British PR profession is there for all to see.

Contemporary public relations practice makes 1973 appear a very long time ago. Although they are not responsible for the voracious media demands of the 24/7 news cycle, the practices of present-day public relations big hitters like Max Clifford and Alastair Campbell would probably have struck Tallents as narrow, disingenuous and short-termist. Here it is worth stressing that Tallents's conception of public relations was related to the rise of a managerial culture that grew up with the slump indented in its collective memory. The organised flow of information was especially important to a culture that emphasised the mediating function of management and which held that the needs of owners, investors and employees must be negotiated into long-term alignment for the good of the nation. In Britain these organisa-tional and ethical norms were severely weakened after 1979 by a shift in the conceptual, ideological and economic assumptions of the governing class. At the very broadest level then, the replacement of what we might term 'the Tallents tradition' with a more aggressive, directive and qualitative iteration of public relations practice appears temptingly correlated with the rise of the 'right to manage', the coarse emphasis on 'shareholder value' and management of the public sector by punitive targets.

Both present academic orthodoxy and common wisdom have it that recent decades have seen an alarming erosion of trust in the media, public life and big business.[4] After a generation focused primarily on the mechanistic *ends* of management, it may be that the crisis of neo-liberal economics signified by the banking bailouts of 2009 once again revives interest in the broader regulatory ethical *means*.[5] If this happens, and the remit of the representative bureaucracy is restored, then perhaps the decline of 'the Tallents tradition' will be reversed.

Indeed, this book was begun in one kind of media crisis and completed in quite another. As News International became embroiled in a series of scandals in the summer of 2011 a debate about the appropriate amount of political power possessed by the media began. The echo of debates held in the aftermath of the First World War was striking.

Methodologically, the approaches pioneered in Tallents's era certainly seem well suited to the age of 'soft power'.[6] The blurring of media forms driven in part by the rise of the internet (along with the widening of participation it theoretically enables) has already revived interest in public relations practice able to engage with a looser associative media culture. 'Good public relations practice emulates that wise bird, the cuckoo', as Gervas Huxley cynically surmised of Tallents's methods, 'it gets other birds to sponsor its eggs and, when really successful, gets the other birds not merely to hatch the egg, but to regard the fledgling as their favourite offspring'.[7]

Historical hand-wringing aside, from the posters of Edward McKnight Kauffer to films such as *Night Mail* and John Betjeman's *Shell Guides*, the material legacy of the early public relations pioneers remains a vital part of the national cultural fabric. Tallents's insistence that good information must be artfully presented has ensured that the publicity output of organisations such as Imperial Airways, London Transport, the GPO and Shell have become as redolent of the 1930s as Agatha Christie novels and Battersea Power Station. As well as being curated, collected and commercially exhibited, this historically specific work begat a lasting heritage of imaginative information that has further been appropriated, embedded and playfully subverted by Britain's wider popular culture. From packed cinemas showing GPO films to office canteens displaying MOI posters, via The Prodigy's *Charly*, the self-conscious humour central to the enterprise of early twentieth-century 'projection' lives on. Indeed, not just the spirit. With established channels of advertising under attack, a new era of enlightened patronage – like the Eurostar-funded *Somers Town*, to take a random example – is apparently dawning.

In 2006, ICONS Online, an independent organisation funded by the government, formulated a list of national icons that included the FA Cup, Oxbridge and the King James Bible as well as less tangible suggestions such as 'our sense of humour' and queuing.[8] What was especially striking about the list (which was voted for by the public) was how many of the selected ICONS owe their existence to Tallents and his peers – from Harry Beck's Tube map to the 'V' sign via the Jubilee telephone kiosk and the Routemaster bus. More contemporary still, any similarity between the promotion of the 2012 Olympics and the approach first drafted by Tallents in 1932 appears entirely intentional. 'Sometimes I think the backdrop to our country tends to be the great heritage images – Beefeaters, Stonehenge, Windsor Castle and so forth', Tessa Jowell (the former Secretary of State of the

Department of Culture, Media and Sport) mused recently 'They are the most wonderful images and they will play a big part in the projection of Britain during the Olympic Games, but Britain is a global centre for creative industry. What we want to see is the modern face of Britain.'[9]

Notes

1 N. Davies, *Flat Earth News: An Award Winning Reporter Exposes Falsehood, Distortion and Propaganda in the Global Media* (London, 2008), p. 159.

2 D. L. LeMahieu, *A Culture for Democracy: Mass Communication and the Cultivated Mind in Britain between the Wars* (Oxford, 1988), p. 140.

3 G. Lewis, 'What Britain Wants', *Public Relations*, May 1973, p. 73.

4 See, for example, J. Lloyd, *What the Media Are Doing to Our Politics* (London, 2004).

5 The broad shape of this argument has been bolstered by the work of Rakesh Khurana, who argues that the moral glue which early (American) twentieth-century 'management' aimed to supply was lost during 'professionalisation'. R. Khurana, *From Higher Aims to Hired Hands: The Social Transformation of American Business Schools and the Unfulfilled Promise of Management as a Profession* (Princeton, NJ, 2007).

6 See J. Nye, *Soft Power: The Means to Success in World Politics* (New York, 2004).

7 Tallents papers, CI34, G. Huxley, 'PR – A Talk Given to the Empire Tea Bureau in 1947'.

8 See http://www.icons.org.uk/.

9 'Business:Life meets Tessa Jowell', *British Airways Business:Life Magazine*, March 2010, p. 34.

THE
PROJECTION OF
ENGLAND

BY SIR STEPHEN TALLENTS
K.C.M.G., C.H., C.B.E.

To

My fellow citizens of the United Kingdom, in Scotland, Wales and Northern Ireland, without apologising for its title, I dedicate this essay. They have cast their shadows – long shadows – across the world in their time. They may be counted on to take their full share in the study and practice of the new art for which these pages plead.

Part of the account of the Barcelona Exhibition is reprinted by courtesy of the 'Spectator'.

I

When Mrs. Gaskell, less than a hundred years ago, depicted in Cranford the life of an English provincial town, she painted a society of ladies whose only contact with the outside world was the *St James's Chronicle*. Four separate households shared the cost of this journal. The honourable Mrs. Jamieson always had the reading of it first, 'in right of her honourableness', and it was a standing annoyance to her fellow subscribers – Miss Matty, Miss Forrester and Miss Pole – to observe through a window as they passed her house the powdered head of Mr. Mulliner, her manservant, tranquilly and composedly studying the issue for which they were waiting. There had been no change in Cranford's external relations since Miss Matty was a girl. The old ladies of Cranford then, she reported. 'had the *St James's Chronicle* three times a week, just as we have now, and we have plenty to say; and I remember the clacking noise there always was when some of the ladies got together'.

To-day a woman living in Miss Matty's house at Cranford reads on seven mornings of the week the world events of the evening before. A single morning's paper will give her the news of revolution in Madrid, of famine and battle in China and of murder in Chicago. Tidings of her relations in Canada and Australia are dropped casually into her letter box. She can telephone to them, if she will, from her fireside. Without moving from her chair, she can listen-in during a single evening to half a dozen European capitals. At the cost of a stroll to the cinema round the corner, she can review the lives and the loves of almost every country but her own. Nor is she merely the passive recipient of news and impressions. Her daily fare is brought to her from four continents, and her diet is modified by the acts of God and the activities of men in Africa and Brazil, in India and New Zealand. Miss Matty's little fortune, it will be remembered, was entrusted to a neighbouring Town and County Bank which defaulted in consequence, it would appear, of unwise management. Her successor's income is much more likely to be affected by the mysterious pilgrimages of gold, backwards and forwards and backwards again, between distant capitals.

These profound changes in the daily life of a provincial Englishwoman have a multiplied significance in the life of the world. The same developments, which have placed her well-being at the mercy of events in distant countries, have made the fortunes of whole peoples mutually dependent. The same inventions, which provide her in her morning paper with the overnight news of the globe, which have enabled her by her fireside to listen and to speak to distant countries, have given to whole nations the power of communing together by new means and in new modes. No great reflection is needed to demonstrate the magnitude of the change. It may be pointed, perhaps, by a single instance. The news of Blenheim, carried by a galloping horse and a sailing ship, took eight days to reach London. The result of last June's Derby was known 12,000 miles away in Australia within five seconds of the finish of the race.

Until this new age of discovery the peoples of the world were largely self-contained. They were independent alike of the products and of the opinions of other countries. In so far as the deeds of a people went beyond its own borders, its fame fell silently like a shadow across other lands. Greece and Rome and Macedon, Spain and Portugal, France and Holland all in their time threw long shadows; and when England by her sea power won her place in the sun, her shadow was the longest of them all. To-day that morning of the world is past, and the sun, standing higher in the heavens, is nearer to filling its traditional role of shining alike on the just and the unjust. The shadows of the peoples are more equal and the long shadows have grown less.

In the era of shadows the reputation of a people outside its own borders depended almost entirely upon personal meetings. India can have had little impression of Macedon until the armies of Alexander appeared over the Himalayas. The fame of Rome among the Picts depended upon the presence of her legions upon Hadrian's Wall. The England of Elizabeth was known only to the Russia of Ivan the Terrible through the merchant adventurers who reached Moscow in the wake of Sir Francis Willoughby's ill-starred voyage, and through the ambassadors who landed at Scarborough and travelled to London in the vain quest for Elizabeth's hand.

To-day, as the result of scientific discovery, a people is known to its fellows by the impression which it makes upon them through the cable and the printing press, on the air and upon the screen. If a nation would be truly known and understood in the world, it must set itself actively to master and employ the new, difficult and swiftly developing modes which science has provided for the projection of national personality. Moreover, whereas in the age of shadows countries were mainly self-contained, and derived from outside prestige little save power, pride and luxury, to-day they depend upon each other alike for their bread and for their peace. No civilized country can today afford either to neglect the projection of its national personality or to resign its projection to others. Least of all countries can England afford either that neglect or that resignation.

In 1580 John Lyly could write approvingly of an old saying that 'all countries stande in neede of Britaine; and Britaine of none'. How singularly untrue of the Britain of to-day, that for four weeks in every five must draw her daily bread from overseas, and maintains one fifth of all her occupied population by her export trade. Lyly could write of the English as 'always though not laughing, yet looking through an Emeraud at others jarres'. That aloofness may have been becoming to her in the sixteenth century. It is tragically unfitted to her situation in the twentieth, when she is partner in an Empire that includes a quarter of the world's surface and a quarter of its populations. Yet it persists sufficiently to allow M. Siegfried to remark drily of England in 1931 that 'she sits in her little island out of contact with the rest of the world'. If his premise be true, we cannot complain of his conclusion: 'If she wishes to continue as one of the Great Powers of the world, or even to exist at all, a complete revision is imperative.'

The seamen of Italy, Portugal and Spain in turn preceded England in the exploration of the new world which was opened to Europe by the discoveries of the fifteenth and sixteenth centuries. Not till after the Pope had divided the new world between Spain and Portugal by a line drawn from pole to pole did England take up the running. But when her seamen, trained by their painful apprenticeship in the search for Northern passages, finally turned their bowsprits south, they swiftly established her supremacy in the newly discovered lands. To-day, as I hope to show in these pages, another new world, less tangible but not less significant, is being rapidly disclosed. England has the need, the obligation and the opportunity of establishing a supremacy within it. That supremacy she can secure only by the exercise of a new and complicated art—the art of national projection. This new art demands an intense study and a continuing apprenticeship. Like every corporate art it demands concentrated planning and organisation. Yet England seems scarcely to have recognized its coming. Certainly in no true sense is she either studying or practicing it. There are some signs that once again other people have got the start of her. It is the business of our generation to see that she masters this new art, and is not content, while other nations are going out 'on the air' and upon the screen, to sit crooning, far from the microphone, the spells and folk songs of her past, or waiting, passively and perplexedly, for the sun to come out and restore her shadow.

2

A friend of mine, travelling lately in Africa and spending the night on a Kenya farm, found that his host often sat up into the early hours of the morning so that he might hear the strike of Big Ben on his wireless. Not long after he told me this story, another friend described to me how in his young days a North American Indian had arrived, after a journey of a thousand miles, to buy at a Canadian trading post an English blanket or two, in preference to the American blankets which he could have got without travelling at all. These two incidents, so diverse in place and in spirit, fittingly introduce some reflections upon the material which England has to project, and certain special advantages which she may look to enjoy in securing a friendly reception for it overseas.

If we want to know what material England should project, it is wise to ask ourselves what are the English characteristics in which the outside world is most interested. It is an entertaining pursuit – this breaking up of the fame of England in to its primary colours. At one end of the spectrum are to be found, I suppose, such national institutions and virtues as:

The Monarchy (with its growing scarcity value).

Parliamentary Institutions (with all the values of a first edition).

The British Navy.

The English Bible, Shakespeare and Dickens.

('What marked and striking excellence', wrote Gerard Hopkins to Patmore nearly fifty years ago, 'has England to show to make her civilization attractive? Her literature is one of her excellences and attractions. This is why I hold that fine works of art are really a great power in the world, an element of strength even to an empire.')

In international affairs – *a reputation for disinterestedness.*

In national affairs – *a tradition of justice, law and order.*

In national character – *a reputation for coolness.*

In commerce – *a reputation for fair dealing.*

In manufacture – *a reputation for quality.*

(How agreeable it was, only last summer, to read of the two astute merchants of Eastern Europe, who were found to be selling their native cloth at a fantastic price by the simple device of calling it English!)

In sport – *a reputation for fair play.*

At the other end of the spectrum might be found such events as the *Derby* and the *Grand National,* the *Trooping of the Colour,* the *Boat Race, Henley, Wimbledon,* the *Test Matches,* and the *Cup Final.* But between these two extremes comes a medley of institutions and excellencies, which every man may compile for himself according to his humour and his ingenuity. My own list would include:

Oxford and *St. Andrews.*

Piccadilly, Bond Street, Big Ben and *Princes Street, Edinburgh.*

The English Countryside, English villages, the *English home* and *English servants.*

The *Lord Mayor of London.*

The Times, Punch, and the *Manchester Guardian.*

The *Metropolitan Police* and *Boy Scouts.*

The *London omnibuses* and *Underground Railways.*

Football and *Foxhunting.*

English bloodstock and *pedigree stock.*

The arts of *gardening* and of *tailoring.*

Of some such elements as these is the standing raw material of England's esteem in the world composed. There should be added to them all those achievements which by a sudden stroke place England from time to time on the world's screen and win her there a favourable reflection. Of such are England's speed records by land, sea and air, Miss Johnson's flight to Australia and Squadron Leader Hinkler's magnificent crossing of the Atlantic to Africa. Striking actions and events such as these need, it may be said, no deliberate projection. Yet among them are some at least of which the excellence could have been enhanced to our advantage in distant eyes, if the arts of national projection had lent them skilled support. How many people in the world, for example, know that Lindbergh's flight, for all its unmatched brilliance, was not the first crossing of the Atlantic by air? How many Canadians, with the newsreels of the United States continually before their eyes, know that not all the athletic championships of the world are held by America? Nor are the materials for England's projection to be found in England alone. Just as a skilled English workman likes to see and to read about the working conditions of men engaged in tasks comparable with his own, so the Canadian or the Australian farmer is interested to learn of the conditions of other farmers, working under different conditions but encountering the same ultimate problems of soil and weather and animal welfare. So too the native of Africa enjoys pictures of other peoples not too far removed from his own manner of living. To satisfy this universal desire of men and women to see and read of the conditions of their fellows, England can summon up the infinite variety of her Empire's resources, and bring that material, however indirectly, within the compass of her own projection.

So much, by way of illustration rather than catalogue, for the more familiar and traditional of the raw materials which can be used in the projection of England. I suspect that the briefest study of our new art and its requirements would disclose a treasure of less familiar excellencies, better fitted to-day than many of these to be flashed upon the screen of a new world. I suspect also – so utterly does our memory of the England of yesterday becloud our perception of the England of to-day – that the same study would discover the need of a preliminary projection of England to herself. What, however, of the special assets upon which England can count to secure favourable conditions for her projection?

She starts with the advantage of a language used by a large section of the world and understood of many who do not habitually use it. Men and women of the same stock as her own are scattered about the world in a unique dispersion. With all of them she shares a common history. She controls or can influence the machinery of Government, including the service of education, in her Colonies, and she has close and sympathetic contacts with the sister Governments of the Dominions. She provides a market for the produce of countless countries, with all the network of commercial and personal relationships and needs, the interdependence in well being, which that provision involves.

Her cable companies and her news agencies girdle the earth. Her shipping companies control one-third of the world's tonnage, and have their agents in every part of the globe. Her steel rails bind whole countries together. Her bankers and merchant houses, her insurance companies and chartered accountants operate the world over. Englishmen are at work in most of the greater English-speaking newspaper offices. Wherever ships are steered or metals won from the earth, there the ships' engineers and the mining engineers of England are posted.

Here surely are conditions very favourable to the effective projection and sympathetic receipt of England's image, would she but master the art of casting it worthily upon the screen.

3

I have claimed that England, reluctant though she seems, must master that art in fulfillment alike of her needs and her responsibilities. Let us consider what those needs and responsibilities are.

In the first place it is essential for England as a world power that she should be able to make herself known to her fellows. Peace itself may at any time depend upon a clear understanding abroad of her actions and her motives. International co-operation is vital; and it is ultimately dependent not merely upon the excursions of statesmen from capital to capital – great though the value of such visits be – but upon a good understanding of each other by the peoples of the world. If we are to play our part in the new world order, we need to master every means and every art by which we can communicate with other peoples. The need is specially urgent between ourselves and the other parts of the Empire. We are experimenting together in a novel political organization, in which are joined together peoples most widely separated from each other in space and in character. Good communications are plainly a first essential for its successful working. On this ground pre-eminently we need to be able to project overseas a full and true presentation of England. We need that ability all the more because it is certain that, if we do not undertake the task ourselves, others will be found to undertake it for us, not always with truth nor always with sympathy.

England to-day is more dependent than any other country in the world upon supplies of food and raw material from other countries, and of overseas markets for her manufactured goods. Is her position in those markets so secure that she can afford to dispense with an up-to-date presentation of her manufacturing power to her customers? Her case has been searchingly analysed within the past year by Mr. Loveday.[1] Here is a short series of the cold statements with which he hammers home his conclusions:

If the share of the United Kingdom in world imports to day were the same as in 1913 it would be between £160 and £170 millions greater than it is ... The great difference between the position of the United Kingdom and that of other leading European countries is that the former has continued to lose status quite steadily from year to year, while the latter, gravely injured at first have for the most part, made a rapid recovery in recent years ... The trade of the world has increased; the share of the United Kingdom has decreased and is decreasing. It is decreasing in the world; it is decreasing in Europe, and as we examine one group of industries after another the same phenomenon presents itself.

No projection of England's ability to serve the world will by itself suffice to remedy so grave a state as is here described. But, in a day when salesmanship is admitted as a cardinal factor in trade, we cannot expect to traffic success fully overseas unless we use every means that we can discover to show our customers that we are still well fitted to supply them. It is not enough to look in at an occasional Exhibition or to dispatch a few trade missions to distant countries. We need a continuous and sustained presentation of our industrial ability and our industrial ambitions, designed with the utmost artistry that we can achieve as a background to the more detailed activities of particular industries and particular firms, and persistently pressed through every channel of communication open to us. All the indications of the time are that England's future export trade will depend upon her ability to sell less her old staple products than the new, highly finished goods which are bought by people living above the subsistence line. Those are the people who are most susceptible to the new art of national presentation. They listen in on the wireless, they go regularly to the cinema, they read of other countries. If we are to win their custom, we must first win their minds; and to win their minds we must set ourselves to project by all the new means of modern international communication a picture of England's industrial qualities.

Again, in a day when nations are reckoning in millions the value to them of their tourist traffic, we cannot afford to neglect the due presentation of England to the world as a desirable and a friendly place. The Travel Association is doing its best with limited resources to attract visitors; but its efforts would be immensely reinforced if its special appeal could be thrown into relief against the more general background of a presentation of the qualities of England. For visitors come to England for a great variety of purposes. They come for pleasure, they come for business and they come for learning. Least of all, perhaps, can we neglect to attract students to England. From every civilized country a certain proportion of the ablest young men and women go abroad to complete or supplement their education. We are well equipped to give such visitors everything that they need except perhaps the facile doctorates which they extract from the United States. It is greatly to our interest – and, especially in the case of students of our own race, we need not be afraid to claim that it is also greatly in theirs – that they should be attracted to our Universities and our research stations. Let us at least not neglect to show them what facilities we can offer.

This reference to research students leads naturally on from the demonstration that England has need of the arts of projection to the demonstration that it is her duty to study them. For it is in the world of scientific research that her responsibilities most patently lie. Within the space of living memory science has opened to us a world incomparably more important than the new territories which opened out before our ancestors in the sixteenth century. She has disclosed to us through the microscope vast populations of minute creatures, whom we have out-stripped in the course of evolution, but whose influence on our happiness and well-being we may come to control but can never escape. She has given us in the X-rays a light infinitely finer than the ordinary light of day, and has enabled us to study with a new intensity the basic structure of all things animate and inanimate.

The swiftness, the range and the intensity of these discoveries have far outstripped our ability to communicate their results to those who might benefit by them. It is commonly said that the applications of science lag at least twenty years behind its discoveries. In the field of medicine alone, a host of simple facts, of the utmost importance to the daily life of whole peoples and long familiar to the worker in the laboratory, remain outside not merely the practice but the knowledge of the populations whom they might profit.

Science itself observes no international frontiers. But the communication of scientific results cannot escape the limitation of differing languages and governments. England is in varying degrees responsible for the welfare of a large part of the world's inhabitants. She has devoted immense care to securing their good government, but she has scarcely thought of her responsibility for securing to them the benefits of scientific discovery. Yet England, with her great traditions in scientific research, her close contact with the thought and work of Europe, is well fitted to convey that knowledge to the whole of her Colonial Empire and far beyond it. It is her plain duty to harness the new methods of international projection to the vital bridging of the gulf between scientific discovery and its application – a gulf which at present divides hundreds of millions of her fellow peoples from well being and happiness. She has the knowledge and the power, and to-day she has the opportunity, to bridge that gulf and to effect a beneficent revolution in the lives of countless human beings. There could be no more compelling call to the study of a new art.

4

I have already sketched, however lightly, some of the raw material which England has at her disposal to meet her general need for a world-wide projection. What of those other, more specialized assets which equip her to fulfil the responsibilities which, as we have seen, rest upon her to communicate the results of scientific research to no small part of the world?

The field of science is too wide for any attempt to be made here to catalogue England's scientific resources. I have touched above very briefly on the profound contribution which England could make to the welfare of her Colonial Empire in particular by a determined projection of the results of research in medicine. Let us now examine in somewhat greater detail the field of agricultural research. Agriculture, in spite of growing industrial developments, especially in Canada and Australia, is still the predominant industry of every overseas Empire country; and agricultural research, upon which their prosperity fundamentally depends, is, most happily, the field in which the Empire has of late co-operated more freely and more fully than in any other branch of activity whatsoever. No group indeed of communities in the world has so nearly approached Burke's ideal of 'a partnership in all science' as have the countries of the Empire in this field. The story of that co-operation still passes almost wholly unrecognized in an England that is accustomed to think in terms of politics and industry and very rarely looks at the world through biological eyes. Its record will one day provide a brilliant page in the history of Empire development. In that record the great research stations of the Empire overseas – the South African Veterinary Station at Onderstepoort leaps to the mind – will fill a part of steadily growing significance, and will justify the splendid faith, now being maintained through days of great discouragement, of the scientific organisations of the Dominions. But for the moment England is naturally ahead of her partner peoples in agricultural research and in other forms of investigation, such as that of low temperature, which closely touch agricultural needs.

I have spoken of England's responsibility for communicating the results of scientific research to her Colonial Empire. But her responsibilities do not end with her Colonies. For years now the Dominions also have joined with us to maintain in England the Imperial Bureaux – more recently entitled the Imperial Institutes – of Entomology and Mycology. The one, housed next to the great entomological collections of the Natural History Museum and recently fortified by the establishment at Slough of the famous 'Parasite Zoo', is admittedly the central point of entomological work in the Empire; and the other, housed in Kew Gardens, the main base of the Empire's mycological research. They have also contributed to the Bureau of Hygiene and Tropical Diseases and to the Imperial Institute. Moreover when the countries of the Empire decided at the Imperial Agricultural Research Conference of 1927 to establish under joint Imperial control, and to maintain at joint Imperial charges, eight new bureaux, each of which would be responsible for keeping the different parts of the Empire in touch with developments in a particular field of research, the centres for these bureaux were all by unanimous agreement found in the research stations of the United Kingdom. Even in branches of science bearing on agriculture, in which no such bureau has yet been established, the Empire countries overseas often look to an English Station as a centre to which they can refer problems arising from their own researches.

Let me give first the bare list of these new inter-Imperial Bureaux which the Empire countries have decided to maintain in England, and the subjects with which they are severally concerned. They are these:

Soil Science – The Rothamsted Experimental Station, Herts.

Animal Nutrition – The Rowett Research Institute, Aberdeen.

Animal Health – The Veterinary Research Laboratory, Weybridge.

Animal Genetics – The Animal Breeding Research Department, Edinburgh University.

Agricultural Parasitology – The Institute of Agricultural Parasitology, St. Albans.

Plant Genetics (for plants other than herbage) – The Plant Breeding Institute, School of Agriculture, Cambridge.

Plant Genetics (for herbage plants) – The Welsh Plant Breeding Station, Aberystwyth.

Fruit Production – The Research Station, East Mailing, Kent.

But while these centres, with the senior Institutes which I have mentioned, are directly recognized and jointly supported by all the countries of the Empire, there are many other stations, not thus directly supported, to which the Empire overseas is accustomed to refer its less familiar problems for advice. To name a few only, the Royal Botanic Gardens, Kew, are recognized as the leading centre of botanical knowledge in the Empire. The Low Temperature Research Station at Cambridge is the Empire's scientific base for studying the problems of cold storage upon the solution of which the great Dominion export industries of meat, fruit and dairy produce cardinally depend. Many parts of the Empire look to the Forest products Research Laboratory at Princes Risborough for the scientific testing of their timbers, and to Leeds for knowledge of those qualities of wool which more specially govern its manufacture.

This list, thus barely recited, will seem, I know, a mere rattling of dry bones to most of those who, like myself, were nourished wholly upon the arts and not at all upon the sciences. Of how much were we deprived! We go about the world of to-day clumsy-eyed and clumsy-fingered; and we observe an ignorance like unto our own at the heart of the affairs of state. When an Imperial Conference gathers, long daylight hours are spent in discussing points of constitutional draftsmanship. Night after night is devoted to overwhelming our visitors with receptions and dinners and again receptions. Of a Saturday they are shown our Fleet or our Army. Of a Sunday we entertain them in our country houses. Yet of all the contributions which England is making to-day to the well-being of the Commonwealth the greatest is probably astir in quarters to which the Conference pays little attention – in stations of research such as I have recorded.

Those forbidding titles conceal secluded guilds of young workers, dotted here and there about England, such as once were dotted the hospitalries of the Order of St John, and happily absorbed in the deft and keen eyed-study of the problems which belong unto our Imperial peace. Here is a worker creating new varieties of wheat and barley; there another bringing forth new breeds of grass – still the greatest of the world's crops. One is studying the incredible lives of the insects – still man's most dangerous rivals for possession of half the world. Another is patiently investigating those agents of disease in man and beast and plant to which no porcelain filter can deny passage. One is measuring the minute quantities of minerals – of calcium and phosphorous and iodine – for the lack of which living creatures in every continent, from schoolchildren in Glasgow to the Kikuyu in Africa, from the sheep of the highlands to the cattle of Australia, New Zealand and South Africa, sicken and may perish. Another is clearing the paths of fish in the ocean; and yet another is recording the minutest details, gathered from forty countries, of the dread movements of the locust swarms.

Of such are the realities which lie behind our forbidding list of inter-Imperial Bureaux. It should be recorded to the honour of many of our most illustrious visitors to the last Imperial Conference that they at least recognized what an Imperial partnership might mean, and stole away, now and again, from the reviews and the receptions, to see for themselves what England was doing in the new and still half secret world of profoundly significant endeavor.

5

What in the fabric and practice of Empire does this young Imperial partnership mean? It has meant, for example, within the last few years alone, that Canada needed a supply of parasites to combat the ravages of the stem sawfly in her wheatfields, she called upon Farnham Royal in Buckinghamshire to supply them; that, when Australia came to tackle the great problems of her pastures, she sent students from her splendid Waite Institute at Adelaide to learn the latest developments at Rothamsted, Aberystwyth and Aberdeen; that, when New Zealand wished to improve the already fine quality of the ten million carcasses of lamb and mutton, which she sends annually to England, she sought at Cambridge the leader of a team in which were happily combined workers of her own and workers from Australia; that, when South Africa wished to have her botanical resources reviewed with a friendly eye, her Prime Minister invited the Director of Kew to visit the Union; that, when Newfoundland wished to develop her fisheries and to prove and improve the fine qualities of her cod liver oil, she sought advice and workers from Edinburgh and London; that, when British Honduras and the Gold Coast wished to try out the qualities of their native timbers, they looked to Princes Risborough for the necessary scientific tests; that, when Cyprus desired to introduce a silk industry, she came to the Imperial Institute for guidance, and that, when India and Australia and Kenya and Tanganyika wanted to discover whether they could grow *Aleurites Fordii* – that tree from the Yangtse valley whose berries produce one of the finest oils known to modern commerce – the collection and distribution of its seeds were entrusted to the Gardens at Kew.

It has meant also that a growing network of personal and impersonal communication has grown up between half a hundred centres of scientific work in this country and their counterparts in the Empire overseas. But the full possibilities of this great partnership have yet to be realized. The results of scientific agricultural research in England still filter slowly and haltingly to the overseas countries which so greatly need them. While the technique of scientific research has enormously advanced, the technique of the communication of its results is still confined for the most part to personal visits, personal correspondence and specialist journals of restricted circulation.

Every director of an English research station who has travelled in the Empire would testify not merely to the warmth of his reception and the hospitality accorded to him but also to the eagerness for new knowledge which he met with on his journeys. Such visits are likely always to remain the most perfect medium of communication. But the Empire is wide and scattered; first-rate research workers are few, and there is a real danger of their being unduly drawn away from their stations by the friendly insistence of the call for their visitations. Every director of agriculture would admit the difficulty of bridging unaided the gulf between the pages of the scientific periodical and the reading of the homestead. In spite of admirable work by agricultural departments throughout the Empire, in spite of machinery, and sometimes elaborate machinery, for circulating to producers the scientific information which they increasingly need and increasingly demand, the great divide between the laboratory on the one side and the farm, the plantation and the forest on the other still remains un-bridged.

England has the patent responsibility of ascertaining by study, by experiment and by continuous observation how the results of her scientific agricultural research may best be communicated, whether it be to the farmers of her own race scattered about the world, to the managers of plantations dispersed in her Colonies, or to the producer cultivating his holding in India or Africa or the West Indies and suffering dumbly from the revolution in agricultural methods which the more advanced parts of the world have achieved. She has at least an equal responsibility in the field of medical research. The capacities and the needs of those, who may benefit by the information about scientific progress which England can give them, differ widely. But England can confer a measureless benefit upon them by applying the new methods and the new art of projection to the dissemination of scientific results.

6

'Your plea', I may be told, 'for the better projection of England is convincing enough. But what evidence have you that her projection is not a straightforward matter of taking pains? What proof have you that it demands the new and difficult art to which you have so constantly, if so vaguely, referred?' I have spoken of signs that other peoples have got the start of England in the mastering and practice of the art of national projection. I can best, perhaps, prove that such an art exists by indicating two of those signs. In so doing I go back to the more general projection of national qualities with which I opened my case.

The greatest agent of international communication at the moment is unquestionably the cinema. It has been calculated that there are some 60,000 picture houses in the world and that their yearly audiences may number some 15,000,000,000 people. Upon the screens of those theatres, feature films, interest films, travel films, news reels, cartoons and comics jostle together. Moreover, there is growing up, outside the picture theatres proper, an immense non-theatrical film circulation. The moral and emotional influence of the cinema is incalculable, and requires no demonstration here. It has been the subject of countless investigations and committees, all of which have recognized the power and most of which have deplored the present manner of its exercise. Its indirect influence is also enormous. 'A foot of film is worth a dollar of trade,' say the Americans, who, enjoying special advantages, have turned every cinema in the world into the equivalent of an American consulate.

They have also forced their own manner of cinematic speech upon other nations.

I am not concerned here to criticize the results. I have always a certain sympathy with those who try to seize new opportunities, however disastrously, as against those who stand by and criticize. But he who desires criticism can find an ample supply of it in the filed reports of despairing Committees. In his preface to the latest of them, the Vice Chancellor of Birmingham University succinctly sums up the decision by referring to 'the abuses and dangers – intellectual, physical and moral ... which at present make what might be an instrument of untold good into an instrument of incalculable and irreparable harm'.

All of us have seen an occasional film of excellence. We have enjoyed '*The Covered Wagon*', '*Nanook of the North*' and '*The Virginian*', and delighted in the earlier Chaplins. More lately we have been charmed by René Clair, with his '*Sous les Toits de Paris*' and '*Le Million*'. We have seen in the '*Secrets of Nature*' series and more recently in such short films as U.F.A.'s 'Turbulent Timber' what possibilities the cinema enjoys in fields hitherto untouched. Such morsels of good fortune, however, are chance finds. With one exception, there is no people in the world that is setting itself to express its point of view and its purposes seriously through the greatest modern medium of international expression. That exception is Russia.

Two or three small schools of Russian producers, working at no great cost and producing a mere handful of films, have done more than all the studios of the world together to show us what an incomparable instrument of national expression the cinema might be. A complete catalogue of these films would not take up more than a dozen lines. Yet this small library, in spite of its relatively scanty theatrical circulation, has established for Russia in the modern world a prestige comparable to that which her novels and her ballets won for her before the War. Let us take four of those films as an illustration – Eisenstein's '*The Cruiser Potemkin*', Pudovkin's '*Storm over Asia*', Turin's '*Turk–Sib*' and Dovjenko's '*Earth*'.

'*The Cruiser Potemkin*' is now a little old-fashioned in technique, and its treatment of life on board a Russian battleship is at a disadvantage in the eyes of those to whom ships mean the ships of the British Navy. Yet can anyone who has seen it deny the moving power of the crowd scenes in Odessa, when the dead revolutionary lies in improvised state upon the quayside,

and the firing Cossacks advance slowly down the long flight of
steps to disperse the mob; or of the scene when the mutineers
of the 'Potemkin', learning that the Black Sea fleet is returning
to destroy them, gradually get her engines going and her guns
trained, and move out to sea to meet it. Over that last scene even
Broadway broke into nightly cheers.

'*Storm over Asia*', grouped round an invented personal story
of some interest, supported by plenty of local material from the
steppes of Eastern Russia and a local fur market, and borrowing
many of the devices of an American 'Western' to add speed to its
story, culminates in the rising of an imaginary people of Turkestan
to drive out an imaginary and unmistakably English suzerainty.
No story in itself could be more antipathetic to an English eye; yet
I have heard an Englishman of wide cinematic experience describe
it as the greatest film that he has seen.

'*Turk–Sib*' treats of the making of the new Turkestan Siberian
railway. It has no personal story, and no individual actors. Its hero
is the slowly advancing railway; its villain the forces of drought
and storm, of ice and rock and flood. I have seen its reception by
a selected audience of English business men and labour representatives, and have heard them describe it as a finer film than any
other that they had viewed.

'*Earth*' is nominally the story of the coming of the new
collective agriculture to an obscure Russian village, with all
the private hopes and agonies engendered by that sudden local
revolution. But in spite of its enforced and tendencious story, the
film is fundamentally a hymn of the soil and of the people who
live by the soil. Its beautiful procession of villagers to the young
man's funeral, its simple and lovely dying fall of rain descending
upon apples, are nearer to true poetry than any other film within
my knowledge.

There are growing up to-day in England scores of small Film
Societies at whose performances week after week throughout the
winter are gathered those whose interest is in cinema as an art
and especially as an art of propaganda. These Russian films are
the mainstay of their performances. They can scarcely find a single
English film of interest to their purpose. Yet the life of England is
rich in material for the making of films at least as remarkable as
those which I have described. Our long sea history could provide
a hundred stories finer than that of the cruiser 'Potemkin', the
wayward representative of a fleet chiefly famous for its inglorious
engagement with our trawlers on the Dogger Bank. We have ready

to our hand all the material to outmatch 'Storm over Asia' by a film that should be entitled 'Dawn over Africa'.

The story of our Imperial development is rich in themes not less great than that of the Turkestan–Siberian Railway. The story of the Hudson Bay Company alone would provide a theme which, incidentally, would not be dependent, as is that of 'Turk–Sib', upon an illusory representation of successful achievement. In the countryside and the country life, which have inspired so noble a body of English poetry and painting, we have themes not less beautiful than that of 'Earth', and we are under no necessity, as was Dovjenko, to disguise them under the appearance of political propaganda.

We are told that England cannot make films of this quality because she can find no basic market at home for them. I doubt the ultimate validity of that contention, though I have a keen sympathy with exhibitors who are criticized for not including in their programmes the often quite amateurish productions which are flung at their heads in the name of better and healthier films. There are signs already of a public demand for a new type of entertainment, in the development both of special theatres devoted to news items and of non-theatrical performances in schools and elsewhere. I suspect that there is a great potential audience, in England and overseas, which could in time be led to add their patronage to the picture houses, if they could count upon finding, at least in some of them, other matter than the sex and crime material of which two-thirds of our present programmes are composed. Such films need not be costly to make. They require little of the elaborate and artificial facilities of the studio, and do not demand the engagement of popular 'stars'. Fundamentally they take and dramatize scenes of ordinary life. Our weakness is that at present we have no one working in this genre, exploring its possibilities and patiently learning its technique. No one, that is, unless I be permitted to follow the admirable critic of the *Observer* in believing that we have in England just one small centre devoted to the fulfilment of this patent need.

7

I turn from the acknowledged medium of international communication, which is Cinema, to a medium which is less often thought of as an instrument of national expression, and still less often as the raw material of an art.

The number of international exhibitions has increased so greatly since the War that it has been found necessary to limit them by international agreement. Here, as in the case of Cinema, I engage in no criticism; for here, too, I appreciate that attempted action, even if unsuccessful, is better than inactive criticism. I will derive my moral from a personal experience.

In December, 1929, I spent the inside of a week in Barcelona, and devoted the whole of my stay to a careful study of the great Exhibition which was then occupying a hillside above the city. I visited in turn the displays which different nations had staged. Of the British display I need say no more than that it was not officially organized, and should have a certain credit as a forlorn hope on the part of private individuals in a field unsuited to individual enterprise. I admired the Hungarian pavilion, with its suggestion of cathedral construction, its great height, its simple lines and a certain beauty in its interior colour and lighting. I paid a passing compliment to the shapely and unpretentious Danish pavilion. I admired the well-designed array of circular steel and glass cases in which Switzerland displayed her clocks and watches. But, to my eye at least, Germany alone demonstrated at Barcelona that there was an art of exhibition display, and that the nation, which realized this fact and acted upon it, secured immense gains without a penny of additional expenditure.

The German national pavilion, designed by Mies van der Rohe, was the outstanding feature of the exhibition. This strange building, covering no considerable space merged insensibly with its immediate surroundings, and yet was in sharp contrast with all the pavilions about it. It is probably impossible to describe it in terms that would bring it before the mind's eye of an Englishman who had not seen it. In it was a gesture rather than a building, deriving its effects from that sense of efficient simplicity more commonly associated with an up-to-date hospital or a modern power house. Its design was throughout rectangular. Its floors and its roof were of white stone. Some of its walls were also of white stone; others of green marble. Along one side of it was a wall that was also a window – a sheet of black glass through which in daylight one might look out without being inspected from outside. It contained a small stone pool, in which was set a single statue. This pool led out to a larger bathing pool, at the extreme end of which a cluster of water plants had been permitted. Here and there about the pavilion a few steel chairs were grouped about a steel table. Otherwise its only decorations were the black-lettered word 'Alemania' upon its front, and the four German flags at the borders of its domain. A visitor remarked that a coloured handkerchief, dropped on its white floor, would have been hastily swept up as an insult to its austerity. One felt in this pavilion the expression of a lonely, powerful and forward-looking spirit – a gesture, incomplete in itself, which was fulfilled in the displays of German industry elsewhere in the Exhibition.

For the same theme was to be followed through fourteen other displays which, in nine different pavilions of the Exhibition, enforced a sense of the industrial power of modern Germany. In some of these the task of the exhibitor had been made difficult by the triviality of the material for the display of which he had been called upon to provide. Certain features, however, were common to them all. The lowered roof of white canvas, the white walls, the single red-lettered inscription 'Alemania', the black-lettered titles of the exhibitors, the steel or aluminum rails which protected or supported the exhibits, the steel tables and chairs, the spaciousness and the absence of irrelevant detail – all these repeated features were common to the fourteen subsidiary German displays. You passed through exhibits of books and typewriters and office furniture, of electrical equipment and toys, till you came to the display of German machinery, black and dustless, displayed in a horizontal and rectangular order which successfully conveyed the sense of a powerful present and a yet more powerful future.

So spoke at Barcelona the industrial ambition of Germany; and the voice was clearly the voice of one who had summoned the arts of architecture and painting and sculpture, of stage design and skilled lighting and fine lettering to the unified projection of a nation's excellence. I sailed from Barcelona at sunset, and looked back upon the city from the Mediterranean. The lights and coloured fountains of her great Exhibition gleamed upon the hills, and I watched them from the deck till the Spanish coast was swallowed up in darkness. Then, divesting myself in imagination of my British nationality, I searched my mind to discover what practical impression my visit to the Exhibition had left with me. I found there the single clear conviction that Germany was the industrial leader of Europe and that, if I wanted to buy efficient, modern manufactured goods, I should look to Germany for them.

8

And now, before we consider what England must do to master and employ the art of national projection, let us reflect for a moment upon the spirit in which she must approach and practise it.

She must in the first place project upon the screen of world opinion such a picture of herself as will create a belief in her ability to serve the world under the new order as she has served it under the old. This role implies neither self-advertisement, as distinct from honest self-expression, nor self-righteousness as distinct from honest confidence.

In her great days of world exploration her pioneers were inspired by a belief that they were called to a religious mission. We cannot approach this new task with the conviction of being a chosen people, elected to lighten the Gentiles. John Davis, pleading in 1595 for English navigation and discovery, could write: 'There is no doubt but that we of England are this saved people, by the eternal and in fallible presence of the Lord predestined to be sent unto these Gentiles in the sea, to those Isles and famous kingdoms, there to preach the peace of the Lord: for are not we only set upon Mount Zion to give light to all the rest of the world?' And Milton himself, fifty years later, could still write of the Almighty, when decreeing to begin some great and new period: 'What does He then but reveal Himself to His servants, and as His manner is, first to His Englishmen?'

There is no place for any such proselytizing spirit in the world of to-day. On the contrary, we must begin by studying the minds – the greatly differing minds – of those to whom our projection is addressed. The peoples of the world are no longer in the resigned mood of the Picts beyond the Roman pale:

> '*Rome never looks where she treads,*
> *Always her heavy hooves fall,*
> *On our stomachs, our hearts or our heads.*'

We must bring to our task a sensitive insight and a keen sympathy, and we must support them by the most carefully acquired knowledge of the different ways and tastes and needs of other people. For different we shall certainly find them. There will be those who are interested in seeing England as an up-to-date and efficient industrial workshop. There will be others to whom she will appeal as a homely country of small fields and farms and familiar breeds of cattle. We must seek to show our different audiences such a picture of England as will win their interest and excite, if possible, their admiration, as will make them desire to know more of England and perhaps to visit her, and certain, if they should do so, of finding themselves at home with England in one at least of her many aspects. We shall find two different misconceptions of England which we must address ourselves to combat. The picture of an England 'down and out' has been widespread during the last few years; while in the younger countries, in particular, England is apt to be regarded, if not as a Shylock and if not as a 'superior person', at any rate as an absentee landlord, with all the indifference attributed to that class.

We must adopt and retain a complete willingness to learn from the successful methods of other nations. We must not delude ourselves into supposing that other peoples wish to copy us, least of all that they want to copy our past history. Nothing, for example, is more clear than that the Dominions want to work out each its own distinctive manner of living, and in each case a very different manner of living from our own. That, however, does not mean that England has no contribution to offer them, or that in their essentially individual tasks they would seek contributions more readily from any other country. The key to success will be a realization that we must represent our point of view and our achievements truthfully to the world and must interest the world in them.

Lastly we must let no reflection of the reproach which once attached to advertising make us ashamed of devoting ourselves with heart and mind to England's projection. We are faced here with a national need and a national responsibility. It is imperative that our national qualities should not remain, in this new sense, 'unexercised and unbreathed', stealing out of a race to which all the world is to-day is compelled. Reticence and modesty are still attractive. The English mode of understatement may be effective, and silence may sometimes even now be golden. It would be none the less intolerable if, when the time had come for speaking, the speech of England should be found of lead.

9

In the cause of good international understanding, within the Empire and without it; for the sake of our export trade; in the interests of our tourist traffic; above all, perhaps, in the discharge of our great responsibilities to the other countries of the Commonwealth of British peoples, we must master the art of national projection and must set ourselves to throw a fitting presentation of England upon the world's screen. The English people must be seen for what it is – a great nation still anxious to serve the world and to secure the world's peace. English industry must be seen for what it is and for what it is determined to be. We must spread through out the world a sense of English industrial quality and ambition, an impression of English adaptability and modernity no less than of English craftsmanship and thoroughness and finish. English science must be known for what it is and for what it might be – an instrument of profound importance to the health and happiness of remote millions of people. England herself must be seen for what she is – still one of the most beautiful, historic and friendly of the world's countrysides.

What then is needed to secure this projection? The fashionable answer leaps out in a demand for the better co-ordination of existing agencies. I dread that familiar prescription, which is forever upon the lips of a generation thinking always in terms of mechanical engineering and never of biology or of art. Too often it has led to the re-enlistment, under a new regimental title, of a familiar stage army of eminent persons, whose time and energies are sorely needed elsewhere. Under that stress and that interference our departments and institutions and industries have already winced too often.

Let us enlist, indeed, the help of every agency that can promote our purpose: but let us also recognize that our first need is for a fresh point of view and a novel quality, that are not to be won by the mere combination of existing agencies. Here too the analogy of sixteenth century discovery is again pertinent. The first cry of those who studied the opportunities of that time was for a school of navigation. In 1410 Prince Henry the Navigator established, as the foundation stone of his policy of exploration, a Naval College at Lisbon. Its establishment led directly to the succession of discoveries which gave Portugal her mastery in the new world. Some fifty years later Columbus, the Genoese, was drawn to Lisbon, which had by then become the world's centre for the study of navigation, and there by patient study fitted himself for the great voyage which only the mischance of pirates prevented from being undertaken in the name of England. When Hakluyt a century afterwards published his plea for the partici-pation of England in world discovery, his first demand was for the better study of navigation. The main need he found to be for 'the increase of knowledge in the arts of navigation and breading of skilfulnesse in the sea men'. By that time he could point to the School of Navigation that had grown up in Seville, and throughout his life he continued to impress upon his countrymen the need for a like development in England. We need, I suggest, to create, in the borderland which lies between Government and private enterprise, a school of national projection. I see the members of this school as a small group, selected less on account of their existing affiliations than by reason of their diverse personal qualifies. It must be their business to study professionally the art of national projection, and to draw for the materials of that art upon all the resources of English life. They must have something of the sense of responsibility, the prestige and the opportunities of Government, and entry to the fields of Government activity; but they must be more free to make experiments and, like all experimenters, to make mistakes, than the ordinary Government Department dares to be. They must enter fully into the ordinary life of the country, avoiding that instinct of withdrawal which has made the Government services of the world the legitimate successors of the monastic orders. On the other hand they must not be subjected to the demand for immediate, tangible results which dogs the undertakings of commercial enterprise. Once again the pages of Hakluyt are suggestive. The story of the great voyages is full of instances in which the demand for gold perverted and hampered the course of discovery. Frobisher, seeking the North West Passage, suffered from the demand of his backers in England for gold ore. Raleigh's disappointing expedition to the Orinoco sprang from his desire to secure a new source of gold. The letters of Columbus himself are full of apologies to the Spanish Court for his delay in providing gold shipments.

I conceive our school of national projection as having several main activities. It must be on the watch for material which can be turned to the advantage of England overseas. Anyone, who in imagination has placed himself even for a short time in that watch tower, knows what a wealth of such material is at present running unheeded to waste. It must watch for, and sometimes it must create, opportunities for using that material, concentrating upon selected screens at favourable moments all the forces of presentation at its disposal. It must be in close touch with all those channels, at home and abroad, through which the material, which it desires to see used, can be projected. It must work, for example, in friendly contact with the press and the news agencies, with a B.B.C. enabled to speak to all our fellow subjects who desire sometimes to listen to England, with the Rugby wireless station, speaking daily to our ships at sea, with the makers of films and of news-reels, with the painters of posters, with all those artists whose gifts, as we have seen, should be enlisted for the planning and designing of exhibitions. To all these agencies it must be able to distribute its material and sometimes to suggest to them appropriate modes for its treatment. It may seek to inspire, but must never attempt to regulate them. It must study new methods of projection, and new means of using and combining old methods; and in certain fields it must experiment until it has devised and mastered the special technique required.

But here I check my bridle. I have sometimes amused myself in moments of speculation by drawing up a scheme for such a school, with its centre for press liaison, its cinema workshop, its bureau of exhibition designs and the like. Pictures of this sort are easy to draw. They can be made to look most impressive on paper, and to suggest a remarkable grasp and prescience on the part of their author. But I shall here attempt no such prospectus. I am convinced, and not without experience, that, when new work has to be under taken in a novel field, the only sensible prescription is to pick out the best team that can be found, to put them to grips with their problem, and to leave them, free of undue pressure or interference, to follow, like Socrates, whithersoever it leads, the argument in which their own intimate handling of the material will quickly engage them.

10

When Hakluyt pleaded for the establishment of a lectureship in navigation, he estimated the cost at £40 a year. Drake offered him half that income, but he never got the rest. A school of national projection should be at the outset neither an ambitious nor a costly foundation; but it will need more than the sum which Hakluyt failed to raise. Our new art is more complicated than the art of navigation, and its components more diverse. Where are the necessary resources to be found?

The essential end is to gather together a small band of picked workers whose main interest shall be devoted to the study and practice of a new national art. Great art has always served the needs of its time, and England needs – most urgently needs – to master the art of national projection. There is no doubt, given the bare opportunity, that the necessary artists can be found to give her that mastery. The artistic instinct finds expression already in many other less commonly recognized ways than in the application of paint to canvas, of words to paper or stones to a building: and it likes to work in response to a definite demand and under definite limitations, provided only that the manner of the solution of the problem presented to it be left uncontrolled.

Here is an enterprise which, in spite of its national importance, in spite of the immense 'invisible export' which it might well create, is not suitable for complete Government maintenance and control. Still less can it be entrusted to private commercial enterprise. The project is such that, once the necessary methods have been worked out, the Government and private interests can very happily and very profitably combine for its advancement. But there is a pioneer stage to be got over.

In the great days of Athens it was the pride of her wealthiest citizens to undertake 'liturgies' on her behalf. Thus one man would present her with a battleship at his own charges and another bear the cost of the staging of a drama before his fellow citizens. Even the earliest English voyages of discovery were partly maintained by private munificence. Michael Lock, a London merchant with a taste for science, supported the voyage which led to the discovery of Cumberland's Island; and John Davis, in his attempt to find the North West Passage, had similar backing. There have always been in England those who regarded wealth as a trust and desired to devote some part of their fortunes to public purposes. In England, too, there have always been patrons who delighted in the encouragement of art. Private art has become a luxury scarcely to be afforded and remote from our manner of living. Already the public patron is yearly superseding the private in the arts of architecture and decoration. The call is for the encouragement of a national rather than a private art, and the patron who gave that encouragement would know that he was not merely satisfying a noble taste but was fulfilling one of the great needs of his country.

What a chance is here for an endowment such as a friend of England has created in the Pilgrim Trust. The appeal after all is not for the support of a mere Cloud Cuckoo Land of the imagination. Anyone who has tried to conceive of the need as a whole could point out creative units already in existence which, given a little more support, could be enabled to become the growing points of just such an artistic development as England needs. Anyone, who has even begun to study the opportunities of the art, could jot down a list of services – some ambitious and some quite modest, but all such as a patron might support with great personal interest to himself. Would it not be a splendid service to provide in a chosen foreign market an artistically conceived exhibition setting for a display for selected English manufactures? I find the answer in my own experience of 1929 at Barcelona. Have we any film record of the English countryside or of the true quality of British industry to show overseas? Only those who have had to deal with requests for such films know how despairing is the search for them. Are there no distinguished scientists whose visits to international conferences abroad might be facilitated? Too often England is inadequately represented at such conferences, or neglects to provide the simple organization which her distinguished delegations need. Are there no experiments to be made in the methods of educating Indian villages or African communities in the practices of hygiene and agriculture? Mr. Brayne's work at Gurgaon in the Punjab and the film displays given by Professor Huxley to a few African schools in 1930 provide a suggestive answer. Are there no research workers abroad anxious to study for a time at our English stations? The very pick of the young scientists of the Empire would come over, if the means – the very modest means – could be found. Do the distant schools of Canada and New Zealand and Africa ask for posters of England to decorate their walls? Are there no oversea countries in need of English books? Are there no remote outposts where English periodicals would be welcomed?

No one whose work has placed him in a listening post for the needs of the countries of the Empire or of foreign countries but could multiply these questions and compile without premeditation a list of needs, such as these, which cry out to be fulfilled by a patron, whether of wealth or of modest means. No would-be patron need be at a loss to know how to direct his 'liturgy'. For the supply of every one of the needs which I have indicated, there exist already agencies, if still working too often in isolation, if in some cases only small growing points of promise, capable of giving successful effect to his intentions.

II

I have tried to show how urgent is the need for England to address herself to the study of the art of national projection. I have tried, too, to show what opportunities there are for public-spirited

Englishmen to come forward as patrons of this new art. But it is not only those who can afford to perform public 'liturgies' for their country who must be enrolled in this service. The projection of England will be fruitless unless there be in England material worthy to be projected. It is no good dramatizing your industry to the world unless your industry is worth dramatizing. It is useless to study the means whereby the results of agricultural research can be conveyed to the farmer unless your scientific research is of a quality that will justify the projection of its results.

In Cranford we began; to Cranford let us return. The effective projection of England depends not merely upon outstanding achievements but in the last resort upon the faithful performance of their daily tasks by Englishmen and Englishwomen. At the back of your projection must lie national excellencies which in large measure, like poetry, will be overheard rather than heard. So only can the tradition of an English excellence be created. But, apart from this universal and indirect opportunity for service, most of us, in one way or another, at one time or another, have means of projecting a fragment of England upon a corner of the world's screen – adding thereby a trifle to England's invisible exports and winning for her if it be but a mite of the world's good opinion. Every customs official or porter, who handles the luggage of a visitor at the susceptible moment of his arrival, creates a lasting impression of his country. Everyone who helps a visitor by courteous directions in the street, every shopman who serves him at the counter, every hotel keeper who entertains him, every telephone girl who handles his calls, every nurse who attends him in sickness, is doing something to project the good name of England beyond the seas. Services such as these, undertaken in the course of the day's work, have indeed a special virtue. Not once or twice only in recent years have they been recognized publicly by departing guests. Everyone who by regular and vivid correspondence keeps up in the minds of relations and friends overseas a lively sense of England, everyone who bears himself worthily in his own travels abroad, is unconsciously serving his country. So too everyone who entertains visitors from abroad in his home. For England viewed from homely windows is a different place from England seen from a solitary lodging or the yet greater solitude of a crowded pavement. Every wisely directed movement for the exchange of visitors between England and other countries, every gift or legacy that enables the selected students of other countries to spend a time in our Universities and research centres, serves the cause. Every action that increases or preserves the beauty of England deserves well of it.

In wartime many English people found an assuaging contentment in the sense that they were working for their country and not for themselves alone. The projection of England affords something of the same opportunity of service and happiness to every English man and woman. 'So that hereby', as John Davis wrote 350 years ago, 'the spiritual benefit arising from this discovery is most apparent; for which, if there were no other cause, we are all bound to labour with purse and mind, for the discovery of this notable passage.'

Note

1 'Britain and World Trade' by A. Loveday

Select bibliography

Archival Sources and private papers

BBC Archive, Caversham, Reading
Files relating to creation of Public Relations department
Files relating to BBC Overseas Service
Files relating to the Festival of Britain
*Files relating to Sir William Crawford, John Grierson, Frank Pick,
    Patrick Ryan and Sir Stephen Tallents*

British Library, St Pancras
Sydney Cockerell letters

British Telecom Archive, Holborn
Files relating to Sir Stephen Tallents
Files relating to Telephone Week
Files relating to the Jubilee Kiosk

Churchill College, University of Cambridge, Cambridge
Leo Amery papers
Sir Winston Churchill papers

The Dessain family, Banbury, Oxon
Sir Stephen Tallents private papers
Interview with Miranda Pemberton-Pigott (née Tallents), 11
    February 2007

History of Advertising Trust, Ravingham, Norfolk
Files relating to the formation of the Institute of Public Relations
The Selfridge archive

Institute of Commonwealth Studies, London
Sir Stephen Tallents papers

King's College, University of Cambridge, Cambridge
Charleston papers
John Maynard Keynes papers

London School of Economics, London
Sir William Beveridge papers
E. H. Lloyd papers
The Markham papers
PEP archive

London Transport Museum, Covent Garden
Frank Pick papers

Modern Records Centre, University of Warwick
FBI papers relating to Empire and public relations
TUC papers relating to the EMB, film and public relations

National Archive, Kew
Cabinet papers
Colonial Office
Home Office
Ministry of Agriculture and Fisheries
Ministry of Health
Ministry of Information
Ministry of Town and Country Planning

Postal Archive, Farringdon
Files relating to the creation of the Public Relations department
Files relating to the GPO Film Unit
Files relating to John Grierson and Stephen Tallents

RIBA Library, London
Files relating to Stephen Tallents and Edward Carter

Syracuse University, New York, United States of America
*Rudyard Kipling correspondence with Sir Stephen Tallents (copies of
    correspondence sent to the UK)*

Toynbee Hall, Whitechapel
The Toynbee Record 1906–1908

University of Stirling, Stirling, Scotland
John Grierson archive

Victoria and Albert Museum Archive, South Kensington
Sir Herbert Baker papers
Sir John Summerson papers
Posters, photographs and shop frontage of the Empire Marketing Board

Primary sources

Journals and periodicals
Advertising World
The Architectural Review
Building: A Journal for Architects, Builders and Specialists
Close-Up
Country Life
The Journal of the Institute of Public Relations
The Listener
The Manchester Guardian
The New Statesman and Nation
The Post Office Magazine
Public Administration
Punch
The Journal of the Royal Institute of British Architects
The Journal of the Royal Society of Arts
The Times
The Times Literary Supplement
The Journal of the Town Planning Institute
TREND: Design of Everyday Things

Published articles

'25th Anniversary of the IPR', *Public Relations*, April 1973, p. 55
'Speaking up for PR', *Public Relations*, May 1973, p. 74
Attlee, C. R., 'Post Office Reform', *New Statesman and Nation*, Vol. II, No. 37, 7 November 1931, pp. 565–566
Baldwin, S., 'Letter from Stanley Baldwin', *Advertising World*, No. 3, January 1927, p. 347
Belloc, P., 'What Use Is All This Impressionist Stuff?', *Advertising World*, Vol. 52, No. 6, May 1927, pp. 21–22
Blennerhassett, L. C., 'Cutting out the Guesswork in Overseas Marketing', *Advertising World*, No. 3, January 1927, pp. 417–422

Boggon, G., '"Eat More Fruit" Campaign', *Advertising World*, No. X, July 1926, pp. 242–243

Bullett, G. W., 'The Dancer and Other Tales', *Times Literary Supplement*, 21 September 1922, p. 598

Cable, B., 'Advertise British Goods', *Advertising World*, No. 8, June 1926, p. 206

Casey, R. D., 'The National Publicity Bureau and British Party Propaganda', *Public Opinion Quarterly*, Vol. 3, No. 4, 1939, pp. 623–634

Child, H., 'Home from the War', *Times Literary Supplement*, 8 January 1918, p. 358

Clark, W., 'Government and the Promotion of Trade', *Public Administration*, Vol. 1, No. 1, 1923, pp. 22–34

Cooke, L., 'The Voice of the Brand: the Value of the Mark of Identity in Overseas Trade', *Advertising World*, No. 12, October 1927, pp. 811–814

Finer, H., 'Officials and the Public', *Public Administration*, Vol. IX, No. 1, January 1931, pp. 22–36

Floud, F., 'The Sphere of the Specialist', *Public Administration*, Vol. 1, No. 2, 1923, pp. 117–126

Forester, M., 'The Coming Revolution in Films', *The Public Opinion Quarterly*, Vol.3, No. 3, July 1939, pp. 502–506

Grierson, J., 'Making a Film of the Actual', *Close-Up*, Vol. V, No. 5, November 1929, pp. 402–409

Grierson, J., 'Films in the Public Service', *Public Administration*, Vol. XIV, No. 4, October 1936, pp. 366–372

Huxley, A., 'Notes on the Way', *Time and Tide*, 7 May 1932, pp. 514–516

Huxley, A., 'Ballyhoo for Nations', *Nash's Pall Mall Magazine*, Vol. XCV, July 1935, pp. 18–21

Huxley, J., 'The State and the Consumer', *Public Administration*, Vol. XIV, No. 3, July 1936, pp. 247–255

Lang, R. T., 'Empire Advertising', *Advertising World*, Vol. XLIX, No. 4, February 1926, pp. 480–484

Leverhulme, Viscount, 'The Real Remedy for Trade Depression', *Advertising World*, Vol. XLIX, No. 1, October 1925, pp. 30–32

Morison, E., 'Why Britain Is Losing Its Dominion Markets', *Advertising World*, Vol. 50, No. 7, October 1926, pp. 534–538

Nash, P., 'Going Modern and Being British', *The Weekend Review*, 12 March 1933, pp. 322–323

Pick, F., 'Art in Modern Life', *The Nineteenth Century and After*, Vol. XCI, No. 540, February 1922, pp. 256–264

Ryan, A. P., 'Intelligence and Public Relations', *Public Administration*, Vol. XIV, No. 1, January 1936, pp. 59–65

Samuel, A. M., 'Goods Do Not Sell Themselves', *Advertising World*, No. 3, January 1927, pp. 350–351

Sharp, W. D., 'Correspondence with the Public', *Public Administration*, Vol. XIV, No. 3, July 1936, pp. 41–48

Stewart, A. C., 'Post Office Publicity and Green Papers', *Public Administration*, Vol. XIV, No. 3, July 1936, p. 70

Tallents, S., 'England on the Screen: A Plea for a New Art, National Projection', *The Times*, 16 April 1932, p. 13

Tallents, S., 'The Progress of Empire Research', *Discovery*, July 1932, pp. 207–211

Tallents, S., 'Salesmanship in the Public Service: Scope and Technique', *Public Administration*, Vol. XI, No. 3, July 1933, pp. 259–266

Tallents, S., 'Introduction', *TREND: Design of Everyday Things*, Vol. 1, No. 1, Spring 1936, p. 2

Tallents, S., 'What's Right with the BBC', *The Spectator*, 24 March 1939, pp. 478–479

Tallents, S., 'The Documentary Film', *The Journal of the Royal Society of Arts*, Vol. XCV, No. 4733, 20 December 1946, pp. 68–85

Tallents, S., 'Review', *Public Administration*, Vol. 27, No. 3, Autumn 1949, p. 218

Tallents, S., 'Who Goes There?', *The Journal of the Institute of Public Relations*, Vol. 5, No. 2, January 1953, pp. 3–5

Tallents, S., 'Advertising and Public Relations To-day', *The Journal of the Royal Society of Arts*, Vol. CIV, No. 4967, 23 December 1955, pp. 94–107

Tallents, S., 'The Birth of the British Documentary (Part I)', *Journal of the University Film Association*, Vol. 20, No. 1, 1968, pp. 14–21

Tallents, S., 'The Birth of the British Documentary (Part II)', *The Journal of the University Film Association*, Vol. 20, No. 2, 1968, pp. 27–32

Whitehead, H., 'Salesmanship in the Public Service', *Public Administration*, Vol. XI, No. 3, July 1933, pp. 267–276

Wood, S. H., 'Intelligence and Public Service', *Public Administration*, Vol. XIV, No. 1, January 1936, pp. 41–48

Wright, B., 'The Cinema', *The Spectator*, Vol. 177, No. 6172, 11 October 1946, p. 364

Published books

Abrams, M. (ed.) *The Home Market* (London, 1939)

Aitken, I. (ed.) *The Documentary Film Movement: An Anthology* (Edinburgh, 1998)

Alexander, S., *Art and the Material* (Manchester, 1925)

Amery, L. S., *Empire and Prosperity* (London, 1929)

Amery, L. S., *The Forward View* (London, 1935)

Amery, L. S., *My Political Life*, 3 Vols (London, 1953 & 1955)

Attlee, C., *As It Happened* (London, 1954)

Balcon, M., *Michael Balcon Presents ... A Lifetime of Ealing* (London, 1969)

Beaverbrook, Lord, *Politicians and War*, 2 Vols (London, 1925 & 1928)

Belfrage, C. (ed.) *All Is Grist* (London, 1988)

Bernays, E., *Propaganda* (New York, 1928 and 2005)

Beveridge, W., *John and Irene: An Anthology of Thoughts on Women* (London, 1912)

Beveridge, W., 'The Ministry of Food under Lord Rhondda' in *DA Thomas: Viscount Rhondda as Remembered by His Daughter and Others* (London, 1921), pp. 218–248

Beveridge, W., *British Food Control* (London, 1928)

Beveridge, W., *Empire Free Trade: A Reply to Lord Beaverbrook* (London, 1931)

Black, S., *Practical Public Relations* (London, 1962)

Black, S., *Public Relations* (London, 1992)

Bowman, P., and Ellis, N. (eds) *The Handbook of Public Relations* (London, 1963)

Boyd Orr, J., *Food, Health and Income* (London, 1936)

Bradshaw, D. (ed.) *The Hidden Huxley* (London, 1994)

Brice, M., *The King's Dogs: The Sporting Dogs of His Majesty King George V* (London, 1935)

Broadley, H., and Crawford, W., *The People's Food* (London, 1938)

Bruce Lockhart, R. H., *Comes the Reckoning* (London, 1947)

Bruntz, G. G., *Allied Propaganda and the Collapse of the German Empire in 1918* (London, 1938)

Buchanan, A., *Films; The Way of the Cinema* (London, 1932)

Calder-Marshall, A., *The Changing Scene* (London, 1937)

Calloway, S. (ed.) *The Golden Age of Shopping, 1910–1940: A Miscellany of Items from Harrods, Gamages and Army & Navy Stores* (London, 1996)

Carter, E., *The Future of London* (London, 1962)

Carter, E., and Goldfinger, E., *The County of London Plan* (London, 1945)

Clark, K., *The Other Half: A Self Portrait* (London, 1977)

Coatman, J., *Magna Britannia* (London, 1936)

Coatman, J., *The British Family of Nations* (London, 1950)

The Commission on Cultural and Educational Film, *The Film in National Life* (London, 1932)

Constantine, S. (ed.) *Buy and Build: The Advertising Posters of the EMB* (London, 1986)

Cooke, A. (ed.) *Garbo and the Night Watchmen: A Selection from the Writings of British and American Film Critics* (London, 1937)

Cooper, D., *Old Men Forget: The Autobiography of Duff Cooper* (London, 1953)

Council of Industrial Design (ed.) *Design in the Festival* (London, 1951)

Crick, B. (ed.) *George Orwell: Essays* (London, 2000)

Crutchley, B., *Ernest Tristram Crutchley: A Memoir* (Cambridge, 1941)

Crutchley, E. T., *GPO* (Cambridge, 1938)

Cutlip, S., and Center, S., *Effective Public Relations* (New York, 1952)

Daily Mail Ideal Home Exhibition Catalogue 1927 (London, 1927)

Davey, C. (ed.) *Footnotes to the Film* (London, 1937)

Davidson, J. C. C., *Memoirs of a Conservative* (London, 1969)

Debenham, E., *A National Milk Marketing Scheme for Great Britain* (London, 1932)

Delmer, S., *Trail Sinister* (London, 1961)

Delmer, S., *Black Boomerang* (London, 1962)

Donald, J., Freidberg, A., and Marcus, L. (eds) *Close-Up 1927–1933: Cinema and Modernism* (London, 1998)

Donaldson, F., *Four Years Harvest* (London, 1945)

Eckersley, R., *The BBC and All That* (London, 1946)

Eliot, T. S., Preface, *The Dark Side of the Moon* (London, 1946)

Elliott, J., and Esau, M., *On and Off the Rails* (London, 1982)

Field, M., and Smith, P., *Secrets of Nature* (London, 1934)

Fincham, H. W., *The Order of the Hospital of St John of Jerusalem and Its Grand Priory of England* (London, 1933)

George, L., *How to Tackle Unemployment: The Liberal Plans as Laid before the Government and the Nation* (London, 1930)

George, W. H., *The Cinema in School* (London, 1935)

Gorham, M., *Sound and Fury* (London, 1948)

Greene, G., *Mornings in the Dark* (London, 1995)

Hardy, F. (ed.) *Grierson on Documentary* (London, 1946)

Hargrave, J., *Propaganda the Mightiest Weapon of All Words Win Wars* (London, 1940)

The Harrods Empire Exhibition (London, 1928)

Hess, A., *The Indianapolis Records* (London, 1949)

Hess, A., *Wheels around the World* (London, 1951)

Hess, A., *Crazy Journey* (London, 1953)

Hitler, A., trans. R. Manheim, *Mein Kampf* (London, 1992)

Huxley, A., *Brave New World* (London, 1932; 2007)

Huxley, G., *Both Hands: An Autobiography* (London, 1970)

Huxley, J., *Scientific Research and Social Needs* (London, 1934)

Jackson, P., *A Retake Please! From Night Mail to Western Approaches* (Liverpool, 1999)

Jeffrey, K. (ed.) *War and Reform: British Politics during the Second World War* (Manchester, 1994)

Jefkins, F., *Public Relations in World Marketing* (London, 1966)

Kipling, R., *The Irish Guards in the Great War: The First Battalion* (London, 1923)

Kirkpatrick, I., *The Inner Circle: The Memoirs of Ivone Kirkpatrick* (London, 1959)

Klingender, J. D., and Legg, S., *Money Behind the Screen* (London, 1937)

Labour Party, *Let Us Face the Future* (London, 1945)

Lasswell, H., *Propaganda Technique in the World War* (New York, 1927)

Lippmann, W., *Public Opinion* (London, 1998)

Lloyd, H., *Teach Yourself Public Relations* (London, 1963)

Macleod, J., *A Job at the BBC: Some Personal Reminiscences* (Glasgow, 1946)

Marchant, J., *The Cinema in Education* (London, 1925)

Merhout, C., Stross, B., Sternberk, E., Lawther, W.; foreword by P. Abercrombie, *Lidice* (London, 1945)

Montagu, I., *With Eisenstein in Hollywood: A Chapter of Autobiography* (Berlin, 1968)

Morgan, H. E., *The Dignity of Business. Thoughts & Theories on Business & Training for Business* (London, 1914)

Morgan, H. E., and Butcher, E. H., *The Retailers' Compendium: A Complete and Practical Guide to Successful Shopkeeping Enterprise* (London, 1924)

Neal, L. E., *Retailing and the Public* (London, 1932)

Nicolson, H., *Diaries and Letters 1939–1945* (London, 1966)

Percy, E., *Some Memories* (London, 1958)

Pevsner, N., *Pioneers of Modern Design: From William Morris to Walter Gropius* (London, 1936)

Pick, F., *Paths to Peace: Two Essays in Aims and Methods* (London, 1941)

Pimlott, J. A. R., *Public Relations and American Democracy* (New York & London, 1951)

Pootle, M. (ed.) *Champion Redoubtable: The Diaries and Letters of Violet Bonham Carter 1914–45* (London, 1998)

Price, H., and Lambert, R. S., *The Haunting of Cashen's Gap: A Modern 'Miracle' Investigated* (London, 1936)

Priestley, J. B., *English Journey* (New York & London, 1934)

Priestley, J. B., *Postscripts* (London, 1940)

Rasmussen, S. E., *London the Unique City* (London, 1935)

Reith, J. C. W., *Into the Wind* (London, 1949)

Robinow, R., *Peter and the Post Office* (London, 1934)

Robinson, W. H., *Railway Ribaldry* (London, 1935)

Rolo, C., *Radio Goes to War* (London, 1943)

Rotha, P., *The Film till Now* (London, 1930)

Rotha, P., *Documentary Diary: An Informal History of the British Documentary Film, 1928–1939* (London, 1973)

Ruskin, J., *The Two Paths: Being Lectures on Art and Its Application to Decoration and Manufacturing Delivered in 1858/9* (Orpington, 1887)

Saxon-Mills, G. H., *There Is a Tide … The Life and Work of Sir William Crawford, Embodying an Historical Study of Modern British Advertising* (London, 1954)

Shaw, A. W., *Simplification* (Chicago & New York, 1927)

Silvey, R., *Who's Listening: The Story of BBC Audience Research* (London, 1975)

Stapledon, G., *The Land Now and To-morrow* (London, 1935)

Stapledon, G., *The Way of the Land* (London, 1942)

Stuart, C. (ed.) *The Reith Diaries* (London, 1975)

Tallents, S., *The Starry Pool* (London, 1918)

Tallents, S., *The Dancer and Other Tales* (London, 1922)

Tallents, S., *The Projection of England* (London, 1932)

Tallents, S., *Post Office Publicity* (London, 1934)

Tallents, S., *Man and Boy* (London, 1943)

Tallents, S., *Green Thoughts* (London, 1952)

Telephone Development Association, *The Strangle-hold on Our Telephones: A Practicable Remedy* (London, 1930)

Tryon, G. C., *A Short History of Imperial Preference* (London, 1931)

Vail, T. N., *Views on Public Questions: A Collection of Papers and Addresses, 1907–1917* (New York, 1917)

Vail, T. N., *In One Man's Life* (New York, 1921)

Wallas, G., *Human Nature in Politics* (London, 1908)

Watt, H., *Don't Look at the Camera* (London, 1974)

Waugh, E., *Put Out More Flags* (London, 1943)

Wells, H. G., *The Work, Wealth and Happiness of Mankind* (London, 1932)

Wendt, L., *Ceylon* (London, 1950)

Williams, F., *Press, Parliament and People* (London, 1946)

Wolmer, R. C. P., *Post Office Reform: Its Importance and Practicability* (London, 1932)

Wright, B., *The Long View: An International History of Cinema* (London, 1974)

Broadcasts

Huxley, A., 'Science and Civilisation', *BBC Radio*, 13 January 1932

Tallents, S., 'Jubilee Stamps', *BBC Radio*, 23 April 1935

Tallents, S., 'Progress of Sixpenny Telegrams', *BBC Radio*, 13 June 1935

Tallents, S., 'Coronation Broadcasts', *BBC Radio*, 11 May 1937

Tallents, S., 'What Every Listener Knows', *BBC Radio*, 2 January 1938

Tallents, S., 'In England Now – The Work of the BBC Overseas Service', *BBC Radio*, 7 May 1940

Tallents, S., 'Letters from Abroad', *BBC Radio*, 11 August 1940

Leslie, S. C., 'Town and Country Planning', *BBC Radio Pacific Service*, 14 December 1945

Your Questions Answered, 'Town Planning in Middlesbrough', *BBC Radio*, 14 December 1945

Tallents, S., 'The Factual Film', *BBC Radio*, 5 February 1947

Tallents, S., 'A Garden of Historic Plants', *BBC Radio*, 10 July 1948

Tallents, S., 'In Britain Now', *BBC Radio*, 10 September 1948

Abrams, M., 'Market Research (British Achievements)', *BBC Radio*, 8 October 1948

Tallents, S., 'Life in Britain', *BBC Radio*, 7 November 1948

Tallents, S., 'Baltic Adventure', *BBC Radio*, 27 March 1949

Tallents, S., 'In My Library', *BBC Radio*, 12 July 1949

London Dialogues, 'The Power of Ideas and Words', *BBC Radio*, 17 July 1951 (Sir Stephen Tallents in discussion with Lady Violet Bonham Carter)

Tallents, S., 'Stage Screen and Studio Film', *BBC Radio*, 13 September 1954

Tallents, S., 'Freedom and the Broadcaster', *BBC Radio*, 17 December 1951

Tallents, S., 'Enjoying My Retirement', *BBC Radio*, 10 November 1954

Tallents, S., 'What I Believe: Improvements in the World's Communications', *BBC Radio*, 2 September 1956

Secondary sources

Published books

Abramovitz, M., and Eliasberg, V., *The Growth of Public Employment in Great Britain* (Princeton, 1957)

Addison, P., *The Road to 1945* (London, 1975)

Addison, P., *British Historians and the Debate over the 'Post-war Consensus'* (Austin, 1996)

Aitken, I., *Film & Reform: John Grierson and the Documentary Film Movement* (London & New York, 1990)

Aldgate, A., and Richards J., *Britain Can Take It* (London, 1986)

Ansoff, I., *Corporate Strategy* (London, 1986)

Ashmore, H. S., *Unseasonable Truths: The Life of Robert Maynard Hutchins* (Boston & London, 1989)

Ashworth, W., *The Genesis of Modern British Town Planning: A Study in Economic and Social History of the Nineteenth and Twentieth Centuries* (London, 1968)

Baker, M., *Marketing Strategy and Management* (Basingstoke, 1992)

Balfe, J. H. (ed.) *Paying the Piper: Causes and Consequences of Art Patronage* (Chicago, 1993)

Balfour, M., *Propaganda in War 1939–1945* (London, 1979)

Bamford, K., *Distorted Images: British National Identity and Film in the 1920s* (London & New York, 1999)

Banham, M., and Hillier, B. (ed.) *A Tonic to the Nation: The Festival of Britain, 1951* (London, 1976)

Barman, C., *The Man Who Built London Transport: A Biography of Frank Pick* (Newton Abbot, 1979)

Barnett, C., *The Collapse of British Power* (London, 1972)

Barnett, C., *The Audit of War: The Illusion and Reality of Britain as a Great Nation* (London, 1986)

Barnouw, E., *Documentary: A History of the Non-fiction Film* (New York & Oxford, 1974)

Barr, C. (ed.) *All Our Yesterdays: 90 Years of British Cinema* (London, 1986)

Beloff, M., 'The Whitehall Factor: The Role of the Higher Civil Service 1919–1939', in Peele, G., and Cook, C. (eds) *The Politics of Reappraisal 1918–1939* (London, 1975), pp. 209–232

Birchall, J., *Co-op: The People's Business* (Manchester, 1994)

Boardman, P., *The Worlds of Patrick Geddes* (London, 1978)

Boon, T., *Films of Fact: A History of Science in Documentary Films and Television* (London, 2008)

Boyle, A., *Only the Wind Will Listen: Reith of the BBC* (London, 1972)

Boyle, A., *Poor, Dear Brendan* (London, 1974)

Briggs, A., *The History of Broadcasting in the United Kingdom Volume I: The Birth of Broadcasting* (Oxford & New York, 1961: 1995)

Briggs, A., *The History of Broadcasting in the United Kingdom Volume II: The Golden Age of Wireless* (Oxford & New York, 1995: 1965)

Briggs, A., *The History of Broadcasting in the United Kingdom Volume III: The War of Words* (Oxford, 1995: 1970)

Briggs, A., and Macartney, A., *Toynbee Hall: The First Hundred Years* (London, Boston & Henley, 1984)

Brownlow, K., *The War, the West and the Wilderness* (New York, 1979)

Butler, D. (ed.) *Coalitions in British Politics* (London, 1978)

Cain, P. J., and Hopkins, A. G., *British Imperialism 1688–2000* (Harlow, 2001)

Calder, A., *The People's War 1939–1945* (London, 1969: 1990)

Cannadine, D., 'Apocalypse When? British Politicians and British "Decline" in the Twentieth Century', in Clarke, P., and Trebilcock, C. (eds) *Understanding Decline: Perceptions and Realities of British Economic Performance* (Cambridge, 1997), pp. 261–284

Cannadine, D., *In Churchill's Shadow: Confronting the Past in Modern Britain* (Harmondsworth, 2001)

Carey, J., *The Intellectuals and the Masses* (London, 1992)

Cherry, G. (ed.) *Pioneers in British Planning* (London, 1981)

Chisholm, A., and Davie, M., *Beaverbrook: A Life* (London, 1993)

Clarke, P., *Hope and Glory: Britain 1900–1990* (London, 1996)

Clarke, P., and Trebilcock, C. (eds) *Understanding Decline: Perceptions and Realities of British Economic Performance* (Cambridge, 1997)

Clinton, A., *Post Office Workers: A Trade Union and Social History* (London, 1984)

Cockett, R., *Twilight of Truth: Chamberlain, Appeasement and the Manipulation of the Press* (London, 1989)

Conekin, B. E., Most, F., Waters, C. (eds) *Moments of Modernity: Reconstructing Britain, 1945–1964* (London & New York, 1999)

Conekin, B. E., *The Autobiography of a Nation: The 1951 Festival of Britain* (Manchester & New York, 2000)

Constantine, S., *The Making of British Colonial Development Policy, 1914–1940* (London, 1984)

Constantine, S., '"Bringing the Empire Alive": The Empire Marketing Board and Imperial Propaganda, 1926–1933', in Mackenzie, J. M. (ed.) *Imperialism and Popular Culture* (Manchester, 1986), pp. 191–231

Cook, D., *A History of Narrative Film* (New York & London, 1990)

Cooper, A, F., *British Agricultural Policy, 1912–1936: A Study in Conservative Politics* (Manchester and New York, 1989)

Crofts, W., *Coercion or Persuasion? Propaganda in Britain after 1945* (London, 1989)

Cronin, J. E., *The Politics of State Expansion* (London and New York, 1991)

Cross, J. A., *Lord Swinton* (Oxford, 1982)

Crossick, G., and Jaumain, S., 'The World of the Department Store: Distribution, Culture and Social Change', in Crossick, G., and Jaumain, S. (eds) *Cathedrals of Consumption: The European Department Store, 1850–1939* (Aldershot, 1999), pp. 1–45

Crossick, G., and Jaumain, S. (eds) *Cathedrals of Consumption: The European Department Store, 1850–1939* (Aldershot, 1999)

Cruickshank, C., *The Fourth Arm: Psychological Warfare 1938–45* (London, 1977)

Cull, N. J., *Selling War: The British Propaganda Campaign against American 'Neutrality' in World War II* (New York & Oxford, 1995)

Cullingworth, J. B., *Town and Country Planning in Britain* (London, 1988)

Curran, C., and Seaton, J., *Power without Responsibility: The Press and Broadcasting in Britain* (London, 1988)

Dale, T., *Harrods: The Store, the Legend* (London, 1981)

Dale, T., *Harrods: A Palace in Knightsbridge* (London, 1995)

Dangerfield, G., *The Strange Death of Liberal England* (London, 1936)

Daunton, M. J., *Royal Mail: The Post Office since 1840* (London & Dover, NH, 1985)

Davenport-Hines, R. T. (ed.) *Markets and Bagmen: Studies in the History of Marketing and British Industrial Performance 1830–1939* (Aldershot, 1986)

Davies, A., *Public Relations Democracy: Public Relations Politics and the Mass Media in Britain* (Manchester & New York, 2002)

Davies, N., *Flat Earth News: An Award Winning Reporter Exposes Falsehood, Distortion and Propaganda in the Global Media* (London, 2008)

Defries, A., *The Interpreter Geddes: The Man and His Gospel* (London, 1927)

Donoughue, B., and Jones, G. W., *Herbert Morrison: Portrait of a Politician* (London, 2001)

Driberg, T., *Beaverbrook: A Study in Power and Frustration* (London, 1956)

Ellis, J. C., and McLane, B. A., *A New History of Documentary Film* (New York & London, 2005)

Everard, S., *The History of The Gas Light and Coke Co. 1812–1949* (London, 1949)

Ewen, S., *PR! A Social History of Spin* (New York, 1996)

Faber, D., *Speaking for England: Leo, Julian and John Amery, The Tragedy of a Political Family* (London, 2005)

Fishwick, N., *English Football and Society, 1910–1950* (Manchester, 1989)

Flanders, J., *Consuming Passions: Leisure and Pleasure in Victorian Britain* (London, 2006)

Forty, A., *Objects of Desire: Design and Society 1750–1980* (London, 1986)

Friedman, L. (ed.) *British Cinema and Thatcherism: Fires Were Started* (London, 1993)

Gienow-Hecht, J. (ed.) *Decentering America* (New York & Oxford, 2007)

Gorham, M., *Sound and Fury* (London, 1948)

Gourvish, T., and O'Day, A. (eds) *Britain Since 1945* (London, 1991)

Grant, K., Levine, P. and Trentmann, F. (eds) *Beyond Sovereignty Britain, Empire and Transnationalism c.1880–1950* (Basingstoke, 2007)

Grant, M., *Propaganda and the Role of the State in Inter-war Britain* (Oxford, 1994)

Greenhalgh, P., *Ephemeral Vistas: The Expositions Universelles, Great Exhibitions and World's Fairs, 1851–1939* (Manchester, 1988)

Grigg, J., *Lloyd George: War Leader 1916–1918* (London, 2003)

Grunig, J. E., and Hunt, T., *Managing Public Relations* (New York & London, 1984)

Habermas, J., *The Structural Transformation of the Public Sphere: An Inquiry into a Category of Bourgeois Society* (Cambridge, 1989)

Hamilton, D., *The Monkey Gland Affair* (London, 1986)

Hardy, F., *John Grierson: A Documentary Biography* (London, 1979)

Harris, J., *William Beveridge: A Biography* (Oxford, 1977; 1997)

Harrison, B., *The Transformation of British Politics, 1860–1995* (Oxford, 1996)

Harrison, S., *Public Relations: An Introduction* (London, 1995)

Hennessy, P., *Never Again: Britain 1945–51* (London, 1992)

Hennessy, P., *Whitehall* (London, 1989; 2001)

Heward, E., *The Great and the Good: A Life of Lord Radcliffe* (Chichester, 1994)

Higson, A., '"Britain's Outstanding Contribution to Film": The Documentary-realist Tradition', in C. Barr (ed.) *All Our Yesterdays: 90 Years of British Cinema* (London, 1986), pp. 72–97

Hobsbawm, E., and Ranger, T. (eds) *The Invention of Tradition* (Cambridge, 1983)

Hoock, H., *Empires of the Imagination: Politics, War and the Arts in the British World, 1750-1850* (London, 2010)

Jenkins, R., *Mr Attlee: An Interim Biography* (London, 1948)

Jobber, D., *Principles and Practices of Marketing* (New York & London, 2004)

Jones, G., and Tedlow, R. (eds) *Adding Value: Brands, and Marketing in Food and Drink* (London, 1994)

Jones, H., and Kandiah, M., *The Myth of Consensus: New Views on British History, 1945–64* (Basingstoke, 1996)

Kennedy, C., *ICI: The Company that Changed Our Lives* (London, 1986)

Khurana, R., *From Higher Aims to Hired Hands: The Social Transformation of American Business Schools and the Unfulfilled Promise of Management as a Profession* (Princeton, NJ, 2007)

Korder, P., *Marketing Management* (London, 1997)

Iriye, A., *Cultural Internationalism and World Order* (Baltimore & London, 1997)

Lancaster, W., *The Department Store: A Social History* (Leicester, 1995)

LeMahieu, D. L., *A Culture for Democracy: Mass Communication* and the Cultivated Mind in Britain between the Wars (Oxford, 1988)

L'Etang, J., Public Relations in Britain: A History of Professional Practice (London, 2004)

L'Etang, J., Public Relations: Concepts, Practice and Critique (Los Angeles & London, 2008)

Lewis, R., In the Name of God Go!: Leo Amery and the British Empire in the Age of Churchill (London, 1992)

Light, A., Forever England: Feminity, Literature and Conservatism between the Wars (London & New York, 1991)

Lloyd H., and Lloyd, P., Public Relations (London, 1984)

Lloyd, J., What the Media Are Doing to Our Politics (London, 2004)

Low, R., The History of the British Film, 1929–1939: Documentary and Educational Films of the 1930s (London, 1997)

MacCarthy, F., All Things Bright and Beautiful: Design in Britain 1830 to Today (London, 1972)

Mackenzie, J., Propaganda and Empire: The Manipulation of Public Opinion, 1880–1960 (Manchester, 1985)

Mackenzie, J. (ed.) Imperialism and Popular Culture (Manchester, 1986)

McKibbin, R., Classes and Cultures: England 1918–1951 (Oxford, 1998; 2000)

MacLaine, I., Ministry of Morale (London, 1979)

Mallinson, B., Public Lies and Private Truths: An Anatomy of Public Relations (London, 1996)

Mandler, P., The English National Character: The History of an Idea from Edmund Burke to Tony Blair (New Haven and London, 2006)

Mansell, G., Let Truth Be Told: 50 Years of BBC External Broadcasting (London, 1982)

Manser, J., Hugh Casson: A Biography (London, 2000)

Mathews, T. D., Censored: What They Didn't Allow You to See, and Why – The Story of Film Censorship in Britain (London, 1994)

Mazower, M., No Enchanted Palace: The End of Empire and the Ideological Origins of the United Nations (New Jersey, 2009)

Meacham, S., Toynbee Hall and Social Reform 1880–1914: The Search for Community (New Haven & London, 1987)

Middlemass, K., Politics in Industrial Society: The Experience of Britain since 1911 (London, 1979)

Moore-Colyer, R. J., Man's Proper Study: A History of Agricultural Science Education in Aberystwyth, 1878–1978 (Llandysul, 1982)

Moore-Colyer, R. J., *Sir George Stapledon and the Landscape of Britain* (Aberystwyth, 1997)

Moran, M., *The Union of Post Office Workers: A Study in Political Sociology* (London & Basingstoke, 1974)

Morgan, K. and J., *Portrait of a Progressive: The Political Career of Viscount Addison* (Oxford, 1980)

Murphy, B. P., *The Origins and Organisation of British Propaganda in Ireland 1920* (Aubane, 2006)

Murray, N., *Aldous Huxley: An English Intellectual* (London, 2002)

Nicholas, S., *The Echo of War: Home Front Propaganda and the Wartime BBC, 1939–1945* (Manchester & New York, 1996)

Nye, J., *Soft Power: The Means to Success in World Politics* (New York, 2004)

Ogilvy-Webb, M., *The Government Explains: A Study of the Information Services* (London, 1965)

O'Halpin, E., *Head of the Civil Service: A Study of Sir Warren Fisher* (London, 1989)

Olasky, M. N., *Corporate Public Relations: A New Historical Perspective* (Hillsdale, 1987)

Olins, W., *The Corporate Personality: An Inquiry into the Nature of Corporate Identity* (London, 1978)

Patvardhan, V. S., *British Agricultural Marketing: A Study in Government Policy* (London, 1965)

Pedersen, S., and Mandler, P. (ed.) *After the Victorians: Private Conscience and Public Duty in Modern Britain* (London & New York, 1994)

Peele, G., and Cook, C. (eds) *The Politics of Reappraisal 1918–1939* (London, 1975)

Perkin, H., *The Rise of Professional Society: England since 1880* (London & New York, 1989)

Perry, G., *The Great British Picture Show* (London, 1985)

Pieczka, M., and L'Etang, J., 'Public Relations and the Question of Professionalism', in Heath, R. L. (ed.) *Handbook of Public Relations* (London, 2001), pp. 223–237

Piette, A., *Imagination at War: British Fiction and Poetry 1939–1945* (London, 1995)

Platt, H. L., *The Electric City: Energy and the Growth of the Chicago Area, 1880–1930* (Chicago & London, 1991)

Porter, B., *The Absent-minded Imperialists: Empire, Society and Culture in Britain* (Oxford, 2004)

Potter, S. J., *News and the British World: The Emergence of an Imperial Press System, 1876–1922* (Oxford, 2003)

Pound, R., *Gordon Selfridge: A Biography* (London, 1960)

Prochaska, F., *Royal Bounty: The Making of a Welfare Monarchy* (New Haven & London, 1995)

Pronay, N. (ed.) *Propaganda, Politics and Film 1918–1945* (London, 1982)

Proudfoot, L., and Roche, M., 'Place, Network, and the Geographies of Empire', in Proudfoot, L., and Roche, M. (eds) *(Dis)Placing Empire: Renegotiating British Colonial Geographies* (Aldershot, 2005), pp. 1–15

Proudfoot, L., and Roche, M. (eds) *(Dis)Placing Empire: Renegotiating British Colonial Geographies* (Aldershot, 2005)

Ramsden, J., *The Making of Conservative Party Policy: The Conservative Research Department since 1929* (London, 1980)

Raucher, A., *Public Relations and Business, 1900–1929* (Baltimore, 1968)

Reader, W. J., *Imperial Chemical Industries: A History. Volume 1: The Forerunners 1870–1926* (London, 1970)

Richards, J., *Films and British National Identity* (Manchester, 1997)

Ross, C., *Twenties London: A City in the Jazz Age* (London, 2003)

Russell, P., and Taylor, J. (eds) *Shadows of Progress: Britain's Forgotten Post-war Documentaries* (London, 2010)

Saler, M., *The Avant-garde in Interwar England: Medieval Modernism and the London Underground* (New York & Oxford, 1999)

Samuel, R., 'Exciting to be English', in Samuel, R. (ed.) *Patriotism: The Making and Unmaking of British National Identity. Vol. 1* (London & New York, 1989), pp. XVIII–LXVII

Samuel, R. (ed.) *Patriotism: The Making and Unmaking of British National Identity. Vol. 1* (London & New York, 1989)

Scannell, P., and Cardiff, D., *A Social History of British Broadcasting. Volume One: 1922–1939* (Oxford and Cambridge, MA, 1991)

Searle, G. R., *Country Before Party: Coalition and the Idea of 'National Government' in Modern Britain, 1885–1987* (London and New York, 1995)

Sissons, M., and French, P. (eds) *The Age of Austerity 1945–1951* (London, 1963)

Smart, N., *The National Government, 1931–1940* (Basingstoke, 1999)

Smith, L. M., *Echoes of Greatness* (Basingstoke, 1988)

Smith, M., *Britain and 1940: History, Myth and Popular Memory* (London & New York, 2000)

Spoor, A., *White-collar Union: Sixty Years of NALGO* (London, 1967)

Stamp, G., *Telephone Boxes* (London, 1989)

Starr, P., *The Creation of the Media: Political Origins of Modern Communications* (New York, 2004)

Steel, R., *Walter Lippmann and the American Century* (Boston, 1980)

Stenton, M., *Radio London and Resistance in Occupied Europe* (Oxford & New York, 2000)

Stevenson, J., 'The Jerusalem that Failed? The Rebuilding of Post-war Britain', in Gourvish, T., and O'Day, A. (eds) *Britain since 1945* (Basingstoke and London, 1991), pp. 89–110

Stollery, M., *Alternative Empires: European Modernist Cinemas and the Culture of Imperialism* (Exeter, 2000)

Sussex, E., *The Rise and Fall of British Documentary* (Berkeley, 1975)

Swann, P., *The British Documentary Movement, 1926–1946* (Cambridge, 1989)

Sweet, M., *Shepperton Babylon: The Lost Worlds of British Cinema* (London, 2005)

Taylor, A. J. P., *Beaverbrook* (London, 1972)

Taylor, A. J. P., *English History 1914–1945* (London, 1965)

Taylor, P. M., *The Projection of Britain: British Overseas Publicity and Propaganda 1919–1939* (Cambridge, 1981)

Taylor, P. M., *Munitions of the Mind* (Glasgow, 1990)

Taylor, S. J., *The Great Outsiders: Northcliffe, Rothermere and The Daily Mail* (London, 1996)

Tench, R., and Yeomans, L. (eds) *Exploring Public Relations* (Harlow & New York, 2006)

Timson, J., *Requiem for a Red Box* (London, 1989)

Trentmann, F., 'Coping with Shortage: the Problem of Food Security and Global Visions of Coordination, c.1890s–1950', in Trentmann, F., and Just, F. (eds) *Food and Conflict in the Age of the Two World Wars* (Basingstoke, 2006), pp. 13–48

Trentmann, F., 'After the Nation State: Citizenship, Empire and Global Coordination in the New Internationalism, 1914–1930', in Grant, K., Levine, P. and Trentmann, F. (eds) *Beyond Sovereignty: Britain, Empire and Transnationalism c.1880–1950* (Basingstoke, 2007), pp. 34–53

Trentmann, F., *Free Trade Nation: Commerce, Consumption, and Civil Society in Modern Britain* (Oxford, 2008)

Trentmann, F., and Just, F. (eds) *Food and Conflict in the Age of the Two World Wars* (Basingstoke, 2006)

Tweedale, G., 'English Versus American Hardware: British

Marketing Techniques and Business Performance in the USA in the Nineteenth and Early-twentieth Centuries', in Davenport-Hines, R. T. (ed.) *Markets and Bagmen: Studies in the History of Marketing and British Industrial Performance 1830–1939* (Aldershot, 1986), pp. 57–81

Vaughan, D., *Portrait of an Invisible Man: The Working Life of Stewart McAllister, Film Editor* (London, 1983)

Vernon, J., *Hunger: A Modern History* (Cambridge, MA, & London, 2007)

Vincent, D., *The Culture of Secrecy, Britain 1832–1998* (Oxford, 1998)

Waller, R., *Prophet of the New Age: The Life and Thought of Sir George Stapledon* (London, 1962)

Walsh, M., *The News from Ireland: Foreign Correspondents and the Irish Revolution* (London & New York, 2008)

Ward, V., 'Marketing Convenience Foods between the Wars', in Jones, G., and Tedlow, R. (eds) *Adding Value: Brands, and Marketing in Food and Drink* (London, 1994), pp. 259–288

Webster, W., *Englishness and Empire 1939–1965* (Oxford & New York, 2005)

Weight, R., *Patriots: National Identity in Britain* (Basingstoke and Oxford, 2002)

Welch, D., *Germany, Propaganda and Total War, 1914–1918* (London, 2000)

Wernick, A., *Promotional Culture: Advertising, Ideology and Symbolic Expression* (London, 1991)

Wheeler-Bennett, J., *John Anderson: Viscount Waverley* (London & New York, 1962)

Wiener, M. J., *English Culture and the Decline of the Industrial Spirit, 1850–1980*, 2nd edition (Cambridge, 2004)

Williams, A. H., *'No Name on the Door': A Memoir of Gordon Selfridge* (London, 1956)

Williams, R., *Culture and Society 1780–1950* (London, 1958)

Williams, T. I., *A History of the British Gas Industry* (Oxford, 1981)

Williamson, P., *Stanley Baldwin: Conservative Leadership and National Values* (Cambridge, 1999)

Wilson, J. F., *British Business History, 1720–1994* (Manchester, 1995)

Wilson, R. B., *Go Go Great Western: A History of GWR Publicity* (Newton Abbot, 1987)

Published articles

Aitken, I., 'John Grierson (1898–1972)', *Dictionary of National Biography*, Oxford University Press, 2004 (http://www.oxforddnb.com/view/article/31173?docPos=8, accessed 14 January 2005)

Anthony, S., 'Crawford, Sir William Smith (1878–1950)', *Dictionary of National Biography*, Oxford University Press, 2004 (http://www.oxforddnb.com/view/printable/40828, accessed 9 October 2008)

Bailkin, J., 'Color Problems: Work, Pathology and Perception in Modern Britain', *International Labor and Working Class History*, No. 68, Fall 2005, pp. 93–111

Church, R., 'New Perspectives on the History of Products, Firms, Marketing, and Consumers in Britain and the United States since the Mid-nineteenth Century' in *The Economic History Review*, New Series, Vol. 52, No. 3, August 1999, pp. 405–435

Clark, A., 'Basil Clark – PR Pioneer', *Public Relations*, Vol. 22, No. 2, 1969, p. 9

Conekin, B. E., 'Barry, Sir Gerald Reid (1898–1968)', *Oxford Dictionary of National Biography*, Oxford University Press, 2004 (http://www.oxforddnb.com/view/articleHL/30623?docPos=6&anchor=match, accessed 18 September 2007)

Constantine, S., 'Tallents, Sir Stephen George (1884–1958)', *Oxford Dictionary of National Biography*, Oxford University Press, 2004 (http://www.oxforddnb.com/view/article/36412?docPos=2, accessed 14 January 2005)

Davenport-Hines, R., 'Kearley, Hudson Ewbanke, First Viscount Devonport (1856–1934)', *Oxford Dictionary of National Biography*, 2008 (http://ezproxy.ouls.ox.ac.uk:2117/view/article/34252, accessed 23 January 2010)

Ellis, J. C., 'The Young Grierson in America, 1924–1927', *Cinema Journal*, 1968, pp. 12–21

Ellis, J. C., 'Grierson at University', *Cinema Journal*, 1973, pp. 39–47

Fox, J., 'John Grierson, his "Documentary Boys" and the British Ministry of information, 1939–1942', *Historical Journal of Film, Radio and Television*, Vol. 25, No. 3, 2005, pp. 345–369

Foxon, G., 'Early Biological Film: The Work of R. G. Canti', *University Vision*, No. 15, December 1976, pp. 5–13

Freeman, J., 'The Publicity of the Empire Marketing Board 1926–1933', *Journal of Advertising History*, No. 1, December 1977, pp. 12–14

Gower, K., 'US Corporate Public Relations in the Progressive Era',

Journal of Communications Management, Vol. 12, No. 4, 2008, pp. 305–318

Greenaway, J.R., 'Warren Fisher and the Transformation of the British Treasury, 1919–1939', *Journal of British Studies*, Vol. 23, 1983, pp. 114–125

Hansen, P. H., 'The Dancing Lamas of Everest: Cinema, Orientalism, and Anglo-Tibetan Relations in the 1920s', *The American Historical Review*, Vol. 101, No. 3, June 1996, pp. 712–747

Hayward, S., '"Good design is largely a matter of common sense": Questioning the Meaning and Ownership of a Twentieth Century Orthodoxy', *Journal of Design History*, Vol. 11, No. 3, 1998, pp. 217–234

Hollins, T. J., 'The Conservative Party and Film Propaganda between the Wars', *English Historical Review*, Vol. 96, No. 379, April, 1981, pp. 359–369

Lebas, E., '"When Every Street Became a Cinema": The Film Work of Bermondsey Borough Council's Public Health Department, 1923–1953', *History Workshop Journal*, Vol. 39, 1995, pp. 42–66

Lee, J. M., 'The Dissolution of the EMB: Reflections in a Diary', *Journal of Imperial and Cultural History*, Vol. 1, No. 1, 1972

Leventhal, F. M.,'"A Tonic to the Nation": The Festival of Britain, 1951', *Albion: A Quarterly Journal Concerned with British Studies*, Vol. 27, No. 3, Autumn 1995, pp. 445–453

McIntyre, I., 'Reith, John Charles Walsham, First Baron Reith (1889–1971)', *Dictionary of National Biography*, Oxford University Press, 2006 (http://www.oxforddnb.com/view/article/31596, accessed 13 June 2006)

Marvick, D., 'The Work of Harold D. Lasswell: His Approach, Concerns and Influence', *Political Behaviour*, 1980, pp. 219–229

Marwick, A., 'Middle Opinion in the Thirties: Planning, Progress and Political "Agreement"', *The English Historical Review*, Vol. LXXIX, No. CCCXI, 1964, pp. 285–298

Matless, D., 'Appropriate Geography: Patrick Abercrombie and the Energy of the World', *Journal of Design History*, Vol. 6, No. 3, 1993, pp. 167–178

Miller, M., 'Abercrombie, Sir (Leslie) Patrick (1879–1957)', *Dictionary of National Biography*, Oxford University Press, 2004 (http://www.oxforddnb.com/view/article/30322?docPos=6, accessed 22 March 2007)

Muir, D., 'The First GPO Logo', *British Philatelic Bulletin*, Vol. 44, September 2006, pp. 11–14

Nicholas, S., '"Sly Demagogues" and Wartime Radio: J. B. Priestley and the BBC', *Twentieth Century British History*, Vol. 6, No. 3, 1995, pp. 247–266

Nottage, R., 'The Post Office: A Pioneer of Big Business', *Public Administration*, Vol. XXXVII, Spring 1959, pp. 54–64

Peet, S., 'John Taylor on Documentary Film Part 1', *Screenonline*, BFI, 2005 (www.screenonline.org.uk/audio/id/945640, accessed 9 September 2005)

Pevsner, N., 'Patient Progress: the Life Work of Frank Pick', *The Architectural Review*, Vol. XCII, 1942, pp. 31–48

Powell, J. M., 'The Empire Meets the New Deal', *Geographical Research: Journal of the Institute of Australian Geographers*, Vol. 43, No. 4, December 2005, pp. 337–360

Pronay, N., 'John Grierson and the Documentary – 60 Years On', *Historical Journal of Film, Radio and Television*, Vol. 9, No. 3, 1989, pp. 227–246

Robbins, M., 'Frank Pick (1878–1941)', *Dictionary of National Biography*, Oxford University Press, 2006 (http://www. oxforddnb.com/view/article/35522, accessed 23 March 2007)

Self, R., 'Treasury Control and the Empire Marketing Board', *Twentieth Century British History*, Vol. 5, No. 2, 1994, pp. 153–181

Simonelli, D., '"Laughing nations of happy children who have never grown up": Race, the Concept of Commonwealth and the 1924–25 British Empire Exhibition', *Journal of Colonialism and Colonial History*, Vol. 10, No. 1, Spring 2009

Smyth, R., 'The Development of British Colonial Film Policy, 1927–1939, with Special Reference to East and Central Africa', *Journal of African History*, Vol. 20, No. 3, 1979, pp. 437–450

Weight, R., 'State, Intelligentsia and the Promotion of National Culture in Britain, 1939–45', *Historical Research*, February 1996, pp. 83–101

Weinstein, M. A., 'Alexander, Samuel (1859–1938)', *Dictionary of National Biography*, Oxford University Press, 2004 (http:// www. oxforddnb.com/view/article/30372?docPos=32, accessed 19 November 2006)

West, D., 'Multinational Competition in the British Advertising Agency Business, 1936–1987', *The Business History Review*, Vol. 62, No. 3, Autumn 1988, pp. 467–501

Wilcox, T., 'Projection or Publicity? Rival Concepts in the Pre-war Planning of the British Ministry of Information', *Journal of Contemporary History*, Vol. 18, 1983, pp. 97–116

Unpublished theses and presentations

Beers, L., 'Learning from Their Mistakes: Labour, the Media and the General Strike', presentation to IHR conference, London, 1 July 2005

Bingham, A., 'Royalty, Celebrity and Privacy in the Popular Press, 1936–55', presentation to IHR conference, London, 30 June 2005

Hunter, J., and Howlett, P., 'Social Compliance in Wartime Britain and Japan: Rationing, the Black Market and Crime', presentation to 'Consumption Constrained: Austerity and Rationing in the 20th Century International Workshop' in Tartu, Estonia, 28 April 2007

Lebas, E., 'Glasgow Corporation as Documentary Pioneer, 1921–1938', presentation to IHR conference, London, 30 June 2005

Nicholas, S., '"Kings or Fellow Human Beings": The Monarchy and the Media in Inter-war Britain', presentation to IHR conference, London, 30 June 2005

Thomas, K.-L., 'A National Correspondence: Postal Reform and Fictions of Communication in Nineteenth Century British Culture', D.Phil. dissertation, University of Oxford, 2002

Whitley, Z., 'Propaganda and Censorship: Examples from the Victoria and Albert Museum's Poster Collections', presentation to IHR conference, London, 1 July 2005

Whitworth, L., 'Constraint as Opportunity: Austerity, Product Standards and Consumer Education: The British Case from 1945', presentation to 'Consumption Constrained: Austerity and Rationing in the 20th Century International Workshop' in Tartu, Estonia, 28 April 2007

Worcester, B., 'History of the Media's Use of Opinion Polls, 1824–2005', presentation to IHR conference, London, 29 June 2005

Index